International Political Economy Series

General Editor: **Timothy M. Shaw**, Professor of Commonwealth Governance and Development, and Director of the Institute of Commonwealth Studies, School of Advanced Study, University of London

Titles include:

Francis Adams, Satya Dev Gupta and Kidane Mengisteab (*editors*)
GLOBALIZATION AND THE DILEMMAS OF THE STATE IN THE SOUTH

Preet S. Aulakh and Michael G. Schechter (*editors*)
RETHINKING GLOBALIZATION(S)
From Corporate Transnationalism to Local Interventions

Elizabeth De Boer-Ashworth
THE GLOBAL POLITICAL ECONOMY AND POST-1989 CHANGE
The Place of the Central European Transition

Edward A. Comor (*editor*)
THE GLOBAL POLITICAL ECONOMY OF COMMUNICATION

Helen A. Garten
US FINANCIAL REGULATION AND THE LEVEL PLAYING FIELD

Randall D.Germain (*editor*)
GLOBALIZATION AND ITS CRITICS
Perspectives from Political Economy

Barry K. Gills (*editor*)
GLOBALIZATION AND THE POLITICS OF RESISTANCE

Richard Grant and John Rennie Short (*editors*)
GLOBALIZATION AND THE MARGINS

Takashi Inoguchi
GLOBAL CHANGE
A Japanese Perspective

Jomo K.S. and Shyamala Nagaraj (*editors*)
GLOBALIZATION VERSUS DEVELOPMENT

Stephen D. McDowell
GLOBALIZATION, LIBERALIZATION AND POLICY CHANGE
A Political Economy of India's Communications Sector

Ronaldo Munck and Peter Waterman (*editors*)
LABOUR WORLDWIDE IN THE ERA OF GLOBALIZATION
Alternative Union Models in the New World Order

Craig N. Murphy (*editor*)
EGALITARIAN POLITICS IN THE AGE OF GLOBALIZATION

Michael Niemann
A SPATIAL APPROACH TO REGIONALISM IN THE GLOBAL ECONOMY

Markus Perkmann and Ngai-Ling Sum (*editors*)
GLOBALIZATION, REGIONALIZATION AND CROSS–BORDER REGIONS

Ted Schrecker (*editor*)
SURVIVING GLOBALISM
The Social and Environmental Challenges

Leonard Seabrooke
US POWER IN INTERNATIONAL FINANCE
The Victory of Dividends

Timothy J. Sinclair and Kenneth P. Thomas (*editors*)
STRUCTURE AND AGENCY IN INTERNATIONAL CAPITAL MOBILITY

Kendall Stiles (*editor*)
GLOBAL INSTITUTIONS AND LOCAL EMPOWERMENT
Competing Theoretical Perspectives

Caroline Thomas and Peter Wilkin (*editors*)
GLOBALIZATION AND THE SOUTH

Kenneth P.Thomas
CAPITAL BEYOND BORDERS
States and Firms in the Auto Industry, 1960–94

Geoffrey R.D. Underhill (*editor*)
THE NEW WORLD ORDER IN INTERNATIONAL FINANCE

Amy Verdun
EUROPEAN RESPONSES TO GLOBALIZATION AND FINANCIAL MARKET
INTEGRATION
Perceptions of Economic and Monetary Union in Britain, France and Germany

Robert Wolfe
FARM WARS
The Political Economy of Agriculture and the International Trade Regime

International Political Economy Series
Series Standing Order ISBN 0–333–71708–2 hardback
Series Standing Order ISBN 0–333–71110–6 paperback
(*outside North America only*)

You can receive future titles in this series as they are published by placing a standing order.
Please contact your bookseller or, in case of difficulty, write to us at the address below with
your name and address, the title of the series and an ISBN quoted above.

Customer Services Department, Macmillan Distribution Ltd, Houndmills, Basingstoke,
Hampshire RG21 6XS, England

Globalization and the Margins

Edited by

Richard Grant
Associate Professor
Department of Geography and Regional Studies
University of Miami, USA

John Rennie Short
Professor and Chair
Department of Geography and Environmental Systems
University of Maryland
Baltimore County, USA

Selection, editorial matter and Chapters 1 and 12
© Richard Grant and John Rennie Short 2002
Chapter 9 © Richard Grant 2002
Chapters 2–8, 10 and 11 © Palgrave Macmillan Ltd 2002

First published 2002 by
PALGRAVE MACMILLAN
Houndmills, Basingstoke, Hampshire RG21 6XS and
175 Fifth Avenue, New York, N.Y. 10010
Companies and representatives throughout the world.

PALGRAVE MACMILLAN is the global academic imprint of the Palgrave
Macmillan division of St Martin's Press, LLC and of Palgrave Macmillan Ltd.
Macmillan® is a registered trademark in the United States, United Kingdom
and other countries. Palgrave is a registered trademark in the European
Union and other countries.

ISBN 0–333–96431–4 hardback
ISBN 0–333–96432–2 paperback

This book is printed on paper suitable for recycling and
made from fully managed and sustained forest sources.

A catalogue record for this book is available
from the British Library.

Library of Congress Cataloging-in-Publication Data
Globalization and the margins/edited by Richard Grant and John Rennie
Short.
    p. cm. – (International political economy series)
Includes bibliographical references and index.
ISBN 0–333–96431–4 (cloth)
    1. International economic relations. 2. Globalization – Economic aspects –
Developing countries. 3. Developing countries – Foreign economic relations.
4. Developing countries – Economic conditions. I. Grant, Richard, 1964–
II. Short, John R. III. International political economy series (Palgrave (Firm))
HF1359 .G5837 2002
330.9172'4–dc21   2002025390

10 9 8 7 6 5 4 3 2 1
11 10 09 08 07 06 05 04 03 02

Printed and bound in Great Britain by
Antony Rowe Ltd, Chippenham and Eastbourne

Contents

List of Maps   vii

List of Tables   viii

List of Figures   ix

Notes on the Contributors   x

List of Abbreviations   xiii

Part I   Theoretical Threads on Globalization   **1**

1   Globalization: An Introduction
    Richard Grant and John Rennie Short   3

2   Globalization and the Formation of Claims
    Saskia Sassen   15

3   Opposition and Resistance to Globalization
    Roland Robertson   25

4   Subduing Globalization: The Challenge of the
    Indigenization Movement
    Mehrzad Boroujerdi   39

Part II   Globalization on the Margins   **51**

5   Globalization or Localization? Rural Advertising
    in India
    Tej K. Bhatia   53

6   Speaking from the Margins: "Postmodernism,"
    Transnationalism, and the Imagining of
    Contemporary Indian Urbanity
    Anthony D. King   72

Part III   Globalization in the Margins   **91**

7   Globalization and Women: Gender and
    Resistance in the Informal Sector of Peru
    Maureen Hays-Mitchell   93

8   Migrant Communities in Accra, Ghana: Marginalizing
    the Margins
    Deborah Pellow   111

9   Foreign Companies and Glocalizations: Evidence
    from Accra, Ghana
    Richard Grant   130

10 The Effects of Economic Globalization: Land Use
    and Land Values in Mumbai, India
    Jan Nijman   150

11 Globalization and Financial Crises in Seoul,
    South Korea
    Yeong-Hyun Kim   170

Part IV: Conclusions   **191**

12 Ordering a Chaotic Concept Based on Evidence
    from the Margins
    Richard Grant and John Rennie Short   193

Index   203

List of Maps

8.1   Map of Accra in 1957 and the location of
      Sabon Zongo (Pellow)   117

8.2   Zongo from "Plan showing Malam Bako's
      area" (Pellow)   119

8.3   Inside Sabon Zongo (Pellow)   122

List of Tables

5.1   Globalization and localization: perceived
        models and linguistic strategies (Bhatia)   60

5.2   Codification of globalization and
        localization (Bhatia)   66

5.3   Parameters of content (Bhatia)   69

11.1   Foreign direct investment in Seoul,
        1982–98 (Kim)   179

List of Figures

10.1   Net office rents in prime business areas in selected Asian cities, 1998 (Nijman)   152

10.2   Peak values of prime office rentals in four Indian cities in 1995/1996 (Nijman)   153

10.3   Commercial real estate values (rentals) across selected areas in Greater Mumbai, 1998 (Nijman)   154

10.4   Capital values of office space in prime business areas of greater Mumbai from 1990 to 1998 (Nijman)   155

10.5   The number of large multinational corporations in four Indian cities, 1998 (Nijman)   157

10.6   The geographical distribution of 606 foreign companies in Greater Mumbai, by pin (zip) code area, 1998 (Nijman)   158

11.1   Overseas travel to/from Korea and the financial crisis (Kim)   183

11.2   Economic trends in post-crisis Korea (Kim)   185

Notes on the Contributors

Tej K. Bhatia is Professor of Linguistics at Syracuse University, Syracuse, New York. He was the recipient of the Chancellor's Citation Award for "exceptional academic achievement". For a number of years he served as the Director of the Linguistic Studies Program and the Acting Director of Cognitive Sciences Program at Syracuse. He has published a number of books and articles in the area of language and cognition, media discourse, the bilingual brain, sociolinguistics, and the structure of English and South Asian languages. His most recent books include: *Advertising in Rural India: Language, Market, Communication, and Consumerism* (2000), *Colloquial Urdu* (2000), *Handbook of Child Language Acquisition* (1999), *Handbook of Second Language Acquisition* (1996) and *Colloquial Hindi* (1996).

Mehrzad Boroujerdi is Associate Professor of Political Science at the Maxwell School of Syracuse University. He received his Ph.D. in International Relations from the American University in Washington, DC. Before joining the faculty of Syracuse University, he was respectively a Post-doctoral fellow and a Rockefeller Foundation fellow at Harvard University and the University of Texas at Austin. Professor Boroujerdi's research interests focus on the intellectual history of the contemporary Middle East, and "Third-World" resistance to modernity and cultural globalization. He is the author of *Iranian Intellectuals and the West: The Tormented Triumph of Nativism* (1996). His articles have appeared in the *Journal of Peace Research*; *international Third World Studies Journal* and *Review: The Oxford Encyclopedia* of *the Modern Islamic World*; *the Middle East Economic Survey*; *critique: Journal* for *Critical Studies of the Middle East* and a variety of edited books and Persian-language journals.

Richard Grant is Associate Professor in the Department of Geography and Regional Studies, University of Miami, Coral Gables, Florida. His research interests include economic globalization, cities in the less-developed world, especially Accra and Mumbai and global trade policy. His research on globalization in the margins has been funded by the National Science Foundation. He is the author of *The Global Crisis in Foreign Aid* (1998), with Jan Nijman.

Maureen Hays-Mitchell is a Associate Professor in the Department of Geography at Colgate University, where she has also served as Coordinator of the Latin American Studies Program. Her ongoing research interests include the gendered dimensions of economic restructuring in Latin America, the role of women's grassroots associations in post-conflict societies, as well as the broader issues of gender relations, human rights, and development. In addition to various book chapters, her publications have appeared in *Environment and Planning D: Society and Space, Environment* and *Planning A: The International Journal of Urban and Regional Planning, The Professional Geographer, the Journal of Latin Americanist Geographers*, and *Grassroots Development Journal*. She has conducted field research in Peru, Mexico, Chile, and Spain.

Yeong-Hyun Kim is a Assistant Professor in the Department of Geography at Ohio University. Her research interests include globalization, development, multinational corporations and the Asian economy. She is a co-author of *Globalization and the City* (with John Rennie Short, 1999). She is currently working on South Korean multinationals' investment in South, Southeast Asia.

Anthony D. King is Professor of Art History and of Sociology at the State University of New York at Binghamton. With Thomas A. Markus he co-edits the Routledge series, ArchiTEXT on architecture and social/cultural theory. His book for this series, Spaces of Transnational Cultures, is in preparation. Other recent titles include two edited collections, *Culture, Globalization and the World-System: Contemporary Conditions for the Representation of Identity* (1991 and second edition in 1997) and *Re-Presenting the City: Ethnicity, Capital and Culture in the 21st Century Metropolis* (1996). A second edition of *The Bungalow: The Production of a Global Culture* (1984) was published.

Jan Nijman is Professor of Geography and Regional Studies in the School of International Studies at the University of Miami. His main interests are in globalization, geopolitics, and urban development. He is preparing a book on the economic and social consequences of globalization in Mumbai, India. He is the author of *The Geopolitics of Power and Conflict* (1993), *The Global Moment in Urban Evolution* (1996) and (with Richard Grant) *The Global Crisis in Foreign Aid* (1998).

Deborah Pellow is Professor of Anthropology at Syracuse University. Trained as an Africanist, her primary geographic area of interest has been West Africa, primarily Ghana; in the 1980s she also did research in Shanghai, China. For the last decade, all of her work has dealt with the mutually constitutive nature of social and physical space. Her most recent publication is Cultural Differences and Urban Spatial Forms: Elements of Boundedness in an Accra Community in *The American Anthropologist*, 2001.

John Rennie Short is Professor of Geography and Chair of the Dept of Geography and Environmental Systems, University of Maryland, Baltimore County. He has research interests in urban issues and globalization. His many publications include *Global Dimensions: Space, Place and The Contemporary World* (2001), *Representing The Republic* (2001); *Alternative Geographies* (2000) *Globalization and The City* (1999), and *New Worlds, New Geographies* (1998).

Roland Robertson is Professor of Sociology and Director of the Centre for the Study of Globalization at the University of Aberdeen, Scotland, his previous position having been that of Distinguished Service Professor of Sociology, University of Pittsburgh. He has held visiting appointments in Japan, Hong Kong, Sweden, England, USA, Brazil and Turkey. Among his many publications (co-editor); *Meaning and Change*; *International Systems and the Modernization of Society* (co-author); and *The Sociological Interpretation of Religion*. His work has been translated into approximately ten languages. His forthcoming books include *Globality and Modernity* and *The Formation of World Society*.

Saskia Sassen is the Ralph Lewis Professor of Sociology at the University of Chicago, and Centennial Visiting Professor at the London School of Economics. She is currently completing her forthcoming book *Denationalization: Territory, Authority and Rights in a Global Digital Age* (2003) based on her five-year project on governance and accountability in a global economy. Most recently she has edited *Global Networks, Linked Cities* (2002). Her books have been translated into twelve languages.

List of Abbreviations

AMA	Accra Metropolitan Assembly
CBD	Central Business District
FDI	Foreign Direct Investment
GATT	General Agreement on Tariffs and Trade
GIPC	Ghana Investment Promotion Center
IMF	International Monetary Fund
IR	International Relations
MAI	Multilateral Agreement on Investment
MNC	Multinational Corporation
NGO	Non-Government Organization
NRI	Non-Resident Indian
NAFTA	North American Free Trade Assocation
OECD	Organisation for Economic Co-operation and Development
SAP	Structural Adjustment Policy
UN	United Nations
UNESCO	United Nations Educational, Scientific and Cultural Organization
US	United States
ULCA	Urban Land Ceiling Act
WTO	World Trade Organization

Part I
Theoretical Threads on Globalization

1
Globalization: An Introduction

Richard Grant and John Rennie Short

In this book we put globalization in place. We focus on the general as well as the particular ways that globalization is embedded in places and analyze how globalization is constituted and situated in a variety of locations from the developing world. We bring together a focused yet diverse group of chapters that examine globalization with particular emphasis on the notion of "the margins." Marginality is defined by the discourse and practices of economic, political, and cultural power. Our use of the term *margins* highlights the ways that global and local processes are imbricated in the less developed world. We see this as a necessary corrective to the overemphasis on the experience of the center – as if globalization only occurs in New York, London, and Tokyo. The debate on globalization is not nearly as global as it ought to be: importantly, there is another story to be told.

A particularly innovative approach of this book is that it does not consider global and local as two distinct analytical categories. Instead, the "global" is conceptualized as already embedded in the local, and the authors seek to clarify as well as give examples on how globalization is constituted in places. We seek to uncover how globalization is mediated locally. We build upon the work of Robertson (1995, p. 28) who has defined glocalization as "the processes that telescope the global and local (scales) to make a blend." Various contributors in this volume examine glocalization phenomena in particular places in an effort to study glocalization(s) from the ground upwards and to clarify the concept of globalization.

The contributors are all established researchers on globalization who have ongoing projects in the less developed areas of the global economy. They presented their research at a symposium on Globalization at the Margins, held at the Global Affairs Institute, at the

Maxwell School of Citizenship and Public Affairs, Syracuse University. This symposium was held in the academic year 1998/99 and was funded by the Dean of the Maxwell School through the School's Global Affairs Institute. For the symposium, researchers were asked to focus on the issue of "the margins," and to ground theoretical concepts in specific case studies. Contributors were selected because they are local experts who have collected local data and evidence on particular globalization trends. Researchers wrote research papers following the symposium and the editors worked with each contributor to produce chapters that made an individual contribution to understanding globalization as well as a collective contribution.

A single author could not write such a book that is global in scope and it is only in an edited volume like this that we can offer such worldwide coverage. We illustrate globalization trends with empirical evidence, much of it only available to researchers with local projects. The book has a tight focus and it explores the geographic dimensions of globalization in specific case studies. Case studies provide a more compelling picture of the range of globalization experiences and allow us to uncover the concrete, localized processes through which globalization exists.

The book is divided into four parts. In Part I, three major social theorists discuss the theoretical threads of the globalization discourse. Saskia Sassen and Roland Robertson examine the discontents and resistances to globalization. Mehrzad Boroujerdi examines the challenges to the discourses of globalization from the perspective of indigenous knowledges. The global triumph of modernity is counterposed to the growth of national identity politics. In Part II researchers examine transnational processes taking shape on the margins. The theorized case studies of globalization on the margins in Part III give both a global coverage and different takes on the notion of margins. Case studies from Peru, Ghana, Mumbai and South Korea uncover the connections between the global and the local and the various ways that glocalization is embedded in particular places. Researchers working in similar cities, for example Accra and Mumbai, detail very different local snapshots of the effects of globalization. For instance, compare Deborah Pellow's chapter on migrant communities in Accra with Richard Grant's chapter on the role of foreign companies in the corporate geography of Accra for an example of the sharp differences between the effects of globalization on the corporate sector and the virtually negligible effects on the informal sector. Similarly, Anthony King's writings emphasize the transnational aspect of globalization in urban India, in Part II whereas Jan Nijman's research emphasizes the role of national and local factors as opposed to global forces in determining land use and land values in Mumbai. The geographic variation even in local economies can be immense in the globalization era. We see this hyper-differentiation across places as an important corollary to the hyper-mobility of capital that has been well documented in the globalization literature. Part IV is a concluding chapter in which we pull the main threads of the findings into a coherent set of conclusions.

Globalization as a chaotic concept

Globalization has become one of the dominant and persuasive images of the twenty-first century. There is an implied assumption that globalization comprises a coherent, causal mechanism. In a world that is constantly changing, and with greater rapidity, there is something reassuring about an idea that can explain many things, providing a sense of order, an understanding of the world in flux. Whether as a promise or as a threat, this image is invoked daily to justify actions and to rationalize policy. Globalization has captured the imaginations of a range of individuals: from policymakers, to politicians, to investors, to individuals who at every scale plug into the global matrix.

Several groups have different stakes in the persistence of the concept of globalization, and like most encompassing terms, it is used in many different ways. Let us consider four of the most salient. First, it is used in the popular press, magazines, and news reports as a sort of shorthand expression of the world becoming more alike. For a counter example see Short (2001a). The business press, in particular, focuses on the development of economic globalization and on the notion that we are moving toward a fully integrated global economy involving complete structural integration and strategic integration across the globe. There is also a particular strain of journalistic analysis that receives a lot of attention and can be identified by its provocative and extensive anecdotal evidence and subjective reporting. This journalistic tourism can be found in the works of Kaplan (1993, 1994) and Friedmann (1999). Kaplan (1994) provided an apocalyptic image of the imploding of West African states and from this event generalized the fate of the rest of the world. Friedmann's (1999, p. 3) explained globalization from the perspective of a "tourist with an attitude" by employing anecdotes (his own as well as his professional contacts) that detailed a "revolution from beyond" (or what he terms "globalution") that is transforming societies by integrating them into a global nexus through global markets, global finance and computer technologies to pursue higher standards of living.

Second, the term is used as a marketing concept to sell goods, commodities, and services. Going global has become the mantra for a whole range of companies, business gurus, and institutions as a marketing strategy and projected goal to position themselves in a new economic order. Globalization has become a necessary myth for management thinkers (Hirst and Thompson, 1996). The business of selling globalization (and associated consulting services and financial services) is itself a business; consultants advise their clients to "think global, act local" and promote "the global market as Prometheus unleashed" (Veseth, 1998, 12). The global business environment has created opportunities for global experts to chart individuals and companies through the chaotic waters of globalization. Individual consumers seem increasingly attracted to globally advertised images and the products associated with them. Consuming global commodities is now closely tied to individual and group identities.

Third, globalization has become a focal point of criticism. In this populist discourse, globalization is the source of unwanted change, an evil influence of the foreign "other." This form of fear – globaphobia – is found around the world. Globalization, as one strain of the populist discourse, is often tied to conspiratorial theories of the new world order. A good example is Pat Buchanan's (US Republican presidential candidate for the 2000 election) rhetoric that the global order is undermining sovereignty by "bleeding the US borders through flows of globalization" (Buchanan, 1999). Globaphobia can also find expression in individuals' musings about the pervasiveness of the global economy, including a Brazilian taxi driver's complaint that traffic in Buenos Aires is much worse because of globalization and a Ghanaian Pentecostalist preacher's fetishizing of imported consumer commodities and claims that the "foreign" imbued in his underpants gives him erotic dreams. All three representations of globalization, which happen to be "true" if not accurate, reveal a growing anxiety with a globalization that is often taken to represent such vague worries as change, the foreign, an incomprehensible process, and a force that is beyond national, let alone individual, control. There are academic analyses that also give credence to the perspective that "globalization has gone too far" already. Rodrik (1997), for example, highlighted the tension between globalization and social cohesion.

Finally, globalization has become the subject of a growing academic debate. Globalization is now the subject of a growing number of books, articles, conferences and even whole careers. There is, however, a distinct bias in this field that reflects the unequal distribution of academic resources. The commentators are overwhelmingly of, or in, the rich countries of Europe and North America, producing a first world elitist bias in the globalization literature. Researchers from the metropolitan center have written largely about their home areas, and have drawn general and often unexamined conclusions about the margins. Furthermore, many are guilty of doing "bad geography" by examining singular representations of the globalization. In many instances, the countries of the world are aggregated into a world characterized by globalized spaces and unglobalized spaces. This division of the world makes little historical or contemporary sense, and it undermines any possibilities for peoples to shape their own histories.

In the non-western world the debates about globalization have reached a fever pitch. Very often these are ideological debates about globalization in which globalization is viewed as either the cause or the cure of all local problems. Proponents have typically adopted polemic positions and it is not clear that they are even speaking about the same globalization. It is understandable and unavoidable yet unfortunate that the local debates have centered on what *ought* to be the effects of globalization rather than undertaking research on what *are* the effects of globalization. Nonetheless, we acknowledge that important research is being conducted locally in the non-western world on the globalization phenomena (for example, *Economic and Political Weekly* in India publishes solid articles on globalization but mainly written by Indian researchers for a South Asian audience). But for the most part, research findings are not being picked up or incorporated into theories by many of the leading researchers in the center. The practical nature of local research in the margins also means that researchers' findings do not connect well with the more abstract and theoretical works on globalization. We acknowledge that all of the contributors to this book work at universities in North America or the UK rather than universities in the non-Western world. But at the same time researchers in this volume have been undertaking research for many years and trying to connect the debates on globalization that are often worlds apart.

In an effort to open up the global debate about globalization we aim to try to connect writings about the margins with writings about globalization in the center. We seek to avoid a simple representation about the contemporary world and aim to provide detailed snapshots of particular places. We seek to critically examine the notion of globalization. We provide a thorough geographical framing of globalization and pay careful attention to the experiences of particular places with it. Our argument is that place is central to many of the circuits through which globalization is constituted. Our objective is to re-center and ground the debates about globalization by placing globalization in a variety of areas in the margins.

Defining globalization

Globalization can be defined as a compression of the world by flows of interaction that are broadening as well as deepening around the world. These flows have brought about a greater degree of interdependence and economic homogenization; a more powerful burgeoning global market, financial institutions, and computer technologies have overwhelmed traditional economic practices. Global markets in finance, trade, and services now operate through a regulatory umbrella that is not state-centered but market-centered. Capital now has more extensive rights than at any time in prior economic history, and capitalists now operate in a new global grid. It is possible to identify two broad spatial trends on this grid that are consistent with globalization arguments. On the one hand, some places have moved closer together in relative space. The trajectories of several national, regional, and local economies have become even more enmeshed within a network of global financial flows and transactions. This is a new geography of centrality cutting across national boundaries and across the old North–South divide.

On the other hand, some places have moved further apart in relative space, as they have been subject to a process of financial exclusion, which has led to a widening of economic and social spaces between such "places of exclusion" and those heavily interconnected in the global economic system. Places of exclusion can even appear in areas that are command centers for economic globalization, such as global cities, where there are low-income areas starved of resources and spaces disconnected and excorporated from the circuits of globalization.

However, in reality the modes of integration into the global economy are not so clear-cut. Time–space compression does not necessarily mean sameness or homogeneity. The world is becoming more interconnected, but it is not necessarily becoming more of the same. Parts of the world may become more different, and other parts may exhibit sameness with difference as they respond and interact with global processes in unique ways. With increasing economic competition and capital mobility, the outcome is often increased uneven development and spatial differentiation rather than homogenization (see Short, 2001a).

There are three processes by which places are shaped by globalization: economic, political, and cultural. It is often assumed that the end state of these processes entails a global economy, a global polity, and a global culture. To date, there has been much more discussion about the end result rather than explaining the processes of transformation.

A global economy has been maturing for some 500 years. Worldwide flows of capital and labor have connected places and integrated them into the world economy since the sixteenth century and the beginnings of colonialism. There is considerable debate about the time frame of the origins of globalization. We have no intention of getting into the precise chronology of globalization, but instead acknowledge that the contemporary period of globalization is unique. The speed, intensity, volume, and reach of capital flows have all grown since the 1970s. We equate the contemporary period of globalization with the widespread introduction of liberalization policies across the developing world since the early 1980s.

A global polity has received a boost with the decline of the Soviet bloc, the increasing importance of international organizations (from NATO to the World Bank), and regimes' (security, trade, human rights, and so on etc.) prominence in organizing political space. For instance, the international human rights regime provides a political and legal framework for promoting a universal or cosmopolitan conception of individual rights. Yet, despite the new forms for political spatial organization, the nation–state has shown a tremendous resilience. The obituary for the nation–state (Ohmae, 1995) is premature. The state still provides legitimation services though social spending and must now mobilize more actively than in the past to keep capital investment within country borders and to open up foreign markets for its producers. The important theoretical issue is to position the state both within the historical relationships between territorial states and within the broader social and economic structures and geopolitical order of the contemporary globalization era.

Cultural, as compared to economic and political globalization, is a much more difficult arena to distinguish. The central problem here is that a global culture is more likely to be chaotic than orderly. It is integrated and connected in ways that the meanings of its components are "relativized" to one another, but it is not unified or centralized. The globalization of culture proceeds through the continuous flow of ideas, information, commitment, values, and tastes across the world, mediated through mobile individuals, signs, symbols, and electronic simulations (Short and Kim, 1999). While the same images and commodities are found around the world, they are interpreted, consumed, and used in different ways. The great challenge is to understand the differences between culture and the consumption of material goods. The heart of a culture involves attachment to place, language, religion, values, tradition, and customs. Drinking Coca-Cola does not make Russians think like Americans any more than eating sushi makes the British think like the Japanese. Throughout human history fashions and material goods have diffused from one cultural realm to another without significantly altering the recipient culture. We do need to acknowledge, however, that the channels for cultural mixing are now more open than ever before.

The three processes vary in intensity and depth around the world and can exhibit idiosyncratic interfaces with local phenomena. Although progress in economic globalization has contributed to cultural globalization, the latter does not necessarily follow from the former. In any one place around the world the precise mix of these three processes produces a markedly different result with other parts of the world. The same yet differentiated is a more accurate characterization of individual globalization experiences.

Globalization and uneven development

Our approach, which clearly implies that globalization develops unevenly across time and space, is linked with the theoretical writings in development theory. Globalization in the form of liberalization policies has replaced modernization theory as the dominant global approach to development. In may ways, modernization has been recast as globalization, but this time around emphasis has shifted from understanding how to achieve national development from global capital toward explaining how global capital harnesses local development. The same logics of capitalism are shown to be central; however, the new narrative puts the emphasis on explaining how the margins are seeded for global capital.

There is both a logic as well as an illogic to globalization. The logic, as articulated in dominant globalization narratives, is the trend toward a single world market dominated by global capitalist and multinational corporations producing globally consumed commodities all under the hegemony of a neoliberal ideology. However, there is an illogic produced by contradictions between an economy of flows and an economy as territorial unit; between the acceleration of flows of capital through a disembodied space and the need for more fixed capital investments in the space–time of global spaces in gateway cities; and, ultimately, between the winners and losers.

Rapid capital flows, the decline of transport costs, and the rise of electronic communications have also made some analysts write of the end of geography (for example, O'Brien, 1992) and the "end of history" (Fukuyama, 1992). The *Economist* put it bluntly by asking, "Does it matter where you are?" and provided a futuristic reply veiled in a world of fantasy:

> The cliché of the information age is that instantaneous global telecommunications, television and computer networks will soon overthrow the ancient tyrannies of time and space. Companies will need no headquarters, workers will toil as effectively from home, car or beach as they could in the offices that need no longer exist, and events half a world away will be seen, heard and felt with the same immediacy as events across the street – if indeed streets still have any point. (*Economist*, 1994, 13)

The friction of distance has been reduced by technological developments, resulting in lower costs for travel, communication, and transportation. In space–time terms the world has shrunk. Some commentators have argued for replacing the notion of place with that of space and have introduced the term "spaces of globalization" (Cox, 1997) to refer to the space of flows intersecting each other. But in the absolute space of economic calculations the relative space of specific places becomes even more important. Place needs to be rethought; our previous notion of "places" as different, separable, bounded, and historically developed in some degree separately from each other is less relevant today. We are witnessing the disarticulation of place-based societies, but at the same time characteristics of place are still important, whether it is in perceived quality of life, quality of environment, variations in wage rates, systems of regulation, business culture, and characteristics of societies (for example, ability to innovate, adopt, integrate, and so forth.). The friction of distance has not yet become the fiction of distance. Even the global jet-setter and the global business consultant are still tied to the land, to the security of familiar territory, and are conditioned by the uncertainty of what lies beyond. The gap between the borderless world of our imaginations and the border-defined world of our daily experiences has shrunk, but not as much as suggested. Against a background of a shrinking world, geography has become more important, not less.

One common image of globalization is as a wave of change sweeping away local distinctiveness. In this scenario, more often assumed than articulated, globalization is a tsunami of change wiping out the uniqueness of localities. However, a more critical view of globalization would acknowledge more complex relationships between the global and the local. The local is not simply a passive recipient of global processes. Globalization flows from the local to the global as much as from the global to the local. Good examples are the growth in ethnic cuisines throughout the world and the appearance of hybrid cuisines. The term "glocalization" refers to this more subtle relationship between the global and the local. Glocalization in the economic realm refers to companies simultaneously going local as well as global. Heineken is a good example of a company that has a global product – "Heineken beer" in its recognizable green bottles – and also a strategy of buying local breweries and marketing and exporting beer from local breweries (for instance, Heineken own and sells Presidente beer from the Dominican Republic and Star beer from Ghana.) Glocalization has a distinctive meaning in the cultural realm. It speaks to the ability of a culture, when it encounters other strong cultures, to absorb influences that naturally fit into and can enrich it, to resist those elements that are truly alien, and to compartmentalize those elements that while different can nonetheless be enjoyed and celebrated as different. One example of a culture that we are not good at glocalizing was that of the Taliban Islamic fundamentalists in Afghanistan: and it is rather ironic that an event beyond their borders was to bring about their eventual decline by a global coalition force. The US culture, by contrast, is perhaps one of the best examples of a glocalizing culture.

Rather than seeing a tidal wave of globalization sweeping away all social differences, a crude global–local juxtaposition, a more appropriate conceptualization of social change would see three scales of resolution: global, national, and local. Questions of scale and issues of causality can be answered only by more careful attention to the appropriate scale of analysis and a more profound sense of the causal links that connect each of the scales. Flows of globalization are sutured at all these scales. It is also important to highlight the spaces of resistance as well as resilience against the processes of globalization. In most writings on globalization investigators focus solely on identifying evidence of globalization; there are dangers of such tunnel vision. There is the possibility of not identifying local resilience to change and not adequately conceptualizing the local–global interface. In the margins, globalization is typically seen as an external force, but this is a far too simplistic conception of the margin.

Much of the literature on globalization takes a curiously ahistorical, aspatial approach, presenting it as a condition devoid of real history and substantive geography. We are eager to move away from the view of globalization as an untethered phenomenon toward a more informed theory that grounds it in time and space. Take a recent example, the book *Global Transformations* (Held *et al.*, 1999), which is reviewed more fully in Short (2001b). The authors are strong on time. They identify four periods of globalization: premodern, early modern (1500–1850), modern (1500 to 1945) and contemporary (post-1945). Their historical description of globalization focuses on the extensity of global networks, the intensity of global interconnectedness, the velocity of global flows and the impact of global interconnectedness. The historical periodization, like all broad brush categorizations, is subject to debate, but they give a good overall picture of globalization as being a continuous, though changing, process for more than five hundred years. They provide a useful corrective to popular arguments of globalization as a brand new phase of human development. They cover a range of topics: the emergence of a global trading order and global finance, international migration, cultural and environmental globalization. The book, like much of the globalization literature, is weak on space. Globalization is discussed primarily as a relationship between states. A more pronounced silence is the lack of material on developing countries. The book is partly based on a series of case studies of the US, UK, Sweden, France, Germany and Japan. In a book on globalization, to restrict your primary data analysis to rich developed countries seems to miss the fundamental point that globalization involves the rich *and* poor. By including only rich countries the authors miss out on a wider arc that would include a more critical account of economic and political globalization. The case study bias reinforces the notion that the globalization debate is still written from a first world perspective. This is globoccidentalism.

A major silence in Held's book, as in many others, is any sense that globalization is a socio-spatial relationship. There is little sense of how globalization unfolds in particular places. National figures are used as if there were a one-to-one relationship between the data and the whole national territory. There is very little discussion of declining and growing regions, world cities, basing points and black holes. The effect of globalization on different groups in different places is never addressed, and this is an important silence, because globalization is uneven and unfair.

References

Buchanan, P. (1999). <http://www.gopatgo2000.org/000-p-pjb-quotes.html> (September 16, 1999).
Cox, K. (ed.). (1997). *Spaces of globalization: Reasserting the power of the local.* New York: Guilford Press.
Economist. (1994). "Does it matter where you are?" July 30, 1994, 13.
Friedmann, T. L. (1999). *The lexus and the olive tree. Understanding globalization.* New York: Farrar, Strauss and Giroux.
Fukuyama, F. (1992). *The end of history and the last man.* New York: Free Press.
David Held and Anthony McGrew, David Goldblatt and Jonathan Perraton (1999). *Global Transformations.* Palo Alto: Stanford University Press.
Hirst, P. and G. Thompson (1996). *Globalization in question.* Cambridge: Polity Press.
Kaplan, R. D. (1993). *Balkan ghosts: A journey through history.* New York: St. Martin's Press.
———. (1994). The coming anarchy. *Atlantic Monthly,* 273 (2), 44–76.
O'Brien, R. (1992). *Global financial integration: The end of geography.* New York: Royal Institute for International Affairs.
Ohmae, K. (1995). *The end of the nation state and the rise of regional economies.* New York: Free Press.
Robertson, R. (1995). "Glocalization: Time–space and homogeneity–hetrogeneity." In M. Featherstone, S. Lash and R. Robertson (eds.). *Global modernities.* California: Sage Publications, pp. 25–44.
Rodrik, D. (1997). *Has globalization gone too far?* Washington, DC: Institute for International Economics.
Short, J. R. (2001a) *Global Dimensions: Space, Place and The Contemporary World.* London: Reaktion Press.
Short, J. R. (2001b) Review of *Global Transformations,* Association of American Geographers. 91: 645–7.
Short, J. R. and Y-H. Kim (1999). *Globalization and the city.* New York: Addison, Wesley, Longman.
Veseth, M. (1998). *Selling globalization. The myth of the global economy.* Boulder: Lynn Rienner.

2
Globalization and the Formation of Claims[1]

Saskia Sassen

The current phase of the world economy – globalization – is characterized by both significant continuities with the preceding periods and radically new arrangements. The latter becomes particularly evident in the impact of globalization on the geography of economic activity and on the organization of political power. There is an incipient unbundling of the exclusive authority over territory we have long associated with the nation–state. The most strategic instantiation of this unbundling is probably the global city, which operates as a partly denationalized platform for global capital. At a different level of complexity, the transnational corporation and global markets in finance can also be seen as such instantiations through their cross-border activities and the new semi-private transnational legal regimes which frame these activities. Sovereignty, the most complex form of that national authority, is also being unbundled by these economic and noneconomic practices, and by new legal regimes.

There are two dynamics I seek to isolate here: the incipient denationalizing of specific types of national settings, particularly global cities, and the formation of conceptual and operational openings for actors other than the national state in cross-border political dynamics, particularly the new global corporate actors and those collectivities whose experience of membership has not been subsumed fully under nationhood in its modern conception; for example, minorities, immigrants, first-nation people, and many feminists.

Recovering place

Including cities in the analysis of economic globalization is not without its consequences. Economic globalization has mostly been conceptualized in terms of the duality of national–global, where the latter gains at the expense of the former. It has also been largely conceptualized in terms of

15

the internationalization of capital and then only the upper circuits of capital. Introducing cities into this analysis allows us to reconceptualize processes of economic globalization as concrete economic complexes situated in specific places, even though place is typically seen as neutralized by the capacity for global communications and control. Also, a focus on cities decomposes the nation–state into a variety of subnational components, some profoundly articulated with the global economy and others not. It signals the declining significance of the national economy as a unitary category in the global economy.

Why does it matter to recover place in analyses of the global economy, particularly place as constituted in major cities? It allows us to see the multiplicity of economies and work cultures in which the global information economy is embedded. It also lets us uncover the concrete, localized processes through which globalization exists, and to argue that much of the multiculturalism in large cities is as much a part of globalization as is international finance. Finally, focusing on cities allows us to specify a geography of strategic places at the global scale, places bound to each other by the dynamics of economic globalization. I refer to this as a geography of centrality. This is a geography that cuts across national borders and the old North–South divide, but it does so along bounded *filières* – a network or set of channels of specific and partial, rather than all-encompassing, dynamics.

The large city of today emerges as a strategic site. It is a nexus where the formation of new claims materializes and assumes concrete forms. The loss of power at the national level produces the possibility for new forms of power and politics at the subnational level. The national as a container of social process and power is cracked. This cracked casing opens up possibilities for a geography of politics that links subnational spaces. Cities are foremost in this new geography. One question this engenders is whether, and how, we are seeing the formation of a new type of transnational politics that localizes in these cities.

The centrality of place in a context of global processes makes possible a transnational economic and political opening for the formation of new claims and hence for the constitution of entitlements, notably rights to place. Eventually, this could be an opening for new forms of "citizenship." The city has indeed emerged as a site for new claims: by global capital, which uses the city as an "organizational commodity," but also by disadvantaged sectors of the urban population. Many of the disadvantaged workers in global cities are women, immigrants, people of color – men and women whose sense of membership is not necessarily adequately captured in terms of the national, and who indeed often evince cross-border solidarities around issues of substance. Both types of actors find in the global city a strategic site for their economic and political operations. Immigration, for instance, is one major process through which a new transnational political economy is being constituted, one that is largely embedded in major cities insofar as most immigrants, whether in the United States, Japan, or Western Europe, are concentrated in major cities. Immigration is, in my reading, one of the constitutive processes of globalization today, even though it is not recognized or represented as such in mainstream accounts of the global economy. (On these issues see Sassen, 1998, Part One, Isin 2000)

The localizations of the global

Economic globalization, then, needs to be understood in its multiple localizations rather than only in terms of the broad, overarching macro level processes that dominate mainstream accounts (e.g. Tardenico and Lungo 1995). We need to see that many of these localizations do not generally get coded as having anything to do with the global economy. The global city is experiencing an expansion of low-wage jobs that do not fit the master images about globalization, yet are part of it. The embeddedness of these workers in the demographic transition evident in all global cities, and their consequent invisibility, contribute to the devalorization of them and their work cultures.

Women and immigrants emerge as the labor supply that facilitates the imposition of low wages and powerlessness under conditions of high-demand for those workers within high-growth sectors. It breaks the historic nexus that would have led to empowering workers, and legitimates this break culturally.

Another localization which is rarely associated with globalization, informalization, reintroduces the community and the household as important economic spaces in global cities. I see informalization in this setting as the low-cost (and often feminized) equivalent of deregulation at the top of the system. Immigrants and women are important actors in the new informal economies of these cities. They absorb the costs of informalizing these activities (see Sassen, 1998, Chapter 8). As with deregulation (for example, financial deregulation), informalization introduces flexibility, reduces the "burdens" of regulation, and lowers costs, in this case especially the costs of labor. Going informal is one way to produce and distribute goods and services at a lower cost and with greater flexibility. Informalization is a multivalent process.

For instance, these transformations contain possibilities, even if limited, for women's autonomy and empowerment. We might ask whether the growth of informalization in advanced urban economies reconfigures some types of economic relations between men and women. Economic downgrading through informalization creates "opportunities" for low-income women entrepreneurs and workers, and therewith reconfigures some of the work and household hierarchies that women find themselves in. This becomes particularly clear in the case of immigrant women who come from countries with rather traditional male-centered cultures. There is a large body of literature showing that immigrant women's regular wage work and improved access to other public realms has an impact on their gender relations. Women gain greater personal autonomy and independence while men lose ground. Women gain more control over budgeting and other domestic decisions, and greater leverage in requesting help from men in domestic chores. Besides the relatively greater empowerment of women in the household associated with waged employment, there is a second important outcome: the potential for their greater participation in the public sphere and their possible emergence as public actors.

There are two arenas where immigrant women are especially active: institutions for public and private assistance, and the immigrant/ethnic community. Hondagneu-Sotelo (1995), for instance, found that immigrant women come to assume more active public and social roles, which further reinforces their status in the household and the settlement process. Once engaged in waged labor, women are more active in community building and community activism and they are positioned differently from men in relation to the broader economy and the state. They are the ones who are likely to have to handle the family's legal vulnerability in maneuvering the logistics of seeking public and social services. Overall, this greater participation by women suggests the possibility that they may well emerge as more forceful and visible actors, making their role in the labor market more visible as well (e.g. Hamilton and Chinchilla, 2001).

There is, to some extent, a joining of two different dynamics in the condition of women in global cities. On the one hand, they are constituted as an invisible and disempowered class of workers in the service of strategic sectors in the global economy. This invisibility keeps them from emerging as a contemporary equivalent of the "labor aristocracy" of earlier forms of economic organization, when a low-wage position in leading sectors had the effect of empowering the worker – through unionizing. On the other hand, the access to (albeit low) wages and salaries, the growing feminization of the job supply, and the growing feminization of business opportunities brought on by informalization, do alter the gender hierarchies in which they find themselves. We, in fact, can detect another important localization of the dynamics of globalization: that of the new stratum of professional women

Although informalization offers increased opportunities and openings for women, what we are seeing is a dynamic of valorization which has sharply increased the distance between the valorized, indeed overvalorized, sectors of the economy and the devalorized sectors, even when the latter are part of leading global industries.

A space of power

Global cities contain powerless and often invisible workers and are potentially constitutive of a new kind of transnational politics, yet they are also sites for the valorization of the new forms of global corporate capital. Global cities are centers for the *servicing* and *financing* of international trade, investment, and headquarter operations. The multiplicity of specialized activities present in global cities are crucial in the valorization, indeed overvalorization, of leading sectors of capital today. And in this sense they are production sites for today's leading economic sectors, a function reflected in the ascendance of these activities in their economies. Elsewhere (Sassen, 2000, Chapter 4) I posit that what is specific about the shift to services is not merely the growth in service jobs but, most importantly, the growing service intensity in the organization of the service sector of advanced economies: firms in all industries, from mining to wholesale, buy more accounting, legal, advertising, financial, economic forecasting services today than they did twenty years ago. Whether at the global or regional level, urban centers – central cities, edge cities – have particularly strong advantages of location. The rapid growth and disproportionate concentration of such specialized services in cities signals that the latter have reemerged as significant production sites after losing this role in the period when mass manufacturing was the dominant sector of the economy.

Further, the vast new economic topography that is being shaped through electronic space is one moment, one fragment, of a vaster economic chain that is in part embedded in nonelectronic spaces. There is no fully dematerialized firm or industry; even the most advanced information industries, such as finance, exist only partly in electronic space. This is also true for industries that produce digital products, such as software designers. The growing digitalization of economic activities has not eliminated the need for major international business and financial centers and all the material resources they bring together, from state-of-the-art telematics infrastructure to brain talent (Castells, 1989; Graham and Marvin, 1996; Sassen, 1998, Chapter 9). These economic topographies contain both virtualization of economic activities and a reconfiguration of the built environment for economic activity.

It is precisely because of the territorial dispersal facilitated by telecommunication advances that the agglomeration of centralizing activities has expanded immensely. This is not a mere continuation of old patterns of agglomeration but, one could posit, a new logic for agglomeration. Many of the leading sectors in the economy operate globally, in uncertain markets, under conditions of rapid change (for example, deregulation and privatization) and under enormous speculative tensions. What glues these conditions together into a new logic for spatial agglomeration is the added pressure of speed.

A focus on the *work* behind command functions, on the actual *production process* in the finance and service complexes, and on global market*places* helps us to join conceptually the material facilities underlying globalization and the whole infrastructure of jobs typically not perceived as belonging to the corporate sector of the economy. An economic configuration very different from that suggested by the concept "information economy" emerges. We uncover the material conditions, production sites, and place-boundedness that are also part of globalization and the information economy.

Making claims on the city

The incorporation of cities into a new cross-border geography of centrality also signals the emergence of a parallel political geography. Major cities have emerged as a site not only for global capital but also for the transnationalization of labor and the formation of translocal communities and identities. In this regard cities are a setting for new types of political operations, a new global grid of politics and engagement (Valle and Torres, 2000; Copjec and Sorkin, 1999; Dunn, 1994; *Journal of Urban Technology*, 1995; King, 1996).

If we consider that large cities concentrate both the leading sectors of global capital and a growing share of disadvantaged populations – immigrants, many of the disadvantaged women, people of color generally, and, in the mega cities of developing countries, masses of shanty dwellers – then we can see them as becoming a strategic terrain for a whole series of conflicts and contradictions. We can then think of cities also as one of the sites for the contradictions of the globalization of capital, even though they cannot be reduced to this dynamic (Fincher and Jacobs, 1998; Allen *et al.*, 1999).

Foreign firms and international business people have increasingly been entitled to do business in whatever country and city they choose

– entitled by new legal regimes, by the new economic culture, and by progressive deregulation of national economies. They are among the new city users, making often immense claims on the city and reconstituting strategic spaces of the city in their image. Their claim to the city is rarely contested, and the costs and benefits to cities have barely been examined. They have profoundly marked the urban landscape. The new city is a fragile one: its survival and successes are centered on an economy of high productivity, advanced technologies, and intensified exchanges. It is a city whose space consists of airports, top-level business districts, top-of-the-line hotels and restaurants – in brief, a sort of urban glamour zone (Orum and Chen, 2002).

Perhaps at the other extreme are those who use urban political violence to make their claims on the city, claims that lack the de facto legitimacy enjoyed by the new "city users." These actors are struggling for recognition, entitlement, and rights to the city (Body-Gendrot, 1999). Their claims have, of course, a long history; every new epoch brings specific conditions to the manner in which the claims are made. The growing weight of "delinquency" (for example, smashing cars and shop windows; robbing and burning stores) in some of these uprisings over the last decade in major cities of the developed world is perhaps an indication of sharpened socioeconomic inequality – the distance, as seen and as lived, between the urban glamour zone and the urban war zone. The extreme visibility of the difference is likely to contribute to further intensification of the conflict: the indifference and greed of the new elites versus the hopelessness and rage of the poor.

There are two aspects in this formation of new claims that have implications for the transnational politics that are increasingly being played out in major cities. One is the sharp, and perhaps sharpening, differences in the representation of claims by different sectors, notably international business and the vast population of low income "others" (immigrants, women, people of color generally). The second aspect is the increasingly transnational element in both types of claims and claimants. It signals a politics of contestation embedded in specific places, but transnational in character.

Globalization and inscription in the urban landscape

The new transnational corporate culture frames how economic globalization is represented in the urban landscape. Yet the city concentrates diversity. Although its spaces are inscribed with the dominant corporate culture there is also a multiplicity of other cultures and identities (King, 1996; Watson and Bridges, 1999; Cordero-Guzman *et al* 2001). The slippage is evident: the dominant culture can encompass only part of the city, and while it inscribes noncorporate cultures and identities with "otherness," thereby devaluing them, they are present everywhere. The immigrant communities and informal economies in cities such as New York and Los Angeles are only two instances.

Once we have recovered the centrality of place and of the multiple work cultures within which economic operations are embedded, we are still left confronting a highly restricted terrain for the inscription of economic globalization. Sennett (1990, p. 36) observes that "the space of authority in Western culture has evolved as a space of precision." Giddens, in turn, notes the centrality of "expertise" in today's society, with the corresponding transfer of authority and trust to expert systems (Giddens, 1990, pp. 88–91). Corporate culture is one representation of precision and expertise. Its space has become one of the main spaces of authority in today's cities. The dense concentrations of tall buildings in major downtowns or in the new "edge" cities are the site for corporate culture (though as I will argue later they are also the site for other forms of inhabitation, but these have been made invisible). The vertical grid of the corporate tower is imbued with the same neutrality and rationality attributed to the horizontal grid of American cities.

Through immigration a proliferation of highly localized cultures has now become present in many large cities, cities whose elites think of themselves as cosmopolitans, yet exclude the former from this representation. Cultures from around the world, each rooted in a particular country or village, now intersect in places such as, New York, Los Angeles, Paris, London, and most recently, Tokyo.

The spaces of the immigrant community, of the black ghetto, and increasingly of the old decaying manufacturing district, emerge as the space of an amalgamated other, constituted as a devalued, downgraded space in the dominant economic narrative about the postindustrial urban economy. Corporate culture collapses differences – some minute, some sharp – among the different sociocultural contexts into one amorphous otherness, an otherness that has no place in the economy, or is, supposedly, only marginally attached to the economy. What is not installed in the corporate center is devalued or will tend to be devalued. What occupies the corporate building in noncorporate ways is made invisible. That most of the people working in the corporate city during the day are low-paid secretaries – mostly women, many immigrants – is not included in the representation of the corporate economy or corporate culture. The whole other work force that installs itself in these spaces at night, including the offices of the chief executives, and inscribes the space with a whole different culture (manual labor, often music, lunch breaks at midnight) is also invisible.

A question here is whether the growing presence of immigrants, of African Americans, of women, in the labor force of large cities is what has facilitated the embedding of this sharp increase in inequality (as expressed in earnings and in culture). New politics of identity and new cultural politics have brought many of these devalorized or marginal sectors into representation and into the forefront of urban life.

There is something to be captured here – a distinction between powerlessness and the condition of being an actor but lacking power – that speaks to the nature of "margins." I use the term "presence" to name this condition. In the context of a strategic space, such as the global city, the disadvantaged people described here are not "marginal"; they acquire presence but in a broader political process that escapes the traditionally defined boundaries of the formal polity. Their presence signals the possibility of a politics. What this politics will be depends on the specific projects and practices of various communities. Insofar as the sense of membership of these communities is not subsumed under the national, it may well signal the possibility of a transnational politics centered in concrete localities and specific, non-cosmopolitan struggles that become part of a new global politics.

Conclusion

Globalization is a contradictory space; it is characterized by contestation, internal differentiation, and continuous border crossings. Global cities are emblematic of this condition. They concentrate a disproportionate share of global corporate power and are one of the key sites for its overvalorization. They also concentrate a disproportionate share of the disadvantaged and are one of the key sites for their devalorization. This dual presence exists in a context where (1) the globalization of the economy has grown sharply and cities have become increasingly strategic for global capital; and (2) marginalized people have found their voice and are making claims on the city. This joint existence is brought into focus by the sharpening of the distance between the two. The center now concentrates immense power, a power that rests on the capabilities for global control and for the production of superprofits. Marginality, notwithstanding little economic and political power, has become an increasingly strong presence through the new politics of culture and identity, and an emergent transnational politics embedded in the new geography of economic globalization. Both sets of actors, increasingly transnational and in contestation, find in the city the strategic terrain for their operations.

Note

1 Text of chapter presented at Syracuse University, 'Globalization and the margins', symposium.

References

Allen, John, Massey, Doreen and Pryke, Michael (eds). (1999). *Unsettling cities.* London: Routledge

Body-Gendrot, S. (1999). *Ville et violence.* Paris: Presses Universitaires de France.

Body-Gendrot, Sophie (1999). *Controlling cities.* Oxford: Blackwll.

Castells, M. (1989). *The informational city.* London: Blackwell.

Copjec, Joan and Sorkin, Michael (eds.). (1999). *Giving ground.* London: Verso.

Cordero-Guzman, Hector R., Robert C. Smith and Ramon Grosfoguel (eds). (2001). *Migration, transnationalization and race in a changing New York.* Philadelphia, Pa: Temple University Press.

Dunn, Seamus (ed.). (1994). *Managing divided cities.* Staffs, UK: Keele University Press.

Fincher, Ruth and Jane M. Jacobs (eds). (1998) *Cities of difference.* New York: Guilford Press.

Garcia, D. Linda (2002). "The Architecture of Global Networking Technologies". In Sassen (ed). *Global network/linked cities* (pp. 39–70). New York and London: Routledge

Giddens, A. (1990). *Consequences of Modernity.* Stanford: Stanford University Press.

Graham, S. and J. Marvin (1996). *Telecommunications and the city: Electronic spaces, urban places.* London: Routledge.

Hamilton, Nora and Norma Stoltz Chinchilla (2001). *Seeking community in a global city: Guatemalans and Salvadorans in Los Angeles.* Philadelphia: Temple University Press.

Hondagneu-Sotelo, I. (1995). *Gendered transitions: Mexican experiences of immigration.* Berkeley and Los Angeles: University of California Press.

Journal of Urban Technology. (1995). Special Issue: *Information technologies and inner-city communities.* vol. 3, no. 1 (Fall).

Isin, Engin F. (ed) (2000). *Democracy, citizenship and the global city.* London and New York: Routledge.

King, A. D. (ed.). (1996). *Representing the city. Ethnicity, capital and culture in the 21st century.* New York: New York University Press.

Orum, Anthony and Xianming Chen (2002) *Urban places.* Malden, Ma: Blackwell.

Sassen, Saskia (2000). *Cities in a world economy.* Thousand Oaks, California: Pine Forge/Sage (New Updated Edition of the original 1994 publication).

———. (1998). *Globalization and its discontents.* New York: New Press.

Sennett, R. (1990). *The conscience of the eye.* New York: Norton.

Tardanico, Richard and Maria Lungo (1995). "Local dimensions of global restructuring in urban Costa Rica." *International Journal of Urban and Regional Research* 19 (2): pp. 223–49.

Valle, Victor M. and Rodolfo D. Torres (2000). *Latino metropolis.* Minneapolis, Mn: University of Minnesota Press.

Watson, S. and G. Bridges, (1999). *Spaces of culture.* London: Sage.

3
Opposition and Resistance to Globalization
Roland Robertson

Globalization as a contested symbol

The public discussion of globalization has reached fever pitch. It is virtually impossible, for example, to read a newspaper without encountering this word. Indeed, it is used so frequently in various media that one would think it had a completely obvious meaning; in fact, it does not. When I first began to write about globalization in earnest about twenty years ago, it was not at all a controversial topic. Indeed, to write about globalization at that time was simply innovative: most had not heard of the word (and those who had, thought that it had something to do with a utopian vision of the world as a whole). Moreover, at that time academic work on globalization (not necessarily using that exact term) was more or less confined to a small cluster of disciplines, particularly sociology, anthropology, religious studies, and – to a lesser extent – international relations and political science. The contrast between the situation in the early 1980s and that of the late 1990s is quite dramatic.

The major change that has occurred centers upon the strong tendency during the last ten years or so for public discussion to involve almost exclusive attention to economic – at best, politicoeconomic – aspects of the globalization process. Indeed, for many people, both lay and academic, globalization now apparently *means* the consolidation of the global economy, deregulation, privatization, and neoliberal marketization, even though sociological, anthropological, comparative literature, and other disciplinary work on globalization has blossomed in the 1990s. In the early 1980s, before economists and business studies professionals began to use the term globalization extensively, most theorists of globalization began to strongly oppose the economic reductionism in much of the talk (although world systems analysts in sociology had promoted in the 1970s a primarily economic view of world formation). We can now see that economists are themselves beginning to consider the extraeconomic aspects of globalization (for example, Rodrik, 1997). As I write (February, 1999), the World Economic Forum in Switzerland is concluding. At this gathering many reservations about the supposed benefits of globalization were expressed, notably by the Secretary General of the United Nations. The general thrust of discussion in Switzerland was to warn of the worldwide threats of globalization and the rapid crystallization of a global economy. As Kofi Annan remarked, until more confidence has been built with respect to the global economy it "will be fragile and vulnerable – vulnerable to backlash from all the 'isms' of a post-Cold-War world: protectionism, populism, nationalism, ethnic chauvinism, fanaticism, and terrorism." A similar kind of sentiment was expressed by other participants, including President Mubarak of Egypt, who said that "our global village has caught fire." Mubarak went on to say that there is presently a worldwide "bitter sentiment of injustice, a sense that there must be something wrong with the system that wipes out years of hard-won development because of changes in market sentiment." (The quotations from Annan and Mubarak are taken from the *New York Times,* February 1, 1999, A10.)

This view of a world out of control is one that has emerged particularly from the experience of globalization in the primarily economic, or politicoeconomic, sense. Indeed, some *sociologists* are now writing about the problematic sociocultural consequences of economic globalization (for example, Bauman, 1998). In addition, some ecologists are in the forefront of those opposing or resisting globalization of the global economy; for example, a recent issue of *The Ecologist* (1998) was titled *How to escape the global economy.* Environmental concerns have greatly contributed to the current preoccupation with globality. In spite of all the enthusiasm in favor of the local economy by leading economists and many politicians of the more powerful economic nations, we are now living through a period of backlash. We are in a situation in which economists and business studies leaders have hijacked the idea of globalization, but very recently there has been a lessening of enthusiasm among this group. Many other social scientists have meanwhile continued to consider the issue of globalization in a much more comprehensive sense. In fact, the literature in this respect is vast and growing.

Economism and antiglobality

The analytic consequences of a shift from a multidimensional sociological approach to globalization to the discussion of *economic* globalization – and its sociocultural consequences – are considerable. I consider this move and, at the same time, focus upon ways in which globalization has been, and is, a target of opposition in various forms. To give a simple example: many people now think about antiglobalization sentiment – what has been called "globaphobia" by some economists opposing protectionsism (Burtless *et al.*, 1998) – as involving such phenomena as political reaction against the International Monetary Fund, the World Trade Organization, and the World Bank. Ironically, these are, of course, very large, worldwide bureaucratic organizations, promoting antibureaucratic, free market principles. Another very recent target of antiglobal orientations has been the Multilateral Agreement on Investment, better known as the MAI. The MAI proposal concerns the lowering of barriers to foreign investment in the same way that GATT (General Agreement on Tariffs and Trade) had liberalized international trade. However, the arguments surrounding MAI have turned into what has been called "a virtual battleground" (Kobrin, 1998). In his discussion of recent MAI deliberations, Kobrin makes the important point that many people of different ideological persuasions have "railed against globalization" (cf. Robertson and Khondker, 1998). In doing so, however, "antiglobalization activists and advocacy groups have become transnational actors themselves" (Kobrin, 1998, p. 99).

The significance of the transnationality or internationality of opposition to globalization cannot be overemphasized. It shows that "globality has no mercy" (Robertson, 1992, p. 172). In using the latter phrase, I mean that it is almost impossible to be directly antiglobal without being at the same time global. Antiglobality enhances global consciousness and the more that people express antiglobal views, the more they contribute – unintentionally for the most part – to the mounting sense across the planet of the world-as-a-whole. This is somewhat similar to the way in which antimodern, so-called fundamentalist, movements have during recent times used distinctly modern methods to promote their ideas. Many movements of the antimodern type (which overlap considerably with antiglobal movements) employ very modern organizational designs, forms of fundraising and persuasion, as well as modern technology, particularly new methods of electronic communication.

Antiglobal movements thus increasingly involve transnational collaboration, and transnational or globewide organization enhances global consciousness. Nevertheless it has to be clearly recognized that globaphobia (in a sociological, extraeconomic sense) has been emphatically expressed by religious and other mainly noneconomic movements for the last twenty or more years. A good example is the fundamentalist–evangelical opposition to the encroachment of "alien" cultures and religions and what is often pejoratively called "one-worldism." Indeed the early years of American religious fundamentalism about one hundred years ago was heavily marked by opposition to the importation of what was considered to be non-American culture; that is, massive immigration from Eastern and Southern Europe. This period I have called the take-off phase of modern globalization (Robertson, 1992, pp. 57–60).

Thus, in thinking of antiglobal trends we must bear clearly in mind that they are multidimensional. Such antiglobal developments have been expressed in reference to cultural, political, economic, and other trends, and we can only fully understand globaphobia in these more-than-economic ways. As I have implied, however, the precise term globaphobia was first used by economists in specific reference to the fear of completely open markets.

Contrary to the famous dictum "think globally, act locally," the reality of the present situation seems to be toward thinking locally and acting globally. A particularly good example of global organization for the promotion of the local is the coming together of organizations across the globe concerned with promoting the traditions and ways of life of indigenous peoples, which has greatly accelerated since the United Nations placed the situation and fate of these on its formal agenda in the early 1980s. Another example is provided by the cross-national initiatives undertaken by labor unions; for example, the Union of Needle Trades, Industrial and Textile employees has been engaged in an attempt to acquaint the American public with global factory matters, with particular reference to Central America (Lin, 1998, pp. 190–91). Similar developments are to be seen with respect to the environment, as in the case of Greenpeace. Ritchie (1996, p. 495) has written that "although global organizing goes as far back as the worldwide antislavery movement of the 1800s, the emergence of widespread cross-border organizing, networking, and coalition building has developed in the last twenty years in direct response to the globalized economy." In saying this, he undoubtedly exaggerates. In any case, in his discussion of the international movement against NAFTA (North American Free Trade Agreement) and GATT, Ritchie remarks that what he calls local–local relations (transnational relations) are often more productive than are those developed between national organizations. It is important, then, to fully recognize that in speaking of antiglobal movements one has to bear in mind that to be as effective as possible much opposition to globalization must be globally organized.

To develop as fully as possible the theme of antiglobalism (to use the pejorative term employed by many antiglobal movements), I must provide a short sketch of my approach to globalization. As I have said, my approach is multidimensional, which means that I regard dimensions of globalization as being, in principle, equal. I do not consider the economic to be a privileged feature. The same applies to political, cultural, and other conceivable dimensions, even though in my own work I have very frequently given special attention to cultural perspectives. My main, but not sole, reason for attending so strongly to culture has been that it was greatly neglected by world systems sociologists. Most of them had in fact talked almost exclusively about the making of the capitalistic world as a whole; although the founder of the world systems school, Wallerstein, has become increasingly interested in cultural matters, to the chagrin of some of his colleagues. In other words, I have been trying to correct an overemphasis on economic aspects, without denying that economic factors have been crucial in propelling the globalization process over a number of centuries. Rather like Max Weber, who wrote his *Protestant Ethic and the Spirit of Capitalism* (1958) at the beginning of the twentieth century in an effort to reduce the one-sidedness of the account of Karl Marx, so I have tried to insert some balance with respect to globalization. Weber claimed that he was seeking to provide a psychocultural account that was just as effective as the highly materialist argument of Marx; but Weber did not claim that the account provided in his famous thesis was the entire story. In fact, he reserved for later a more complete and multi-dimensional analysis of the rise of modern capitalism (Weber, 1961).

I have insisted that globalization must be regarded as a very long his-torical process, going back at the very least to the so-called Axial Period, a term coined by the German philosopher Karl Jaspers to refer to the almost simultaneous rise of the great world religions about 2000 years ago. Thus, contrary to the writings and discussion of many con-temporary commentators, I do not see how, other than by pure con-vention, we can possibly confine the globalization process to the last few decades. In the course of elaborating my own theory of globaliza-tion (Robertson, 1992) I have had occasion to pinpoint the major refer-ence points of the globalization process regardless of whether we are talking about culture, politics, economics, or any other feature of the human condition. These reference points, I have argued, are the nation–state; the self; international relations; and humankind. I have argued that these constitute the very basic touchstones, and over recent centuries the concrete "components", of the human condition. Along these lines, I have attempted to specify the forms in which antiglobal movements have developed (Hannerz, 1996, 92–5 Robertson, 1992, pp. 61–84;).

Undoubtedly, the most comprehensive type of opposition to the present nature of the global scene is that provided some years ago by Wallerstein (for example, 1982; cf. Robertson, 1992, pp. 60–84) who, in his writings, touched on the theme of what he called antisystemic movements. These are movements seeking to eliminate the "metaphysical presuppositions" of the modern world system. There does seem by now an extensive worldwide series of independent, but overlapping, movements expressing considerable militant opposition to the ethos of what Wallerstein calls the modern world-system. Undoubtedly, a great deal of this worldwide opposition has been created by the perceived negative consequences of globalization in the neoliberal economic sense, as well as of "the new world order" of alleged American design. In this regard, it is necessary to say that when we speak of economic globalization it does not require that we equate this idea with marketization, deregulation, privatization, and so on. In principle, the notion of economic globalization could just as meaningfully refer to the linking or integration of socialist economies on a worldwide basis. Nevertheless, globalization is indeed thought of around much of the world as involving capitalistic developments. (This was certainly not a central theme in my own early writings on globalization – nor is it now, except that I presently feel obliged to write about it, mainly in a critical way.)

It is frequently stated that globalization is an American phenomenon – indeed, that it is a form of Americanization. I myself thoroughly object to this thesis; what is generally neglected in such discussion is that American society is replete with various forms, some of them extremely militant, of antiglobal sentiment. One has only to think of the opposition to the new world order or the apocalyptic opposition to global phenomena found in the Militia movement. Other examples would include some labor unions, Buchananites, and a number of religious movements and people who stress that communal, local life is the most viable and moral way of living (Robertson, 1997). One should also recall that various school systems have been pressured into expressing in pedagogical terms the superiority of American culture. Nor should one neglect the recent strength of anti-immigration sentiment in the United States and other societies. And although this seems to be fading somewhat, there is a considerable decline of interest in news from and about other countries in US newspapers and other media. To give just two examples: CNN, which proudly proclaims its global focus, had 70 correspondents covering the O. J. Simpson trial and devoted 630 hours of viewing time to it, even though Simpson was at the outset hardly known outside the United States; in 1987 *Time* devoted eleven of its cover stories to international news, while ten years later, in 1997, there was only one (Halimi, 1998). In sharp contrast, US and European business schools are putting increasing emphasis on international or global issues (Weinstein, 1997).

While I have not studied in any detail antiglobal movements and trends in countries other than the United States (although I am not unfamiliar with such phenomena), it seems to be that the United States is, ironically, the home of so-called antiglobalism. Thus, when we find leaders of governments and NGOs outside the United States speaking in a mixture of antiglobal and anti-American rhetoric, we should remember that in the United States itself there is probably as much, if not more, antiglobal sentiment than in those other countries. The conclusion to be drawn from this is that the United States may have much to teach the rest of the world about opposition to globalization! This idea, of course, stands in an uneasy relationship to the proposition that American cultural imperialism is leading to the homogenization of world culture.

The homogenization thesis and antiglobality

In addressing directly oppositional movements relating to globalization, it is necessary to emphasize that perhaps the most frequently expressed opposition is in support of so-called indigenous or national culture, identity, and tradition. Much of the concern with the preservation of these has resulted from "the invention of tradition" (Hobsbawm and Ranger, 1983). Although the subject of the invention of tradition during the nineteenth and early twentieth centuries cannot be discussed at any length here, we must be conscious of it, because the idea of the invention, or construction, of tradition raises important and problematic questions about authenticity. We have heard much during the last twenty years or so about the contamination, or even the destruction, of "native" cultures by the processes of globalization. This perceived threat to the purity of local culture is not simply a matter of a global culture destroying local cultures, for economic, political, and media processes have played a crucial role in the crystallization of this perception. The concern with the preservation of allegedly indigenous cultures has in a sense been simply cultural, but other dimensions of the globalization process are involved.

One of the most controversial issues in the debate about globalization and related matters is whether global culture is becoming more homogeneous or more heterogeneous. Some people see the world as a whole as being in the grips of a conflict or contradiction between homogenizing and difference-inducing forces. Barber (1995), most notably, expresses this with his well-known phrase "Jihad vs. McWorld." On the whole, Barber's thesis has to be placed, nonetheless, in the homogenizing camp. The homogenizing view is expressed particularly strongly in the writings of Ritzer (for example, 1996). This alleged homogenization into a kind of global culture is the target of much opposition around the world. (This debate has led to much discussion of what is meant by the term culture, with a number of anthropologists and sociologists emphasizing the essentially *contested* nature of culture.) A number of scholars, however, are writing persuasively against the homogenization thesis. One particularly good recent example is the book edited by Watson (1997) entitled *Golden Arches East: McDonald's in East Asia* (see also, *inter alia*, Robertson, 1995; Tomlinson, 1991; Hannerz, 1996, pp. 56–64). The contributors to this book, notably Watson himself, emphasize that McDonald's is a vehicle for *localization* and for the consolidation of sociocultural difference. The same point is made in more strictly business terms by Barboza in his newspaper article entitled "Pluralism under Golden Arches" (1999). Somewhat paradoxically, students of global marketing and advertising are particularly conscious of the phenomenon of glo*cal*ization (Robertson, 1995; de Mooij, 1998). The adaptation of global goods and services to local – including national – circumstances is the crucial issue here.

Global variety

The view to which I subscribe – namely that globalization is a difference-enhancing process – is one which would take us too far from the main theme of this book. However, it is worth repeating an argument that I have made on a number of other occasions; namely, in the contemporary world there is increasingly a near-global expectation of difference and uniqueness. We live in a world where there has been a virtual institutionalization, on a global basis, of difference, ranging from differences among national identities to those among personal identities. This development makes it something of a puzzle as to why there should be so much opposition or resistance to globalization on the grounds that it homogenizes. In due course, perhaps, people generally will come to realize that globalization does not mean homogenization or standardization anywhere near to the extent elleged by this view. What we now have is difference-within-sameness (Robertson, 1995) meaning, *inter alia,* that there are trends in both directions, each facilitating the other.

Having said this, I must emphasize that there are indeed negative consequences of globalization, particularly in its economic sense. Undoubtedly, globalization, particularly via the policies and demands of the IMF (International Monetary Fund) and other supranational agencies, has brought, and is still bringing, an intensification of inequality in a number of countries. Not infrequently the IMF demands that – as is currently the case in Brazil – welfare spending to be greatly reduced, as well as expenditures on various projects affecting the quality of life of the already poverty stricken as well as the middle class. We have seen in recent years much protest against globewide agencies like the IMF both from grassroots movements and from intellectuals. The attitudes exhibited in these antiglobal projects are, as I have emphasized, consolidating globewide antiglobality. Here, however, is the great irony that I have already touched upon. It could be said that these protests from the margins are, when all is said and done, an aspect of the process of globalization. One can say this only if adhering to a comprehensive, multidimensional – as opposed to a simply economic – conception of globalization. In other words, were one to think of globalization as increasingly open markets, deregulation, and so forth, then protests from the margins and other sources could not safely be classified as aspects of the globalization process.

The view advanced in this chapter is that globalization consists of both the compression of the world as a whole in a number of different ways *and* the rapidly increasing consciousness of the world. In this light, antiglobality can be just as much an aspect of globalization as the more restricted conceptions of globalization of economists, journalists, and a number of politicians and intellectuals. I do not wish to press this point too hard, but it is certainly worth reflecting upon the possibility that marginality is a significant feature of contemporary globality. There are most definitely exploited people across the world at the margins of contemporary society, but this observation should not lead to a simplistic conception of globalization producing sets of people or societies unambiguously at the margin or, as some would say, the periphery.

Particularly relevant are the very significant cultural flows from the periphery to the center. I think especially of cuisine, of which the flow from the periphery is increasingly evident all over the northern hemisphere; that flow is evident as well in the areas of music, fashion–including models–art, alternative medicine, religious practices, and so on. Although there may be clear-cut marginality with respect to socioeconomic phenomena, this is not the case with these cultural phenomena. In fact, an argument could well be made that simply as far as cuisine is concerned the flow from the so-called Third World is just as significant globally as the alleged homogenizing consequences of McDonald's, Kentucky Fried Chicken, and Coca Cola. Indian, Thai, Japanese, Moroccan, Afghan, and other "exotic" foods have made great inroads into Western/Northern cuisine, not to speak of the inroads previously made by Italian and Chinese cuisines.

Of great significance also is the flow of religiosity to Europe and English-speaking North America from other parts of the world, notably from Asia and Islamic countries. Although much studied by scholars of religion, this flow takes a somewhat different direction when we look at the various religious "cults" that have developed in recent times in Brazil, especially in Brasilia. As Brazil's recession has deepened, its unemployment risen, and its financial system destabilized, religious "cults" have become increasingly evident. While this may have something to do with the changing millennium and the idea that Brasilia will be the capital of the Third Millennium, there seems little doubt that the financial crisis has contributed to the remarkable increase in religiosity (Scoffield, 1999). (It should be said that this idea has some opponents in Brazil on the grounds that it is an allegedly Marxist viewpoint.)

One should not, of course, equate antiglobality or antiglobalization with marginality. There are many developments in the contemporary world, as we have already seen, that could well be classified as antiglobal which are not driven by the interests of the oppressed. Take again the example of the rapidly declining concern with news of other parts of the world in US newspapers and television news programs. The precipitous decline in the column inches of US newspapers devoted to non-US affairs in recent years may show the United States to be one of the most isolated countries in the entire world. The decline is to a considerable extent a reaction of owners and editors of newspapers to the tastes of the populace at large (determined largely through surveys). There is, then, a contribution from the margins within the United States to this disinterest as expressed in various forms of journalism. It is, in any case, a very striking feature of the contemporary world that in what is widely regarded as the dominant country there is rapidly declining focus upon the rest of the world. The United States is a marginal country in other aspects of life as well, including its enthusiasm for capital punishment and violence generally, although violent US movies find fascinated audiences in other parts of the world. Thus, the issue of antiglobalization and antiglobality, not to speak of marginality and peripherality, is complex.

Concluding remarks

I have not dealt here with the vital issue of the contemporary resurgence of nationalism. I can only say that the dichotomy and antagonistic relationship between nationalism and globalization has been greatly exaggerated. Nationalism grew in the nineteenth century as an *international* phenomenon, while the twentieth-century nation–state gained ground as an aspect of what Meyer (for example, 1980) has called world political culture. This is by no means to say that modern nationalism is not, at least partly, driven by protectionist antiglobality, but it is an issue of great complexity. We should recall that the institutionalization of the notion of national self-determination has been, since the mid-nineteenth century, a *global* phenomenon. The relationship between globality and nationalism is not unlike that between global and local ecology. As Sachs (1993, p. xvii) has written, "global ecology can easily be at odds with local ecologies, since global resource planning protects nature as environment around the economy, while local conservation efforts protect nature around the home." Here again we find the local being clearly opposed to the global, without any recognition of the possibility that the local is globally produced (Appaduri, 1996, pp. 178–99; Robertson, 1995).

Since the preceeding was written in early 1999, there have been numerous developments that would appear to have confirmed my arguments. Here I can only draw attention to some of the most salient. First, much more clearly than before, there has emerged in various parts of the world a strong "anti-globalization" movement, particularly since the demonstrations directed at, or surrounding, the meetings of the World Trade Organization (WTO) in Seattle at the very end of 1999. This movement is not, by any means, unified. Rather, it is very diffuse, drawing in groups of people from various countries with different agendas.

Second, there has been a concomitant surge of books, articles, TV and radio commentaries, Internet and web communication concerning anti-globalization – a notion which, although still used (in 2001), is in some quarters being replaced by the very interesting idea of "globalization from below," the latter being closely related to themes of global, postnational, or transnational citizenship, on the one hand, and global or transnational governance, on the other.

Third, even though the forgiveness of Third World debt has been central to the much reported demonstrations in North and South America, Europe, East Asia and elsewhere, concrete targets have included not only the WTO but also the World Bank, the International Monetary Fund (IMF), the World Economic Forum, and various transnational corporations (notably, of course, McDonald's, but also Nike, Starbucks, Gap, and so on). Of particular significance has been hostility towards pharmaceutical corporations concerning the latter's resistance – now overcome – to allowing relatively cheap anti-AIDS drugs to be sold in South Africa. Much more broadly, "global capitalism" has been the focus of considerable opposition. The September attacks on the World Trade Center and the Pentagon are striking examples of the assault on the symbols of global power.

Fourth, much of the fight against globalization, or "globalization from above," in the somewhat, but not entirely, reductionist manner that it has taken, has increasingly included opposition to environmental degradation, the crushing of local cultural variety, and so on. To put this another way, a significant element of the diffuse movement against globalization ("from above") has in fact *broadened* the conception of globalization so as to include not only dimensions other than the economic – the cultural, the political, the social-communicative, and so on – but also individuals, localities, and other "small scale" phenomena.

It is in the latter respect that there has been a "reconciliation" between the early-1980s academic conception of globalization (that was very anti-economic-reductionist) and the shape that globalization-from-below movements have taken in recent years. For the leaders and activists involved in these have come to realize that the scope of their objections to "globalization" is inadequately expressed in the sloganic form of "anti-globalization." Rather quickly, "being anti-global" has in creasis become recognized by many as being oxymoronic. One cannot "be" anti-global without simultaneously global.

Finally, a word about the relationship between globalization and Americanization. The equation of these two motifs is very common. However, to put it all too polemically at this point, this equation is, emphatically, *wrong* – unless we all want to play the role of victim and to subscribe, unthinkingly, to the (mainly right-wing) American thesis that this century too is an American century. Besides being grotesquely unfair and insulting to millions of US citizens or residents, just a little historical knowledge will inform us of the indisputable fact that the USA was itself *born* out of the globalization process and that, in a number of respects, still remains relatively marginal to the mainstream of global change.

References

Appaduri, A. (1996). *Modernity at large*. Minneapolis: University of Minnesota Press.

Barber, B. (1995). *Jihad vs. McWorld: How globalism and tribalism are reshaping the world*. New York: Ballantine Books.

Barboza, D. (1999). "Pluralism under golden arches." *New York Times,* February 12: C1, C7.

Bauman, Z. (1998). *Globalization: The human consequences,* New York: Columbia University Press.

Burtless, G., R. Lawrence, R. Litan, and R. Shapiro (1998). *Globaphobia: Confronting fears about open trade*. Washington, DC: Brookings Institution Press.

de Mooij, M. (1998). *Global marketing and advertising: Understanding cultural paradoxes,* Thousand Oaks, California: Sage.

Ecologist. (1998). Special Issue: *How to escape the global economy,* 28 (no. 4) July/August.

Halimi, S. (1998). "Myopic and cheapskate journalism." *Guardian Weekly (Le Monde diplomatique),* November: 14–15.

Hannerz, U. (1996). *Transnational connections: Cultures, people, places*. London: Routledge.

Hobsbawm, E. and T. Ranger. (eds.). (1983). *The invention of tradition*. Cambridge: Cambridge University Press.

Kobrin, S. J. (1998). "The MAI and the clash of globalizations." *Foreign Policy* 112 (Fall): pp. 97–109.

Lin, J. (1998). *Reconstructing Chinatown: Ethnic enclave, global change*. Minneapolis: University of Minnesota Press.

Meyer, J. W. (1980). "The world polity and the authority of the nation–state." In A. Bergesen, (ed.). *Studies of the modern world system* (pp. 109–37). New York: Academic Press.

Nettl, J. P. and R. Robertson (1968). *International systems and the modernization of societies: The formation of national goals and attitudes*. London: Faber/New York: Basic Books.

Ritchie, M. (1996). "Cross-Border organizing." In J. Mander and E. Goldsmith (eds.). *The case against the global economy and for a turn toward the local* (pp. 494–500). San Francisco: Sierra Club Books.

Ritzer, G. (1996). *The McDonaldization of society*. Thousand Oaks, California: Pine Forge Press.

Robertson, R. (1997). "Values and globalization: Communitarianism and global-ity." In L. E. Soares (ed.). *Identity, culture and globalization* (pp. 73–97). Rio de Janeiro: UNESCO.

———. (1995). "Globalization: Time–space and homogeneity–heterogeneity." In M. Featherstone, S. Lash, and R. Robertson (eds.). *Global modernities* (pp. 25–44). London: Sage.

———. (1992). *Globalization: Social theory and global culture.* London: Sage.

Roberston, R. and H. H. Khondker, (1998). "Discourses of globalization: Preliminary considerations." *International Sociology* 13 (1): pp. 25–40.

Rodrik, D. (1997). *Has globalization gone too far?* Washington, DC: Institute for International Economics.

Sachs, W. (1993). "Introduction." In W. Sachs (ed.). *Global ecology: A new arena of political conflict* (p. xvii). London: Zed Books.

Scoffield, H. (1999). "Battered Brazil's spiritual hotbed." *Globe and Mail,* February 9: pp. 1, 13.

Tomlinson, J. (1991). *Cultural imperialism.* Baltimore: Johns Hopkins University Press.

Wallerstein, I. (1982). "Crisis as transitions." In S. Amin, G. Arrighi, A. G. Frank, and I. Wallerstein (eds.). *Dynamics of global crisis.* New York: Monthly Review Press.

Watson, J. L. (ed.). (1997). *Golden arches east: McDonald's in East Asia.* Stanford: Stanford University Press.

Weber, M. (1958). *The Protestant ethic and the spirit of capitalism.* New York: Charles Scribner's Sons.

———. (1961). *General economic history.* New York: Collier Books.

Weinstein, S. (1997). "Globalization: Here to stay." *International Herald Tribune,* May 19: p. 18.

4
Subduing Globalization: The Challenge of the Indigenization Movement

Mehrzad Boroujerdi

More than two decades ago, Stanley Hoffmann described the discipline of international relations (IR) as a peculiarly "American social science" (Hoffmann, 1977). He maintained that, traditionally, analysis of the international system had been equated with the study of US foreign policy – not surprising us, given that scholars residing in the United States do much of the theorizing in IR. Ironically, however, IR scholars continue to view their discipline as a "global" social science within which theories and research methodologies can supposedly travel from one culture and location to others with little difficulty. Of late, postmodernist IR theorists have questioned the notion of IR as a "global" social science, insisting that all scholarship is radically situated within cultural and temporal frameworks. Postmodernists claim that there is no neutral vantage point or absolute standard of scientific objectivity from which scholars can observe human behavior.

Meanwhile, another emerging body of literature, not necessarily always in tune with postmodernism, has also challenged IR in particular, and Euro-American-centered social sciences in general. I refer here to the authors of this literature as members of the "indigenization" movement. Proponents of indigenization argue that Eurocentric premises have, alas, colonized the social sciences and, in turn, helped to secure and perpetuate a Western-dominated world order. They argue that Third World intellectuals have to be wary of "Western," disguised as "universal," theories and research methodologies in the social sciences. Proponents of the indigenization have also attacked such cherished assumptions and axiomatic principles of Western philosophy as objective reason, humanism, the idea of progress, culture-transcending knowledge, and the radical dualism between religion and science. They maintain that social scientists in the Third World should generate and use concepts and theories rooted in indigenous intellectual traditions, historical experiences, and cultural practices to explain in a more comprehensive fashion the worldviews, sociohistorical contexts, and scholarship of their people.[1] Indigenization theorists maintain that social science is universal in so far as concepts and theories developed in one civilization are available to scholars in another civilization. However, they caution that we should not confuse universalization with generalization[2] and that we should aspire to make social sciences more transcultural.

The brazen nature of indigenization scholars' attacks on Western scholarship, combined with Euro-American scholars' intellectual arrogance, has not endeared the former to Western academic circles. In fact, some Western opponents of knowledge indigenization have branded this movement as apologetic, chauvinist, essentialist, ideological, antimodern, particularistic, and xenophobic. I argue that the project of knowledge indigenization should not be readily dismissed as obscurantism, atavism, militant particularism, or an invidious and compulsive tendency to fetishize and celebrate difference. Instead, I maintain that it is a largely genuine, albeit conflict-ridden, project by partisans of erstwhile civilizations seeking to end their condition of intellectual docility while negotiating with a compulsive and restless modernity. By looking at the ideological efficacy and travails of the indigenization project, I demonstrate how Third World intellectuals form their own discursive repertoire, not wanting to be a prolegomenon to Western philosophy. As a case study, I briefly survey the "Islamization of knowledge" as one such enterprise.

Indigenization: historical battle cry for third world scholars

The calls of Third World thinkers for knowledge indigenization came on the heels of demands for political independence and cultural authenticity during the post–World War II era. A host of movements – for example, Rastafaris and Négritude – and activist intellectuals – such as Samir Amin, Aimé Césaire, Frantz Fanon, C. L. R. James, Albert Memmi, and Léopold Sédar Senghor – argued that "intellectual decolonization" must accompany political liberation if the Third World is not to remain a nodal point on the Western imperialist map. The rise of "Third Worldism," starting in the mid-1950s, strengthened the calls for cultural authenticity because mimicry and submission were considered fraudulent and counterfeit modes of existence. Hence, the "decoloniza-tion" of Egyptian, Ghanaian, Indian, Indonesian, and numerous other national histories and historiographies began in earnest with much fanfare and vociferous rhetoric.

In 1972, Malaysian scholar Syed Hussein Alatas lamented the "captive mind" of Third World social scientists, defining it as "the product of higher institutions of learning, either at home or abroad, whose way of thinking is dominated by Western thought in an imitative and uncriti-cal manner" (Alatas, 1993, p. 691). He contended that Asians needed to create their own autonomous social science tradition. A few years later one of Alatas's counterparts in India, C. T. Kurien, wrote:

> We are neither Asian nor scientists. Our knowledge about the prob-lems of our own societies is largely bookish, and the books that we read are mainly from the West ... . We are beggars, all of us – we sneak under many an academic table to gather the crumbs under them. And we mix these bits and make a hash which we pretend to relish, but which we can hardly digest. We have hardly made a con-tribution to academic cuisine, and have thought it impossible to prepare a dish of our own, with a recipe we have made, using ingre-dients we have (cited in Atal, 1981, p. 191).

Such developments as the precipitous decline of Third Worldist soli-darity, the end of the Cold War, and the swift globalization of capital-ism and modernity have moderated the rhetoric of authenticity and indigenization movements. Yet the indigenization movement has not fallen into the dustbin of history; on the contrary, at a time when all cultures are experiencing the impact of globalization – the expansion of financial markets, the growing importance of information technol-ogy, and soon – the calls for knowledge indigenization and cultural authenticity are intensifying. While the global commodification of culture tends to homogenize the particulars, a robust countermove-ment of local identity politics is concurrently rising. As Third World societies try to engage, finesse, or incorporate Western modernity into their everyday life practices, they simultaneously alter that modernity by drawing upon their own reservoir of "cultural capital" and "habitus" (Bourdieu, 1977).[3] Because the prerequisite for the realization of the ethos of Western modernity is the loss of non-Western peoples' former ontological identity, globalization and local resistance(s) to the process often go hand in hand.

Knowledge indigenization: the project's utility

The movement to indigenize knowledge raises the following questions:
(1) Is indigenization of knowledge a pernicious intellectual project? (2)
How legitimate are the non-Western charges against the precepts and
ethos of the meta-narrative of Euro-American–centered social sciences?
(3) Should criticisms of Eurocentric ideologies lead to incrimination of
Enlightenment principles or actual realization of some of them? (4)
How have non-Western intellectuals historicized and delimited
Western thought? (5) Have Third World intellectuals formulated judi-
cious "indigenous" epistemological principles in such fields as anthropology, economics, political science, psychology, and sociology?
Finally, (6) what are some of the obstacles to knowledge indigenization
in the Third World? The brevity of this chapter does not allow me to
address all these questions; in fact, I shall tackle these issues in a book
about the sociology of social sciences in the Third World. For now, I
focus on the definition of indigenization, the rationale for this movement, the risks involved in this project, and its limitations.

According to Syed Farid Alatas,

> The call to indigenization does not simply suggest approaching
> specifically indigenous problems in a social scientific manner with a
> view to developing suitable concepts and methods, and modifying
> what has been developed in Western settings. It goes beyond this
> and refers to the idea that social scientific theories, concepts, and
> methodologies can be derived from the histories and cultures of the
> various non-Western civilizations (1993, p. 309).

The calls for indigenization gained particular momentum during the
1970s when numerous African, Asian, Latin American, and Middle
Eastern intellectuals argued that Western culture and social sciences are
not the only relevant and valid models. These intellectuals sought to
narrate their respective societies' historical trajectories by developing a
new conceptual vocabulary rooted in their own local conditions,
needs, practices, and problems – yet obviously mediated through their
exposure to the West. As dependency theorists (for example Amin,
1976; Baran, 1957; Frank, 1969) and advocates of the New
International Economic Order (NIEO) attacked the assumptions and
arguments of modernization theory in the 1970s, Third World intellectuals called for an end to the sociocultural subjugation of Africa, Asia,
Latin America, and the Middle East. Years of Western intellectual impe-

rialism had produced a predominantly borrowed consciousness that rendered most social sciences esoteric and irrelevant in much of the Third World. As such, social scientists could play at best an ancillary role in Third World societies; typically, however, the masses regarded social scientists as alienated from local realities.

Advocates of knowledge indigenization insisted that they did not see themselves through the Western gaze or mirror which had reduced them to mere echoes of American, British, and French scholarship under the false pretense of scientific universality. Intellectuals in the Third World had to focus on the historical and cultural specificities of their societies to offer theories and research methods reflective of their own goals, worldviews, and sociocultural experience. Responding to those skeptics who denounced this "self-awareness" as too subjective, the proponents of knowledge indigenization questioned the totalizing master narrative of Western modernity, which is based on an East–West binary construction, and the disguised partiality of Western science. These advocates claim that they have the right to criticize the ideals, norms, and prescriptions of Western social scientists, who are the children of the Enlightenment. Third World intellectuals maintain that while "selective" and "constructive" integration of Western sciences is perfectly legitimate, one should not lose sight of the inherent ethnocentrism of Western academicians and their analysis.[4] Furthermore, these intellectuals underscore the intersubjective meanings between Western and non-Western settings that must not be minimized if social sciences are to become truly intercultural. Finally, the advocates of indigenization assert that like charity, social scientific research should begin at home. When local social scientists analyze their own realities, they expand both the substance and methodologies of their disciplines, offering alternative perspectives on human behavior.

While knowledge indigenization is fraught with epistemological difficulties and marked by vitriolic rhetoric, I cannot dismiss this project as a homogeneously rhetorical plot by Third World demagogues. Central to the indigenization project are qualms about such pillars of Western intellectual tradition as objective reality, universal rationality and value-free science. Ironically, Western thinkers have raised similar objections, inspiring – albeit perhaps inadvertently – their counterparts in the Third World. For example, Peter Winch (1958) argued that various societies have different standards of "rationality." Roy Mottahedeh (1985) described "reason" as "a notorious weasel word [which] appears to designate a sanitized, universal area of discourse and yet in practice turns out to be as culturally determined and idiosyncratic [to say nothing of its gendered nature] as most of our ideas." As for the neutrality of science, the collective works of Jurgen Habermas and the Frankfurt School theorists demonstrate that all knowledge is rooted in some underlying interest or ideology. In addition, Michel Foucault and postmodernist scholars substantiate the claim that social sciences are not power-free, value-free, or interest-free.

The proponents of indigenization remind scholars: (a) that, in science, they need to distinguish the universal from the particular; (b) that while the aim and method of science may be uniform throughout the world, its relation to society is not; (c) that what constitutes science at a given period is determined by the prevailing system of values; and (d) that the radical dualisms of body and soul, fact and value, reason and faith so central to Western ontology and epistemology are not universally shared.[5] In other words, the protestation of positivists notwithstanding, indigenization theorists object to the scientism and epistemological/methodological imperialism of Western sciences. For example, a group of cross-cultural psychologists from the United States, New Zealand, Turkey, and India have maintained that instead of "thinking globally, acting locally," American psychology is largely "thinking locally, acting globally." The strong commitments of Western psychology to foundationalism, empiricism, and the model of the self-contained individual often leads to the negation or ignorance of the "local intelligibilities" of non-Westerners. Significantly, these psychologists have concluded:

> We see particular dangers inhering in the traditional attempt to establish culture free knowledge of human functioning regardless of the particular methods chosen for study. Not only do such attempts obscure or denigrate myriad traditions, in favor of the culture which "calls the truth." But, such inquiry does not appear to have significant promise in terms of the enormous practical problems confronting the world–both in local and international terms. Theories and methods with a strong grounding in or applicability to practical contexts are much to be sought (Gergen *et al.* 2001).

Contrary to the prophecy of modernization theorists, who contended that a priori identities (ethnic, religious, linguistic, and so forth) would dissipate with exposure to "the West," these identities have endured. Western social scientists must recognize and read the self-reflexive narrative of scholars seeking to build between cultures. Ignoring these narrative in fact reduces the explanatory power of Western social science.

Worse yet, to underestimate non-Western scholars while the latter become increasingly self-assured and assertive in articulating their own historical narratives runs the risk of turning the principles of "intercultural interchange" and the "global village" into mere slogans. Humanity has overcome the condition of "historical pseudomorphosis" (Spengler, 1939) – that situation in which an older alien culture's extensive hegemony hampers a young indigenous culture from developing self-consciousness. As Fred Dallmayr (1996) contends, humanity is in dire need of a new mode of cross-cultural encounter based on a "deconstructive dialogue or a hermeneutics of difference which respects otherness beyond assimilation."

Finally, a number of indigenization theorists pose the following questions: To what extent should reason and its corresponding values and goals be considered globally uniform and universal considering the absence of ideological syncretism or ecumenical brotherhood in the world today?[6] Even if reason were perceived as universal, to what extent should scholars embrace the scientific analysis that flows from reason without compromising cultural authenticity and specificity? Western thinkers such as Rousseau, Nietzsche, Heidegger, Sartre, Gramsci, and Kierkegaard would not favor the loss of authenticity, for they championed in one way or another the "be yourself" motto of authenticity. As Daniel J. Boorstin, former Librarian of Congress, inquires:

> Can such an idea [the idea of progress], that grew from distinctively Western memory, experience, and imagination, take root and flourish elsewhere? Can it be credible in parts of the world that do not share the Judeo-Christian belief in a Creator God, a God of Novelty, and in a Creator Man, Apostle of Novelty? Can the idea of progress survive in societies that lack the melodramatic Western triumphs of science and technology? Can people be expected to share the intellectual product when they had not shared the process from which it came? ... Would we not, perhaps, profit more from the diversity of human experience if we encouraged all people to make their own metaphor? (Boorstin, 1993, p. 60).

Risks and limitations of indigenization: the islamic experiment

The process of retrieving heritage while at the same time reckoning with modernity has rendered the knowledge indigenization project at once heroic and disjunctive. Yet hauteur toward the indigenization project should not necessarily translate into a blind acceptance of its fetishism of difference, cult of authenticity, or rancorous rhetoric. The efforts of certain indigenization theorists to short-circuit modernity through recourse to historical amnesia, exaltation of plebeian values, and invidious polarizing is ill advised. Nor is "nativism" – the doctrine calling for the resurgence, reinstatement, or continuance of native or indigenous cultural customs, beliefs, and values especially in opposition to acculturation – a viable alternative to a modernity that has been simultaneously prodigious and perfidious (elaborated on in Boroujerdi, 1996). In other words, countering the counterfeit "universalism" of the West can no longer be accomplished by embracing an arbitrary and intolerant "particularism."

We can take as an example the Islamization of knowledge presently pursued by various Muslim intellectuals who present Islam as a faith for all seasons: it is an endeavor riven by epistemological flaws.[7] The hybrid which results from mutation of Islam into an ideology supposedly capable of guiding Muslims, through a shortcut, to the blessed land of an indigenous postmodern enlightenment often produces nothing but "cultural schizophrenia" (Shayegan, 1997). While Islamization of knowledge is an effort by Muslim intellectuals not to suffocate in a secularist universe, where the commodification of everyday life is threatening the tenets of faith,[8] the thought of religiously sanctioned social sciences is disturbing.[9]

More troubling is that the ardent appeals for Islamization have not produced rigorous theoretical alternatives to Western social sciences. Besides parochial and pedestrian critiques of Western models, and essentialist or indigenously ethnocentric alternatives, there is not much there. "Islamic economics," for example, is nothing but neoclassical economic theory in religious guise. Developing an authentically Islamic theory of sociohistorical change – not to speak of actual political practice based on such a new idea – has been extremely difficult. (For expositions and discussions of such efforts, see Lee, 1997; Mutahhari, 1986; Safi, 1994.)

I do not wish to suggest that all Muslim intellectuals have wholeheartedly embraced the Islamization of knowledge project; far from it, many have become rather critical of this whole endeavor. For example, a leading contemporary Iranian intellectual considers the attempt of the Muslim new Aristotelians to Islamicize sociology, economics, and law to be rather futile. He writes:

> Water, for example, has a peculiar structure and essence. As such, we do not have religious and non-religious water or religious and

non-religious wine. The same is true for justice, government, science, and philosophy. Even if these subjects were to have an essence then their Islamization would be rather meaningless. As such we can not have a science of sociology that is essentially religious or a philosophy that is essentially Islamic or Christian, the same way we can not have a system of government that is essentially religious (Sorush, 1995, p. 11).

In short, for the time being, to speak of indigenizing the substance of various social sciences is possible. However, I am skeptical about efforts to formulate an indigenous social science "methodology" because this entails altering and presumably improving the very logic of inquiry. Making allowance for the distinction between substance and methodology may expedite the closure of the Third World's scientific and technological gap with the West. In this way, Third World intellectuals may pursue a homegrown rereading of sciences and redefine separate paths to development without resorting to invidious language, engaging demagogy, and stigmatizing the 'other'.

Notes

1 For example, the ideas of the fourteenth century Arab historical sociologist Ibn Khaldun on the rise and fall of states, Amin's "tributary mode of production," "the rentier-state" argument, and Asiatic mode of production.
2 We should remember Raymond Williams's idea of "keywords" (words whose meanings change over time and differ across cultures). For example, some of the keywords in the liberal lexicon ("Liberalism," "individualism," "equality" "democracy," and "civilization") can be contested. Democracy may be a universal concept, but its specific applicability often is not. You can have democracy in a Lockean form (checks and balances), as in Britain and the United States, or in a Rousseauian form (organic, centralized, unified rule), as in France or Latin America.
3 For example, the neo-Confucian cultural movement of Asia stresses the ethics of the bureaucratic public sphere by extracting from the cherished ideals of the family. The movement considers the individual an instrument of the group rather than an autonomous agent.
4 For example, during the 1970s, estimates put the number of American political scientist at 75 percent of the total worldwide. Similarly, Susan Strange maintains that in 1971, nine-tenths of the world's living economists were Americans (Strange, 1971, p. 223).
5 The cosmopolitanism of Diderot – who believed that without the unity of physics, ethics and poetry humans face a new "barbarianism" – exemplifies a Western idea not universally shared.

6   As I have argued elsewhere (Boroujerdi, 1997), Francis Fukuyama's argument (1992) that the growing appeal of economic and political liberalism in the Third World is tantamount to the "end of history" is shortsighted.

7   For two such examples, see Moten, 1996 and the International Institute of Islamic Thought, 1989.

8   For a discussion of how trends in the postmodern world have influenced Islam, see Ahmed, 1992.

9   The heavy-handed nature of government-sponsored research in Muslim societies in particular, and the Third World in general, is of special concern. Because governments finance most research projects in the Third World, they often use the rhetoric of indigenization as a means to persuade or pressure social scientists to tailor their research to meet the state's needs for social engineering or its standards of public morality. Consequently, Third World social scientists must often confront the vexing questions: What do I know? What should I think? What shall I do?

References

Ahmed, Akbar S. (1992). *Postmodernism and Islam: Predicament and promise*. New York: Routledge.

Alatas, Syed Farid (1993). "On the indigenization of academic discourse." *Alternatives*, 18: pp. 307–38.

Alatas, Syed Hussein (1972). "The captive mind in development studies." *International Social Science Journal*, 24 (no. 1): pp. 9–25.

Amin, Samir (1976). *Unequal development: An essay on the social formations of peripheral capitalism*. Hassocks: Harvester Press.

Atal, Yogesh (1981). "The call for indigenization." *International Social Science Journal*, 33 (no. 1): pp. 189–197.

Baran, Paul (1957). *The political economy of growth*. New York: Monthly Review Press.

Boorstin, Daniel J. (1993). "Apostles of novelty." *New Perspectives Quarterly*, 10 (no. 3, Summer): pp. 60.

Boroujerdi, Mehrzad (1997). "Iranian Islam and the Faustian bargain of Western modernity." *Journal of Peace Research*, 34 (no. 1, February): pp. 1–5.

———. (1996). *Iranian intellectuals and the West: The tormented triumph of nativism*. Syracuse, N.Y.: Syracuse University Press.

Bourdieu, Pierre (1977). *Outline of a theory of practice*. Cambridge: Cambridge University Press.

Dallmayr, Fred (1996). *Beyond Orientalism: Essays on cross-cultural encounter*. Albany: State University of New York Press.

Frank, A. G. (1969). *Capitalism and underdevelopment in Latin America*. New York: Monthly Review Press.

Fukuyama, Francis (1992). *The end of history and the last man*. New York: Free Press.

Gergen, Kenneth, Aydan Gulerce, Andrew Lock, and Girishwar Misra Psychological science in cultural context. <http://www.massey.ac.nz/~ALock/culture/culture.htm>

Hoffmann, Stanley (1977). "An American social science: International relations." *Daedalus*, 106 (no. 3, Summer): pp. 41–60.

International Institute of Islamic Thought. (1989). *Islamization of knowledge: General principles and work plan*. Herndon, VA: International Institute of Islamic Thought.

Lee, Robert D. (1997) *Overcoming tradition and modernity: The search for Islamic authenticity*. Boulder: Westview Press.

Moten, Abdul Rashid (1996). *Political science: An Islamic perspective*. New York: St. Martin's Press.

Mottahedeh, Roy (1985). *The mantle of the Prophet: Religion and politics in Iran*. New York: Pantheon Books.

Mutahhari, Ayatullah Murtaza (1986). *Social and historical change: An Islamic perspective*. Berkeley: Mizan Press.

Safi, Louay M. (1994). *The challenge of modernity: The quest for authenticity in the Arab world*. Lanham, MD.: University Press of America.

Shayegan, Daryush (1997). *Cultural schizophrenia: Islamic societies confronting the West*. Syracuse, N.Y.: Syracuse University Press.

Sorush, Abdolkarim (1995). Mana va Mabnay-e Sekularism. [The meaning and basis of secularism]. *Kiyan*, 26 (August–September): pp. 11.

Spengler, Oswald (1939). *The decline of the West*. New York: Knopf.

Strange, Susan (1971). "The politics of international currencies." *World Politics*, 22 (January): pp. 24–39.

Winch, Peter (1958). *The idea of a social science and its relation to philosophy*. 2nd edition. London: Routledge.

Part II
Globalization on The Margins

5
Globalization or Localization? Rural Advertising in India

Tej K. Bhatia

In the aftermath of the post-Cold War era, globalization has brought about, and continues to bring about, profound changes to economic, political, social, developmental, communication, and governance arenas (as well as to others) at both conceptual and concrete levels (Baylis and Smith, 1997; Chomsky and McChesney, 1998; Fingleton, 1999; Friedmann, 1999; Hoogvelt, 1997; James, 1999; Razin and Sadka, 1999). In terms of global communication, some changes have been noted in the choice of language and its role in shaping and reshaping global market discourse. There is no doubt that English has effectively dethroned competitor languages, such as French and Russian, and continues to do so with more vigor and dynamics than ever before. Importantly, English has become the single most important language of globalization. At the same time, English itself is undergoing some dynamic changes in the process of engendering and shaping global market discourse, with ramifications for international advertising media and marketing (Crystal, 1997; Goodman and Graddol, 1996, McArthur, 1998). Even in the globalization era, however, English cannot be deployed without regard for locality. This is especially the case in the "margins," where earlier experiences under colonialism involved the hegemony of the English language and the subversion of native languages.

One of the main concerns of globalization for international advertisers is how to resolve the paradox between globalization and localization (national and regional interests, appeals, affiliations, and so forth) in their formal and functional linguistic manifestations. This concern has shown itself in terms of the "standardization" versus "adaptation" debate in international advertising, media, and marketing (see Hite and Fraser, 1988; Kanso, 1991; Kujala and Lehtinen, 1989; Mueller,

1992; Onkvisit and Shaw, 1987; Ryans and Ratz, 1987; among others). Although the lively debate has led to a productive exchange of ideas over the past three decades, the marketing and media literature is dominated by the underlying approach best characterized as the "either-or" language choice approach. I argue here that international advertisers can use and, in fact, do use, an approach that goes beyond the simplistic either-or approach and that aims at mediating the two-pronged (globalization versus localization) problem. Consequently, advertisers solve the paradox between globalization and localization in a more productive and optimal fashion by following an innovative approach known as "glocalization." This approach stresses cooperation and integration of global diversity over competition and homogenization (or hyperglobalization).

To date, globalization debates have concentrated on the homogenization of conventional advertising, particularly on the role of high-profile companies like McDonald's, Time–Warner (especially CNN), and so forth (Robertson, 1995; de Mooij, 1998). In India, but also globally, in the advertising industry a distinction is made between "conventional" and "nonconventional" in advertising media forms. Conventional media forms include print and electronic media, such as radio and TV advertising; nonconventional media forms include wall or wall paintings and video-van advertising. Although the terms conventional and nonconventional certainly suggest the marginality of wall paintings (and video-van advertising), that form of advertising is, ironically, more traditional and more predominant in rural settings than conventional advertising, as discussed later in this chapter. Wall advertising is treated as a marginal phenomenon in marginal areas; yet for another reason – that is, its integral relationship with rural settings – it is still beyond the easy reach of globalization in comparison to advertising in urban areas. Although it is one of the most effective media forms of advertising, because of its perceived marginality no systematic study has been conducted on it. Moreover, elitist attitudes of media experts and their preference for glamour in advertising further lead to the neglect of this topic in advertising research in general and in Indian media research in particular. I attempt to fill this gap by focusing on wall advertising.

My specific aim in this chapter is to seek answers to the following questions:

(1) How is the tension between globalization and localization resolved by advertisers?

(2) How are paradoxical roles of globalization and localization allocated in terms of language choice? In other words, how do globalization and localization (both themes and appeals) get coded through the choice of languages, scripts, and linguistic structures in the body of advertisements?
(3) How does the media reach the "unreachable" in the "margins" by coming to terms with the geographical and linguistic dispersion phenomena?

I search for the answers through a content and structural analysis of nonconventional rural advertising in India. I selected three types of products for this study: commercial, social/developmental, and service. The selection of *commercial products* was based on the findings of the Indian Market Research Bureau (1991), Social and Rural Research Institute (1991), and National Council of Applied Economic Research (1996), which reveal that the following product-types reach every village in India: toiletries, washing soaps and powders, basic food items (tea, rice, and flour), batteries, cement, farming and transportation equipment, and cold and headache medicines. The *social and development campaigns* included AIDS, immunization, family planning, infant mortality, mother and child welfare, rural employment, and clean water. These campaigns were run jointly through the efforts of the government of India, NGOs (nongovernmental organizations), UNESCO (United Nations Educational, Scientific, and Cultural Organization), and other developmental agencies in cooperation with private advertising agencies. The *service industry* advertisements included repair (for example, kitchen stoves), medical, and recycling services.

The sample size consisted of approximately 400 advertisements in English, Hindi, Bengali, and Marathi. Although I focus mainly on Hindi and English advertisements, the generalizations I draw may well be valid for other Indian languages as well. Texts of advertisements were coded for the following content parameters: product information (name, distributor/contact information, nature/content), physical properties (packing, color, spokesperson), utility (price/value, quality), research (assurance, safety), and evaluation (ranking, novelty).

Before I attempt to identify the defining and salient features of wall advertising. together with its relationship to the rural setting of India, some remarks are in order about rural India and the pattern of communication there. These remarks, in turn, single out the importance of rural India to advertisers and, at the same time, answer in part the third question dealing with the media reach to geographically and linguistically dispersed masses of India.

Rural India: interpreting global marketing in the margins

Unchanged for centuries, rural India constitutes "the heart of India." A rural area is here defined as a nonurban area with a population less than 5000 and a population density less than 400 people per square kilometer. Approximately 78 percent of Indians still live in more than half a million villages (approximately 627 000 villages). Rural India generates more than half of the national income, and 94 million middle-class rural Indians have more disposable income than urban Indians (Rao and Natrajan, 1996). The growing economic power of rural India, the forces of globalization, and the influence of the electronic media – in particular TV, videos, and the vibrant Hindi movie industry, Bollywood – are adding to growing rural aspirations, which are being felt in the form of growing consumerism. Advertisers are thus naturally turning their attention to rural India. Many recent articles devoted to strategic probing into the Indian market, such as Kaul (1997, p. 97), ask marketers, "Are you in tune with the beat of the 200-million strong rural market?" – an important question to ask in terms of consumption, economic power, output, literacy, etc.

The most important challenge that advertisers face, however, is how to cope with the problem of geographic and linguistic dispersion. The rural market is scattered over many small villages, all beyond the conventional media and rural corporate giants, such as Hindustan Lever (McDonald, 1993–94, p. 47). The problem of geographical dispersion is compounded by the active presence of linguistic dispersion. India is a multilingual country where at least seventeen languages and countless dialects are spoken. Hindi–Urdu serves as a lingua franca, whereas English serves as a link language for approximately 2 percent of the Indian population. This linguistic dispersion adds new significance to the classic standardization versus specialization debate in marketing: whether to use a uniform standardized advertisement or a customized advertisement tailored to the individual taste of a particular village. (For details about the standardization and specialization debate in international media and marketing, see Bhatia and Bhargava, 2000).

The advertisers' solution is to go to where rural India actually lives, socializes, and entertains itself. The two most common approaches to reach the masses are wall and video-van advertising. Wall advertising enables Indian and global advertisers to reach inaccessible areas and to tailor their messages to the needs of a rural audience using either the lingua franca Hindi–Urdu (with or without local dialectal coloring) or other regional languages. In spite of the low incidence of literacy in general, and the extremely low incidence of bilingualism with English in particular, English is not ruled out. By mixing and accommodating different linguistic forms with pictures, advertisers overcome the delimitation of linguistic dispersion. While conducting this research in a village in Rajasthan, I came across a woman who was trying very hard to decipher a wall painting, which contained a social message. When she was asked whether she understood the advertisement, her answer was negative. With further probing about the utility of such advertisements and her strained efforts to read the advertisement, her response was revealing: "If I like an ad, I can always ask someone. But if there is no such ad, how on this earth will I ever know the content of the message?" The response was good enough to silence this skeptic. Wall paintings have a dominating long-term presence in rural India and can help villagers to overcome linguistic and literacy (even pictorial) barriers by their engagement in cooperative learning. In short, wall advertisements are main attention-getters and provide signs and signals to connect rural people in the margins with global products.

Wall advertising: its characteristics and effectiveness[1]

Before isolating the salient nonlinguistic features of wall advertisements, I describe them in general terms. If one travels from an urban area, the rural landscape presents both green space and open farms. Along railroad tracks and highways, however, one finds that every standing structure is covered with bright yellow, red, green, pink, or white colors and has something written on it. To an uninitiated foreign eye, these appear to be graffiti. But, in fact, the "graffiti" is actually advertising. Remarkably, even private structures are not spared; the outer wall of a private house or shop might be painted, with or without the permission of its owner. The same scene is repeated over and over again, with greater intensity as one goes deeper into the rural heartland of India. From rural market centers to a village, any brick or mud wall in sight is painted with some kind of commercial, social, or service message. Wall paintings are a mark of a vibrant economic and social life. They represent the most widespread form of advertising and are the favorite of Indian rural masses. Furthermore, wall paintings are very traditional in nature. An illustration might clarify the concept of wall advertising and its roots in Indian history, mythology, politics, motifs, literature, and fine arts.

Consider the advertisement for an upscale restaurant in the state of Rajasthan. The advertisement makes use of a character from the Ramayana, one of the two most prominent classical epics of India. The character is depicted as a puppet, highlighting puppeteering, a famous art form in the region of Rajasthan. The calligraphic style of handwriting and the language use are from Hindi, but with a local Rajasthani touch. The header carries a greeting that is not from standard Hindi, which would typically be used by companies like Air India and Indian Airlines, but a local greeting that highlights the main epic character, Lord Rama.

In addition to being an integral part of the rural Indian landscape, wall advertising is the most economical; all one needs is some paint and a low-wage painter from a local area. It can be customized with relative ease for the purpose of segment marketing. Also, an old advertisement can be replaced by a new one in a matter of hours, or be allowed to stay until it takes its natural death. The form is innovative and artistic with indigenous verbal and visual appeal. Wall paintings are rich in ethnic motifs and are the visual vocabulary of the region. Moreover, their ability to reach to the illiterate as well as the literate segments of society cannot be underestimated.

It is not surprising that a study on "audience recall" by Jethwaney and Dayal (1992) found wall advertising to be one of the most effective media advertising forms. These researchers, devoted to the effectiveness and impact of various advertising media forms in India, reveal that wall paintings ranked third among advertising forms for recall by subjects; hoarding and kiosk advertising forms ranked first and second, respectively. Their study was designed to evaluate the relative impact of advertising campaigns with seven media forms: hoarding, kiosk, wall painting, film, song/dance/drama, print, and bus-panel advertising. This multimedia campaign was launched by the Ministry of Information and Broadcasting to reach millions of visitors to Hardwar and Ujjain to attend the sacred Ardha Kubh Mela. Jethwaney and Dayal's 1992 study, in most ways excellent, is however blemished by methodological shortcomings that particularly affect the ranking of wall advertising. (I hasten to emphasize though that the Ministry of Information and Broadcasting commissioned the study; the investigators, therefore, are not directly responsible for the methodological flaw.) Notably, of all the media forms selected for the study, only wall advertising was not within the easy reach of viewers in places over-crowded with millions of people. Such a selection puts wall paintings at a disadvantage in terms of appropriate and necessary exposure required to arrive at an accurate and comparative rating. However, the inescapable conclusion from the study is that wall advertising is a very effective, and the most economic, form of advertising.

The structure of wall advertisements

Treating printed advertisements as a single (verbal) discourse unit, I show, in an earlier work (1992), that printed advertisements exhibit the following four structural components: (1) attention-getters/header/captions, subheaders, and elaborations of these in title form; (2) body copy/main text, outlining the significant properties and reasoning promoting the use of the product; (3) product name/signature lines, giving the name of the product and/or its manufacturer; and (4) slogans. An advertisement may or may not incorporate all four components, which represent its general schema. Also, the components are not necessarily sequentially ordered; although there is a clear preference for ordering between the attention-getter and the main text, slogans and signature lines do not always follow the main text.

Wall advertising differs from printed advertising in that it usually does not involve the body copy or main text component. This is a natural consequence of wall advertising's inclination toward conciseness rather than an elaborate explanation about the properties of the product. This component's function is filled by providing an evolutionary statement about the product. As such, wall advertising comes closer to the banner-type of advertising witnessed in Western sport arenas than to that found in elaborate printed advertising magazines. The only difference with banner advertising is that wall advertising contains an invitational closing structure that often gives information about the availability of the product and its distributor. While such a structure is invariably absent from the banner advertisements, it is sometimes present in printed advertisements.

The color schemes and physical properties of a wall are exploited to impose structure on an advertisement and, at the same time, distinguish its different structural properties. Consider, for example, the soap advertisement for *Fenaa* (derived from Hindi *fena* 'foam, lather'). The advertisement carries a Hindi attention-getting phrase, *daam hai kam safedii camacame* 'the price is less (and yet the soap makes clothes) glitter white', which is separated from the prominent display of the product name on the package using the blue background. A subheader, *naii* 'new' is also displayed on the package. The third structural property, slogan, is distinguished by using a different color scheme (blue) within the rectangular border. The slogan is in Hindi: *fenaa hii lenaa* 'Take/buy only the Fena'. The verb *lenaa* 'take/buy' rhymes with the product name, *Fenaa*. The slogan is further highlighted with a visual cue, the fairy, to give a magical touch to the product. *Fenaa* is a local product; therefore, local appeal is created entirely by means of the Hindi language and the Devanagari script in which the Hindi is written. The color scheme is not only used to impose structure on the advertisement, but is also in agreement with the sensory perception of the Indian culture. The white color carries an ultra-whiteness in Indian context and is different from the perception of whiteness in Western advertising.

Globalization: two views and underlying strategies

It is intriguing to observe that advertisers, either unconsciously or by design, have developed two distinct models of globalization and its relation to localization which, in turn, govern their linguistic representational strategies and linguistic choices. These two models, characterized as the "competitive" and "cooperative" views, naturally lead to two distinct underlying linguistic representational strategies: the competitive view leads to language segregation, whereas the integrative and cooperative view yields to language mixing (Table 5.1). Language segregation is a natural outcome of the perception of globalization and localization as oppositions, while language integration is the consequence of the perceived accommodation between the two. The pattern of language choice and language use within an advertisement is accounted for in the discussion below.

Table 5.1   Globalization and localization: perceived models and linguistic strategies

	Model	
	Competitive	*Cooperative*
Approach	either-or	mixed
Language/script	one	two or more
Text	monolingual	bilingual or multilingual

The competitive model: patterns of globalization and localization codification

Based on research findings on the social psychological patterns of communication in India, it is assumed that English and Hindi are not interchangeable. For advertisers, English considered more appropriate to voice the theme of globalization, whereas Hindi is found more suitable for national and local themes. Such a language allocation pattern can be witnessed in the language choice of rural advertisers. For highly localized themes or appeals, either local dialects, Hindi–Urdu, or other regional languages are molded to create dialectal mood. (For more details about how different languages – Hindi, Sanskrit, Persian, and English – carry different functional loads in Indian advertising, see Bhatia, 1987, p. 33; Bhatia, 1992, p. 201).

Two specific patterns of language choice and their use to mark globalization and localization in rural advertising are rendered by the competition model: (1) Think Global, Act Global and (2) Think Local, Act Local. The following discussion details these two patterns in commercial, social/developmental, and service advertisements.

Think Global, Act Global Pattern

The Think Global, Act Global pattern is carried out by means of English only. Here are some examples found in rural Indian wall advertisements.

(1)   Pennzoil
      Castro (oil)
      Coca-Cola
      Pepsi
      Gulf Lubricants, worldwide since 1901 (oil)
      Kellogg's Frosties: The energy to win

The linguistic composition of such messages is restricted to either the product name and/or its logo in English. The text rarely goes beyond one word in length. The script chosen for the products is Roman. The content transmission beyond product name and logo is not deemed necessary by advertisers, because they perceive that villagers will process an English word as a visual image and will retain it as such. In other words, language use is primarily symbolic, and the appeal is exclusively global or Western in character.

The only two exceptions in (1) are the Gulf and Kellogg advertisements, which use more than one word. The Gulf oil advertisement adds a slogan as a sub-attention-getter, in very small letters next to the prominent display of the product name. A century-old history in India enables Gulf to go beyond the product name. Nonessential products, such as Kellogg's breakfast cereal, do show a larger text size, but such advertisements usually end up as a communication failure, because the text has no relevance in the rural setting and there is no effort to create bilingualism with English to reach the rural audience.

Only the commercial products with international product positioning in mind follow the Think Global, Act Global pattern. The commercial products with local appeal adopt the Think Local, Act Local pattern; this pattern is also dominant in service and social advertisements.

Think Local, Act Local Pattern

The Think Local, Act Local pattern represents the reversal of the Think Global, Act Global pattern, as shown in the following examples:

(2) *kraanti   saabun*
     revolution   soap
     'Kranti (revolution) soap'

     anuraadhaa   masaale
     Anuradha   spices
     'Anuradha spices'

     griin   hilz   caay
     Green   Hills   tea
     'Green Hills tea'

     penza   aail
     'Pennzoil'

     apnaa   baasmatii   caaval
     Apnaa/self   Basmati   rice
     '*Apnaa* Basmati rice' ('your own Basmati rice')

This pattern is carried out essentially in the Hindi language and in Devanagari script.

The Think Local, Act Local approach enables rural advertisers to increase text size and make effective use of slogans by beefing up their content. Compare the following advertisement for a tractor (3) with the advertisements in (2):

(3)   *nayaa*   *htm*   *TrekTor* ...
       new   HTM   tractor
       'The new HTM tractor'

       ab   *taakat*   *aap*   *kii*   *muTThi*   *men*
       now   strength   you   of   fist   in
       'Now the strength (is) in your fist/hands.'

Notice that the text size is relatively large in advertisements using the Think Local, Act Local approach, as exemplified in (2) and (3). In fact, the Think Local, Act Local text sizes are at least four to six times larger than the text in advertisements employing the Think Global, Act Global approach. In example (3), the attention-getter introduces the new product: an HTM tractor. The attention-getter is followed by a slogan: 'Now the strength is in your hands'. The consideration of lexical economy motivates the deletion of the copular verb form 'is' (Hindi: *hai*). The advertisement ends with contact information about the distributor. The following advertisement is about *biRi* (a twist of tobacco rolled in a tobacco leaf; the most popular form of rural cigarette smoking and becoming very popular among youths in the United States):

(4)   *502*   *pataakaa*   *biiRii*
       502   Pataka   Biri

       502   *kaa*   *vaadaa,*   *daam*   *vaajib,*   *svaad*   *zyaadaa*
       502   of   promise   price   reasonable   taste   more
       'The promise of 502, the price reasonable (and) more taste'

Regionality can be highlighted linguistically by overt use of a regional language or a dialect on the one hand, and by adapting Hindi to the phonological (or morphological/syntactic) scheme of the regional variety on the other. (5) exemplifies the latter:

(5)   *caTpaTo*   *svaad,*   *rasoii*   *kii*   *shaan*
       spicy   taste   kitchen   of   grandeur
       'Lively in taste; the pride of a kitchen'

Although the language of the advertisement is essentially Hindi, the phonological adaptation of the adjective introduces the regional Rajasthani touch. The change of the final vowel from *aa* (standard Hindi, *caTpaTaa* 'spicy') to *o* (i.e., *caTpaTo*) brings a highly dialectal tone to the advertisement.

The color scheme can perform and/or highlight local functions. Consider the following advertisement from the state of Rajasthan:

(6) *naval* *kocing* *senTar*
    Naval Coaching center
    'Naval training center'

The advertisement is entirely in Devanagari script. The English words are made to look like Hindi by means of phonetic adaptation. The message is written in a pink to identify the school with the local region: pink is the color of the state of Rajasthan, which houses a well-known tourist place, Jaipur, popularly known as "Pink City."

The Think Local, Act Local approach is preferred by social development and service advertisers, who depend on Hindi or regional dialects for transmitting the message. Consider the following three ads:

(7a) *graamiiN* *vikaas* *aur* *rozgaar* *kaa* *vaaydaa*
     rural development employment of promise
     'Rural development and the promise of employment'

     javaahar *rozgaar* *yojnaa* *kaa* *dohraa* *faaydaa*
     Jawahar employment plan of double benefit
     'The double benefit of the Jawahar Employment Plan'

(7b) *pancaayatii* *raaj ...* *jantaa* *kaa* *apnaa* *raaj*
     Panchayati rule ... people of self rule
     'Panchayati Rule, people's self rule'

(7c) *surakshit* *yaun* *sambandh ...* *eDs* *se* *savaadhaan*
     safe sex relation(s) AIDS from beaware
     'SaFe sex relation(s) ... Beware of AIDS'

All three advertisements lean slightly toward a Sanskritized style of Hindi. The themes are highly local in character; thus the natural choice is Hindi and Devanagari script over English. The rural employment plan (advertisement [7a]; is named after the first Prime Minister of India (Jawahal Lal Nehru). The advertisement in (7b) reinforces the Gandhian concept of self-government rural rule. Both advertisements (7a) and (7b) stress rurality by means of visual cues, providing a desired visual context for the messages. Because of the taboo involving AIDS, advertisements associated with it are usually short and without visual aids. The message in (7c) is slightly Sanskritized Hindi and is written in Devanagari script.

Now consider some service industry advertisements:

(8a) *gais*   *cuulhaa,*   *preshar*   *kukkar*   *ripeyar*
      gas   stove   pressure   cooker   repair
      'Gas stove (and) pressure cooker repairs'

(8b) *minii*   *Tiffan*   *sarvis*
      Mini   Tiffin   Service

(8c) *vaidya*   *ruup*   *kishor*   *raaThii ...*   *strii*   *purush*   *rog,*
      Doctor   Roop   Kishore   Rathi ...   female   male   disease

      mardaanaa   *kamzori,*   *svapan-dosh*   *virya*   *kii*
      male   weakness   nocturnal emission   virility   of

      kami   *viirya-skraaNu–[sperm]*   *kii*   *kamii*
      shortage   sperm count   of   shortage

      joRon   *kaa*   *dard [gaThiyaa],*   *safed*   *daag*   *ke liye...*   *maile*
      joints of   pain   white   spots   for   meet

'Meet Vaidaya (Dr.) Rup Kishor Rathi for (the treatment of) female, male diseases, masculine weakness, nocturnal emission, shortage of virility, sperm (count) shortage, arthritis, (and) white spots'

Advertisement (8a) advertises a repair service. Although all of the words except for *cuulhaa* 'stove' are from English, they are assimilated into Indian languages and are thus written in local scripts (Devanagari in this case). Advertisement (8b) advertises hot lunch delivery service. Taking its cues from the renowned hot lunch delivery service in Bombay (Mumbai) the advertisement targets lunch delivery to rural workers working in urban areas in the vicinity of the advertisement. Most of the service advertisements (including commercial advertisements) shown in (7a–8b) are gender neutral. The only exception is the alternative medicine advertisement in (8c). These types of advertisements are placed by doctors (called *vaidya* or *hakim*) practicing indigenous medicine. They are overwhelmingly aimed at males and the topic is generally male impotence. Such advertisements are heavily indigenous in content, appeal, and approach. Within the monolingual framework of the advertisement, advertisers sometimes strive for bilingual strategies. Notice the paraphrasing in advertisement (8c). The concept of the low sperm count is paraphrased as *virya kii kami* 'short-age of virility' in colloquial Hindi, and then with a more Sanskritized Hindi *(viirya-skraaNu*–[sperm] *kii kamii)*. This time the Sanksrit word is followed by its English translational equivalent in square brackets. Similarly, arthritis is first mentioned in colloquial Hindi as *joRon kaa dard* 'pain of the joints' and then in a rural form as [*gaThiyaa*].

The codification of the competitive model in Indian wall advertising is summarized in Table 5.2.

Globalization and localization: bridging the gap

Some advertisements, such as Pennzoil (1), depart from the exclusive Think Global, Act Global strategy and make room for globalization by way of localization. Reaching masses by means of local languages and scripts paves a less risky route for globalization appeal. Although the competitive approaches are overtly mutually exclusive in both concep-tual and linguistic terms, the localization–globalization gap is bridged primarily by nonlinguistic means – either by sharing logographic prop-erties of the product or by maintaining the common color scheme. The yellow color and logographic imposition around the Hindi text in the Pennzoil advertisement in (2) provide a critical linkage between local and global appeals. Needless to say, the audience needs two separate advertisements to arrive at such a crucial linkage and, thus, bypasses the barrier created by the complementary linguistic choices.

Table 5.2 Codification of globalization and localization

	Think global, act global	*approach*	*Think local, act local*	
Ad type	Commercial	Commercial	Social	Service
Language	English	Hindi/ reg. lgs.*	Hindi/ reg. lgs.	Hindi/ reg. lgs.
Script	Roman	Devanagari/ reg. scripts	Devanagari/ reg. scripts	Devanagari/ reg. scripts
Structure	Attention-getter	Attention-getter, slogans, invitation	Attention-getter, slogans, invitation	Attention-getter, slogans, invitation
Text size	One word	6–8 words	8–12 words	6–10 words

*reg. lgs. = regional languages

Rather than relying on visual cues and indirect, segmented approaches, some advertisements rely on content-sensitive means to induce some degree of globalization. A case in point is the advertisement for Aral engine oil (9):

(9)	*araal – jarmanii*	*kaa*	*nambar*	*ek*	*injan*	*ail*
	Aral Germany	of	number	one	engine	oil

'Aral – the number one German engine oil'

The message has a topic-comment type of structure. The topic, Aral (the product name), is separated from the comment – the number one German engine oil – by the slightly rising wall dividing the two portions of the wall. The entire advertisement is in Hindi and is written in Devanagari script. The suggestion of global appeal is brought about by the content of the comment structure, which contains two content-sensitive parts: the affiliation and the evaluatory. The affiliation part contains information about the German association of the product, and the evaluatory part reveals the product being the number one product. The comment structure is entirely in the Devanagari script.

The cooperation model: codification of glocalization

With the cooperative (or integrative) model in mind, advertisers break the barriers posed by linguistic segregation and attempt to integrate the globalization and localization themes with participating linguistic systems. This is an optimization strategy that subscribes to the Think and Act Both Globally and Locally at the Same Time approach, "glocalization." The following advertisements are illustrative of glocalization by language and script mixing.

(10a)	*Brook Bond A1 ...*	*kaRak*	*chaap*	*caay*
	Brook Bond A1	KaRak (thunder)	brand	tea

'Brook Bond A1 ... the KaRak brand tea'

(10b)   Philips ... In service to the service

	TV ...	*saalon*	*saloon*	*aap*	*saath ...*	*Radio*
	TV	years	years	you	with	radio

'Philips ... in service to the service ... for years and years with you ...TV (and) Radio'

(10c)	TATA	*pesh*	*karte*	*hain – injan*	*aayal*	*kaa*	*shanshaa ...*
	TATA	present	do	are	engine	oil	of king

BP   superior engine oil
'TATA presents the king of the engine oil – BP superior
engine oil'

The Brook Bond advertisement achieves glocalization by displaying the
package of the Karak tea. The company pictorial logo is on the top of the
advertisement and is embedded with the English text 'Brook Bond A1'.
Below the English text is the Hindi text in Devanagari script, with a larger
font in a semicircle above a picture of a hot cup of tea. The Phillip's Radio
and TV advertisement (10b), in contrast, displays the company's name
with prominent fonts followed by the slogan "in service to the service" in
English with a smaller font size. In the third line, there is a TV on the left
and a radio on the right, with 'TV' and 'radio' written in English.
Sandwiched between the two images is the Hindi text 'years and years
with you'. The Whirlpool home appliance advertisement follows essentially the same strategy, the only difference being that the pictures of the
refrigerator and washing machine in the Whirlpool advertisement have
the words 'refrigerator' and 'washing machine' written in Devanagari
script. In advertisement (10c), the collaboration of TATA and BP is highlighted by the use of English, while the localization appeal is carried out
by means of Hindi. The Indian company's name appears as part of the
attention-getter 'presents', which is in Hindi. The evaluatory statement
'the king of the engine oil' is also in Hindi. Hindi text is enclosed at both
ends with English lettering.

   In sum, glocalization is achieved by mixing two languages and
scripts within a single advertisement. The language and script allocation process is not random; it appears that the onset and termination
points are presented in English, connected by a long content-sensitive
string of Hindi text. The mixing of different languages and scripts sets
the stage of bilingualism, which enables the masses to overcome the
limitation of content transmission when English is used. Furthermore,
the interface of verbal and visual cues promotes and maximizes the
degree of bilingualism and, thus, enables a relatively easier grasp of the
content of an advertisement. By linking the visual message with the
verbal message, social campaigns overcome the limitations presented
by low literacy in rural India.

Content analysis and marketization of discourse

As I have attempted to show in the preceding two subsections, the
theme of globalization is expressed by means of English, and the pre-

ferred vehicles of localization themes are regional languages and scripts. By making these linguistic choices, advertisers position their products at either the global or the local ends of the spectrum.

My analysis of the parameters of content analysis mentioned in this chapter's Introduction is summarized in Table 5.3. The analysis focuses on the presence versus absence of the parameters with reference to the types of wall advertising campaigns investigated in this study.

English is the single most important linguistic tool for the promotion of globalization. In addition, rural advertising, in spite of its local character, is undergoing globalization, in both overt and covert ways: overtly by product naming, logos, and colors, and covertly by marketization of the rural discourse. Take, for example, the expression "Number 1." Before the onset of globalization, the concept was expressed by means of the native expression *avval darza* 'excellent/first

Table 5.3   Parameters of content

Parameters	English Commercial	Hindi Commercial	Social	Service	Mixed Commercial
Product information					
Name	+*	+	+	+	+
Logo	+	+	−	−	+
Distributor/ Contact info	−	+	+	+	+
Nature/content	+	+	+	+	+
Physical properties					
Packing	+	+	−	−	+
Color	+	+	+	−	+
Spokesperson	−	+	+	−	+
Utility					
Price/value	−	+	−	−	+
Quality	−	+	−	−	+
Research					
Assurance	−	+	+	+	−
Safety	−	−	+	+	−
Evaluation					
Ranking	−	+	−	−	+
Novelty	−	+	−	−	+

* The signs + (presence) and − (absence) represent dominant rather than absolute trends. Sometimes absence is the result of a lack of relevance; for instance, price is not relevant for most social ads.

class', but it has been completely replaced by either "No. 1" or the expression *nambar* 'number' *ek* 'one' (or by the numeric substitution).

Conclusions

Globalization in the margin as well in the center should be conceived of as the integration of localization and globalization. Any view of these processes as oppositions is shortsighted and thus subject to serious questioning. The analysis of wall advertising data reveals that globalization, even marginally, favors an integrative view, which is best termed glocalization. The best practice of globalization would take its cues from glocalization rather than from (hyper)globalization. Advertisers can optimize the strength and appeal of their messages by mixing languages and scripts. Although advertisers are remarkably homogeneous in their choice of English as the language of globalization and marketization of discourse, rather than creating a black-and-white piece of work, they prefer to create mosaics with different languages and scripts. Such integration is achieved through insightful accommodations of the different linguistic systems in the structure of an advertisement. The deeper need of glocalization compels the use of bridging techniques to undercut its intrinsic limitations.

Note

1 Photographs of the wall advertisements discussed in this chapter are available in Bhatia, Tej K. 2000. *Advertising in Rural India: Language, Marketing Communication, and Consumerism*. Institute for the Study of Languages and Cultures of Asia and Africa, Tokyo University of Foreign Studies, Tokyo: Japan. pp. 139–172).

References

Baylis, J. and S. Smith (eds.). (1997). *The globalization of world politics: An introduction to international relations*. Oxford/New York: Oxford University Press.

Bhatia, T. (1992). "Discourse functions and pragmatics of mixing: Advertising across cultures." *World Englishes*, 11 (2/3), pp. 195–215.

———. (1987). "English in advertising: Multiple mixing and media." *World Englishes*, 6 (1), pp. 33–48.

Bhatia, T. and Bhargava, C. (2000). "Adaptation, standardization, or fusion? Innovative linguistic trends in Japanese advertising." *Journal of Asian and African Studies* (Tokyo University of Foreign Studies), March.

Chomsky, N. and R. McChesney (1998). *Profits over people*. New York: Seven Stories Press.

Crystal, D. (1997). *English as a global language*. Cambridge/New York: Cambridge University Press.

de Mooij, M. (1998). *Global marketing and advertising. Understanding cultural paradoxes*. Thousand Oaks, California: Sage.

Fingleton, E. (1999). *In praise of hard industries: Why manufacturing, not the information economy is the key to future prosperity*. Boston, Mass.: Houghton Mifflin.

Friedmann, T. L. (1999). *The lexus and the olive tree*. New York: Farrar, Straus, Giroux.

Goodman, S. and D. Graddol (eds.). (1996). *Redesigning English: New texts, new identities*. London: Routledge.

Hite, R. E. and C. Fraser (1988). 'International advertising strategies." *Journal of Advertising Research*, 28 (5), pp. 9–17.

Hoogvelt, A. (1997). *Globalization and the postcolonial world: The new political economy of development*. Baltimore, MD.: Johns Hopkins University Press.

Indian Marketing Research Bureau. (1991). *Census digest*. New Delhi: Indian Marketing Research Bureau.

James, J. (1999). *Globalization, information technology and development*. New York: St. Martin's Press.

Jethwaney, J. and R. Dayal (1992). *'Impact' of the multi-media publicity campaign at Ardh Kumbh Mela 1992–An analysis*. New Delhi: Indian Institute of Mass Communication.

Kanso, A. "(1991). The use of advertising agencies from foreign markets: Decentralized decisions and localized approaches?" *International Journal of Advertising*, 10, pp. 129–36.

Kaul, P. (1997). "Are you adding value through rural selling." *Business Today*, January 7–21, pp. 98–102.

Kujala, A. and U. Lehtinen (1989). "A new structural method for analyzing linguistic significance in market communications." *International Journal of Advertising*, 8, pp. 219–136.

McArthur, T. (1998). *The English languages*. Cambridge/New York: Cambridge University Press.

McDonald, H. (1993–94). "Cleaning up." *Far Eastern Economic Review,* December 30, 1993 and January 6, 1994, p. 46–47.

Mueller, B. (1992). "Standardization vs. specialization: An examination of westernization in Japanese advertising." *Journal of Advertising Research*, 1, p. 15–24.

Onkvisit, S. and J. Shaw (1987). "Standardized international advertising: A review and critical evaluation of theoretical and empirical evidence." *Columbia Journal of World Business*, Fall, pp. 43–55.

Rao, S. L. and I. Natrajan (1996). *Indian market demographics: Consumer classes*. Delhi: Global Business Press, National Council of Applied Economic Research (NCAER).

Razin, A. and E. Sadka (eds.). (1999). *The economics of globalization: Policy perspectives from public economics*. Cambridge/New York: Cambridge University Press.

Robertson, R (1993) "Glocalization: Time-space and homogeneity-heterogeneity." In M. Featherstone, S. Lash, and R. Rosertson (eds.) *Global modernities*, pp. 25–44. London: Sage.

Ryans, J. and D. Ratz (1987). "Advertising standardization: A re-examination." *International Journal of Advertising*, 6, pp. 145–58.

6
Speaking from the Margins: "Postmodernism," Transnationalism, and the Imagining of Contemporary Indian Urbanity[1]

Anthony D. King

However we understand the nature of globalization – perhaps "the compression of the world and the intensification of consciousness of the world as a whole" (Robertson, 1992, p. 8) or "the stretching of similar economic, cultural and political activities across the globe" (Short and Kim, 1999, p. 3) – we must acknowledge that the term "global," referring to the globe as such, is being used metaphorically rather than literally. We need hardly be reminded that three-fifths of the globe's surface is water and much of the rest uninhabited or uninhabitable. And if the globe is a sphere, where are the margins? I can only think here of the concept of the noosphere, the layer of knowledge encircling the globe, a concept imagined half a century ago by French philosopher and paleontologist Teilhard de Chardin. Alternatively, I would be quite happy to accept the notion of being, myself, on the margins of (the discourse on) globalization for, like many academics who jumped onto this rolling band wagon fifteen or more years ago, I am now, as I shall explain, constantly rethinking just what it means.

More difficult was the request from the editors to explore the topic of "postmodernity and urbanization, with particular emphasis on the notion of the margins." I have elsewhere (King, 1995) spelled out why I have problems with the idea of postmodernism, which, like Gayatri Spivak and others, I find a totally Eurocentric, or Euro-Americancentric notion (even though it occasionally has its uses). The manner in which it has come to be deployed from the late 1970s, not only denies, or ignores, the whole history of the West's 500-year-old complicity through the colonial relationship, with the rest of the world in the construction of what is conventionally accepted as "modernity" but, equally Eurocentrically, refuses to recognize that there are, and have been in history, many different forms of modernity, positioned in regard to many different social, political, and religiocultural systems.

These views have not been much changed by Perry Anderson's *The Origins of Postmodernity* (1998), in which (based partly by reference to the work of some 335 scholars he cites, all but two dozen of whom originate in "the West") he extols the merits of Jameson's (1992) paradigm and the way in which this has now been exported both to Latin America as well as to China. If postcolonialism, as a contestatory paradigm to the postmodern, has as its goal the prioritizing of the voice of the once-colonized peoples and, to quote Chakrabarty, "the provincializing of Europe," then Anderson, referring to a mere three or four Chinese scholars and about the same number from India and Africa together, clearly does not have much sympathy for that paradigm. Indeed, in a brief three-page discussion in which he cites all of three sources, he largely dismisses the postcolonial paradigm as lacking "a critical edge" (p. 119). More surprisingly for a book with this title, in referring to Toynbee's use of the term, he omits reference to what Jencks (1986) sees as a central theme of the postmodern (at least, in 1947):

> For Toynbee, the term was an encompassing category describing the new historical cycle which started in 1875 with the end of Western dominance, the decline of individualism, capitalism and Christianity and the rise to power of Non-Western cultures. In addition, it referred to a pluralism and world culture, meanings which are still essential to its definition today, and positively so (Jencks, 1986, p. 8).

My own preference for foregrounding the political realities of colonialism is not only because this prioritizes historical realities, including the introduction of colonial forms of European modernities, but also because the inherent *spatiality* assumed in the concept of colonialism enables us to recognize the existence of culturally different conceptions of what is called modernity. As the attributes of modernity (and postmodernity) are inherently temporal (modern refers to what is now, postmodern, to what is after now), it implicitly takes the spatial for granted.

Having therefore sidestepped the editors' request, what I address in this chapter are some recent developments in relation to urbanization in one of the world's two largest states in terms of population, namely,

India. I do this mainly though the medium of a widely distributed, India-based weekly magazine which arrives regularly in my home in upstate New York. It is also this, therefore, that accounts for my title, "Speaking from the Margins." Rather than grand narratives – such as, contradictorily, postmodernism – I shall make use of a few small ones.

Imagination

In his book *Modernity at Large: Cultural Dimensions of Globalization* (1996), Arjun Appadurai explores the joint effects of "media and migration" on "the work of the imagination as a constitutive feature of modern subjectivity." He writes:

> The media offer new disciplines for the construction of imagined selves and imagined worlds ... [they] are resources for experiments with self-making in all sorts of societies for all sorts of purposes ... moving images meet deterritorialized viewers. These create diasporic public spheres, phenomena that confound theories that depend on the continued salience of the nation state as the key arbiter of social changes. (1996, pp. 3–4)

In this chapter, I want to extend Appaduri's insights into the relationship between media, migration, and imagination in the constitution of modern subjectivity. I want to show how the outcome of these interrelated phenomena is – with the help of other agencies and processes – currently influencing material form in the architecture and suburban spaces of some of India's most rapidly developing cities. However, I also take issue with Appadurai; not only does the nation–state continue to be a major player in contributing to social change, but it is critical to the construction of what he calls the "diasporic public sphere."

The research I report here is part of a larger project which I've titled "The Spaces of Transnational Cultures." In this, my aim is to examine different disciplinary as well as popular discourses dealing with the "transnationalization of cultures" (including theoretical ideas and concepts on, for example, globalization, transnationalism, global culture, postcolonial criticism, and so forth) and to assess their effectiveness in helping to interpret spatial transformations over the last two or three decades in the realms of architecture, urbanism, and the larger built environment, particularly in major world cities. My chapter here is in two parts. I first address the larger theoretical frame and elaborate some of the concepts used before examining, in the second part, the particular instance of transnational cultures as represented in contemporary advertising of suburban housing in specific Indian cities.

I use the term "space" in two senses: first, metaphorically, to refer to the discursive space in which notions of the transcultural are being constructed; but also, second, in a materialist, realist sense to refer to those phenomena signified by these discourses – physical and spatial urban form, architecture, the larger built environment. Space here also implies addressing the *production* of space – to use Lefebvre's (1991) phrase – and the economic, social, political, and, especially, cultural conditions in which space is produced.

"Transnational cultures" is more problematic. If we can accept that transnational means "extending beyond national bounds or frontiers," trans*national culture* perhaps suggests not only that cultures are normally somehow "national," that is, that they somehow belong to nations (that is, peoples, not nation–states) but that they are also confined within the territorial boundaries of the nation–state. Not only do cultures – by which I refer to socially organized systems of meaning and identity which are not necessarily coherent or even stable – increasingly exist far from their places of origin but, as Gupta and Ferguson (1992) have argued, cultures are not necessarily confined or situated in a particular space or place. Moreover, cultures are constantly being transformed as well as being created.

Here it is tempting to explore the substantial literature which speculates about the existence of "global culture(s)"; for example, Appaduri (1996), Featherstone (1990), Robertson (1992), and others. There is, however, a problem about cultures being "global." While it is possible for people, ideas, memories, images, or movable objects to be located (almost) anywhere and to move around at will, immovable objects, such as property, and the spaces of city squares, have to be fixed and located. They are fixed in particular places, frequently in cities, which are situated in nation–states. I take this, therefore, as my first assumption: that transnational culture can be understood only when it is "practiced," and becomes meaningful, when seen from a particular place. There is this basic contradiction; namely, that if there are transnational spaces in a realist, physicalist sense, they still have to be located in the space of a nation–state, although, as I shall argue here, such spaces have been produced transnationally prior to, or in the course of, the process of that location.

There are, therefore, two components to the project. The first is the discursive construction and representation of the spaces of transnational culture. This includes the concepts, images, and visual representations, and the meanings attached to them by different people – for example, by academics (Appaduri, 1996; Breckenridge, 1995; Clifford, 1992), media specialists, and, as is this case here, architects, advertisers, developers, and others: ideas about the "international," the "global," about what is "modern," "world class," or about nationalism, cultural flows, and the rest. These concepts are what people use to talk about transnational phenomena and, through these discourses, bring transnational spaces into representation.

The second component is what I have already hinted at: the "fixed spaces" of transnational culture. These require that we give attention to the processes by which transnational cultures are constructed, whether these are political, economic, demographic, financial, techno-logical, and so on. I refer here to movements of both capital and people, migrations and transmigrations[2] (Schiller, Basch, and Blanc, 1995), decisions and legislation of governments, activities of the ser-vices industry such as legal or real estate professionals, and use of media technology (the press, television, fax, Internet, the Web). We can cite here Arjun Appadurai's notion of global cultural flows in their various dimensions – ethnoscapes, technoscapes, finanscapes, medias-capes (1990) – and, as I have suggested elsewhere (King, 1997), extend these to the production of particular landscapes.

Diasporic designs: constructed dream cultures of (or for) the NRI

To put some concrete substance into these ideas I address what might be described as a good example of transnational culture, as previously discussed. This is the diasporic culture (or better, cultures) of the "NRI," the Non-Resident Indian, as it is (partly, but significantly) con-stituted by the Indian state. I speak about some of its institutions and, also, some of the spaces produced in its name. These are some brief observations on this phenomenon as it manifests itself in a key institu-tion of that culture, the international (US) edition of *India Today*.[3]

Given my earlier definition of transnational, the category of the Non-Resident Indian is one that might be closely related to the idea of a transnational culture. On the one hand, the legal status of the iden-tity is established by the government of India through various tax, citi-zenship, and financial regulations such that Indian subjectivity is firmly centered in a powerful sense of nation and culture, an essence where the notion of *home* (as residence from which *Non*-Resident takes its logic and meaning) is ultimately located in India. Non-Resident

Indian refers to a *personal* identity as Indian (to be one, to be able to speak, feel, and probably also look like one) but *not,* however, to reside like one.[4] The negation of this particular identity here is in the fact of residence; Indian residence is denied because, just like the definition of transnational, the NRI lives "beyond national bounds and frontiers."[5]

If living in the United States, the NRI or, for that matter, the British expatriate (note the difference in terminology) can, of course, be a *Resident Alien.* This, however, completely opposite to the status of the NRI, gives the right of *residence,* but only as an *alien* (defined in the *Oxford English Dictionary* as a subject of another country in which he or she resides). Here it is not residence that is denied, but one's national, cultural, personal, and, indeed, political (that is, voting) identity.[6]

Being resident in a country implies at least three conditions. We reside in a particular territorial nation–state, as well as a particular part of that state (perhaps a city, town, and a neighborhood); we occupy some kind of accommodation or dwelling; and we are in some social and/or tenurial relationship – as tenant, paying guest, visitor, or owner – to that dwelling, in which case the residence is also property. As this dwelling or residence always involves different levels of choice, in terms of location, cost, size, type, image, it is also part of our identity – whether that identity is professional, class, social, ethnic, cultural, or, in particular places, racial. The location and dwelling where we live is one (important) way of how we either choose to, or are seen to, represent ourselves to others. In the section that follows, I examine how some recent developments in domestic architectural culture in India are currently being represented in the pages of *India Today* and, not least, how this is being done in the name of the NRI. First, however, some background.

Architecture, property, and consumerism in contemporary India

With the decline, if not the end, of over forty years of a predominantly state-regulated economy in the late 1980s, and the formal liberalization of India's economy and opening to foreign direct investment in 1991, the space of particular cities in India has been increasingly exposed to the winds of economic globalization; the acceleration of the denationalization of industry under Rajiv Gandhi was followed by the shift of multi- and transnational corporations into India (Breckenridge, 1995) and the outward spread of the diasporic culture of the NRI.

After half a century of bureaucratic building by the state and a varying output of private enterprise, there have been vast changes in the production of domestic space over the last few years. In terms of India's urban and architectural history, these have not only been of revolutionary proportions but also of revolutionary architectural design. The combination of India's booming economy and the much-publicized growth in the size of its urban middle class (estimates range between 60 to 100 million significant new consumers in a total population approaching 1 billion) are two important factors. Two others have been the influx of investment capital from NRIs abroad and the establishment of multinational companies (MNCs), especially in Delhi, Bangalore, and Mumbai (Bombay). A further factor, despite the ups and downs, is the overall continuing rise in Indian real estate prices in what, from the mid-1980s, has become a global commercial and residential property market. According to the director of one Delhi development company, unlike in other parts of the world, real estate prices had not fallen in Indian cities in recent years (in the United States and the United Kingdom values went down by 30–40 percent in the years after 1987) (*India Today,* June 15, 1995, p. 77). In Mumbai, Bangalore, Delhi, and elsewhere they increased (in Delhi, by a factor of *nine* between 1985 and 1995). Since June 1994, following the relaxation of government regulations, NRIs (including foreign citizens of Indian origin as well as non-residents holding Indian passports) have been allowed to repatriate the original investment of up to two houses in foreign exchange after a three year lock-in period. They have also been exempt from wealth tax for seven years. What this has meant, according to journalist Monica Raina, writing in *India Today* (May 15, 1995, p. 70) is that "luxury living" has become the new buzzword in Delhi, represented especially by the upmarket condominium – fully furnished, air-conditioned, and with high security, club, gym, pool, and so forth. In mid-1995, over 50 percent of condominium buyers were said to be NRIs.

A hundred years ago, under the influences of capitalist imperialism and the historically distinctive forms of a bureaucratic colonial culture (Scriver, 1995), local versions of European and especially British architectural paradigms helped to shape the city centers and suburbs of England, India, Egypt, and elsewhere (Abel, 1997; Crinson, 1996; Evenson, 1989; King, 1976, 1995; Metcalf, 1989). In the 1990s – if we can believe the advertisements in *India Today* – the rapidly expanding suburbs of particular Indian cities are now being transformed by an equally historically, culturally, and geographically specific interpretation of transnational culture, though one in which local processes of adaptation "translate" Euro-American suburban models. Before addressing this situation, however, I elaborate on why I stress the specificity of the Indian case.

Thinking about "global" cultures of consumption[7]

The phenomenon I describe, namely, the international advertising and marketing of substantial "Western-style" suburban residential property,[8] has, with other forms of property development, increasingly become a form of globalized practice (Thrift 1986). And though viewed through different theoretical optics, it has been addressed in places as far apart as Australia and California (Dovey, 1999), Indonesia (Leaf, 1994; Kusno, 2000), and Turkey (Oncu, 1997).

In Ayse Oncu's account of how different segments of Istanbul's "middle strata" were "initiated into the fantasy world of the ideal home as the quintessential dream, symbol and embodiment of middle class identity ... on the outskirts of the city" (p. 58), she offers three potential ways of thinking about the phenomenon as "a 'global' culture of consumption." The first is "the universal language of money, interpenetrating ... into an ever larger sphere of meanings, adding a new level of signification to 'local' habits, standards, beliefs or practices, by attaching to them a monetary sign." Money "establishes a universally valid equivalence, undermining a plethora of local logics by drawing them into the sphere of exchange, thus 'commodifying' them." Second, she draws on Bourdieu (1984) to address the symbolic significance of cultural practices: "it is possible to think of 'globalization' as the erosion of referential hierarchies from which goods derive their meanings ... consumption practices lose their anchoring in the class system, become footloose so to speak, ceasing to signify categorical differences." In this sense, "globalization ... creates a world of movement and mixture, to evoke the 'global ecumene' of Hannerz (1989) in which the global and the local are moments in the same process." Third, Oncu draws on Barthes (1972) to think about consumer culture as "the realm of contemporary myth-making." Here, "a culture of consumption would mean a culture in which goods become the embodiment of desires, dreams, emotions; wherein subjective experiences of love, excitement, pleasure or freedom are objictified in goods... . Such mythical properties of goods ... are universalsed in global culture." These different ways of understanding consumer culture, Oncu suggests, "need not be thought of as mutually exclusive" (Oncu, 1997, pp. 58–9).

In discussing the conditions surrounding the marketing and intro-duction of the "ideal home" into Istanbul suburbs, Oncu emphasizes the internationalization (through joint ventures) of the advertising industry in the mid-1980s, which brings the same language and con-cepts into the process ("we are not selling a house, we're selling a lifestyle") and also the "initiation into the global myth of the ideal home as the embodiment of a middle class way of life", p. 59).

Oncu's valuable account of the Turkish phenomenon helps to point up the differences in the Indian case. As she writes, "consumer myths which circulate across the globe acquire facticity in response to differ-ent sets of circumstances in different, historically-specific sites" (p. 70). The most obvious difference in India is the existence of the NRI, a social, cultural, legal, and financial category which (as far as I know) does not exist in relation to other nation–states. This gives the new suburban phenomenon three historically distinctive characteristics: (1) it secures a flow of investment which, in the context of changing exchange rates between India and other countries (especially the United States and the United Kingdom, and generally to the disadvan-tage of the rupee) encourages ever-higher investments of capital in ever-more luxurious and larger levels of construction; (2) it helps to explain the culturally distinctive visual, spatial, typological, architec-tural, and naming practices of new suburban developments; and, not least (3) contrary to Appaduri's suggestion, it reaffirms the power of the state as a major contributor to the making of India's contemporary public culture. I turn now to the empirical material of my study.

Worlds of (and for) the NRI

The first issue concerns the way (local) Indian developers construct the relationship – and bridge the gap – between what they see as the world of the NRI and the world of India. As one developer suggests, "You've seen the finest of luxuries, in foreign lands. And enjoyed the best life has to offer. C-Homes[9] [is] perhaps the first concerted effort in India to create not just luxury homes, but a complete luxury world for sophisti-cated people like you. Enriched with international luxuries and sur-rounded with advanced facilities that have already attracted several important personalities – both Indians and NRI's – to this address ... the elite neighborhood of Delhi." Or others: "You've traveled across the world, acquiring a taste for the international while balancing it with the Indian ... . that's why all our complexes combine the very best world standards with values uniquely Indian"; "The world is an oyster for you. You breakfast in New York, lunch in London, and have dinner in Singapore. But your heart reaches out to India. Now [XY Projects] offers to fulfil that long-cherished dream with world-class apartments ... minutes away from Delhi." In Bangalore, one developer announces, "Live the way the world does ... . (We offer) International style houses ... [and] exclusive locations in Asia's fastest growing city." In Delhi, Palam Vihar apartments are built to "global specifications"; other developments offer what they state are "world class homes," "exclusively for Non-Resident Indians"; in Pune, houses in a new development are of "international quality and style" (*India Today*, passim, 1995, 1996). How is this sense of "international style and standards," of "global specifications" (not terms one normally sees, for example, in German, US, or British real estate ads) constructed?

One construction is that one lives in a jet-set world, linked by global airways. Architectural critic Deyan Sudjic (1992) has suggested that the symbolic center of the contemporary metropolitan city has shifted from the city hall and market square to the airport plaza. In India, NRI-favored properties are, for example, represented as "ten minutes drive from the India Gandhi International (IGI) Airport" in Delhi; "close to the international airport in Powaii" in Mumbai; "near the planned new airport in Bangalore." Manhattan apartments (*sic*) ("exclusively for non-resident Indians") are more specific about what they see as "world class amenities," that is, "exclusive club – pool, sauna, Jacuzzi, shopping complex, covered parking, remote controlled security systems" – or their "international" features: paneled teakwood doors, powdered coated aluminum windows, colored fittings and single lever mixers in toilets. Other advertisers just offer "Western-style amenities."

Prominently featured facilities in the ads for these new developments include a greater or lesser selection of swimming pools (with spiral splashdowns, or slides) or "Beverly Hills style pools," jogging tracks, dish antennae, supermarkets, vegetarian restaurants, party lawns, creche (childcare) facilities, libraries, tennis courts, croquet lawns, indoor badminton courts, putting greens, discotheques, boat clubs, eighteen-hole golf courses, private airstrips, shopping malls, multi-cuisine restaurants, laundromats, gyms, table tennis and billiard rooms, party rooms, health clubs, saunas, landscaped gardens, waterfalls, and inside, individual Jacuzzis, video entry phone security systems, marble floors, teakwood floors, designer toilets, and air-conditioning.

The "international" nature of facilities is matched by the "international" (though mainly Euro-American) signifying nomenclature used to market the developments – Bel Air, La Hacienda, Villa Del Mar, Belvedere, Riviera, Manhattan – as well as a rich sprinkling of Anglicized pseudo-aristocratic names – Burlington, Somerville, Sinclair, Eden Gardens. On this evidence, "international standards" are clearly *less than* international and rather those of the "first world's" wealthiest states and of the most privileged class within them.

Similarly, though Indian names are also in evidence, the nomenclature is often less international than post- or neocolonial. It constructs a type of imperial nostalgia where colonial mimicry is strong. On the outskirts of Bangalore in a "premier residential locale," appropriately named Impero and signifying "The Imperial Revival," "the essence of British architecture is about to make its presence felt, with Oxford Impero, with motifs and elements from different styles of early seventeenth century architecture spanning 350 years." This "mega project ... is sprawling across 13 prime acres of which 75 per cent is devoted to traditional English style of landscape." The twenty-six buildings (with 550 premium apartments) sport appropriate signifying labels designed to appeal to the social and spatial memories of the diasporic NRI in London's West End and inner as well as outer suburbs of South Asian London: Hampstead, Regent's Park, Royal Crescent House, Bedford, Dorset, but also Drayton, Shelburne, and Bristol (though not Dubai, Dharan, Saudi Arabia).

The same Bangalore company is also developing Oxford Hermitage (with a club called The Scottish Glade), Oxford Suites, Oxford Studios, Oxford Chambers, Oxford Palazzo, Oxford Ambience, Oxford Manor, and, expectedly, Oxford Spires. Nostalgia is used to feed the imagination of the NRI (though also, perhaps, other readers of *India Today*, possibly British and other managers sent in with the MNCs). "Come! Experience the English splendor amidst the sprawling countryside" is the caption attached to the second phase of development for Oxford Hermitage. "Doddaballapu might not sound as evocative of the English countryside as, say, Kent. Or Sussex. But it looks just as picturesque." Bangalore–developed as a cantonment city by the British in the days of the Raj–offers, to the developers, the "hypnotic beauty of a green expanse" in which they build their "English country houses." In New Delhi, potential customers for a new series of "independent villas" are hailed with "Come, crown yourself with the distinction of the Scottish and Continental Villas."

In the symbolic construction of the "international" with which I began this section, presumably meaning *all* the world's nation–states including India (almost 200 in all), there is a peculiar disjuncture in that "international" and "India" are positioned as being mutually exclusive, rather than inclusive of each other. Thus, advertisements for the Manhattan apartments in Delhi suggest that "when you come home to India, you don't have to leave your international lifestyle behind." "International" here, therefore, is "other" than, or different from, India. Take, for example, "Draw the curtains and you could be in one of London's fashionable designer homes" (but not, apparently, in India), or the Premier Park View apartments in Madras, "that would easily belong in Park Avenue, New York; Mayfair, London and Bel-Air, Los Angeles" (but again, apparently not in India). Or "Men and women of the world may now [*sic*] feel perfectly at home in India."

Other appeals are to the social imaginary, linking architectural representation and status. For new, high-rise apartments in Delhi's South City ("Ivory Towers," "exclusively for NRI's"), buyers can "Live above the Rest" in "Homes the World Will Look Up To." In Mumbai, the Chesterfield apartments stand "Tall and proud, on a hill 100 feet above everybody else." Also near Mumbai, a "plush residential complex" is being developed, known as "Milestone (to symbolize your success)". If height is one status indicator, distance from the city is another. "As cities grow, become over-populated, polluted and real estate prices shoot up, more and more builders are shifting to the suburbs," according to the marketing manager of a major Indian developer. As in Istanbul inner-city exhaust pollution is now a major stimulant to the wealthy's desire to move away:

> Some things are just too good to be left to your imagination … . Like a luxurious lifestyle finding expression in elegant surroundings … and the deep satisfaction of breathing in clean, unpolluted air as the breeze blows gently by you … . Yet knowing that you are just 15 minutes from New Delhi airport (Oncu, 1997).

What is also remarkable about all these advertisements is the way that the space is gendered. None refers to the domestic realm of eating, dining, or cooking; none makes reference to kitchens, presumably because this is not within the normal spatial realm of the male owner or because it is still seen as the space of servants.[10]

Although most advertisements are specifically targeted at NRIs, it is not evident to whom else they are addressed. Some demand for apartments with high specifications certainly comes from representatives of MNCs resident in India on corporate lease who, like NRI investors, seek large, high-rise flats both for logistic convenience and security, though this clientele (unless Indian) is hardly likely to read *India*

Today. Other potential buyers could be institutional or private investors, or even drug lords. One might surmise that, whatever their nationality, they could belong to one class, namely, Sklair's "transnational global elite" (Sklair, 1989). Yet anecdotal evidence from India suggests the opposite, at least for some houses; space is bought by members of the new middle class and then split up according to family requirements. Moreover, for many projects, the exotic specifications described in the advertisements are often not executed in the event. It is largely for NRIs acquiring properties for their own occupation that developments provide all facilities prevalent in the West.[11] Irrespective of ownership, however, where new developments of such "international standards" are indeed built, they are likely to have a significant impact both as models of domestic consumption, on the new upper middle class, and as an example of overlap of financial, economic, cultural, discursive, and architectural globalization. Liberalization and globalization have clearly brought many MNCs into India. Indeed, MNCs and NRIs are acknowledged, both in adverts and accompanying articles in *India Today,* as the principal forces giving "a new impetus to building activity"; it is these who are associated with "selling lifestyles." In Chenai (Madras), "Spencer Plaza is already home to some of the best corporate names like Citibank, Cathay Pacific, American Express, Nestle etc." (The irony of the recent Indianization of the [previously Anglicized] names of major cities – Chenai [Madras], Mumbai [Bombay] – and what I describe is not hard to grasp.) In Bangalore, "the list [of MNCs] is mind boggling: Nike, Reebok, Adidas, Sanyo, Samsung, Asea Brown Boveri, 3M, Motorola Siemens, Hewlett-Packard ... IBM, ... AT&T, Compaq, British Aerospace, Rolls-Royce, Coats Viyella, Nestle, Unilever" (*India Today,* January 15, 1997). According to one property company in Delhi, "the country is moving to the central stage of the world-economy. Ushering in an era of plenty and prosperity. Nurturing many new aspirations and many new dreams," which Ansal Plaza, the "international shopping cum-office complex," is meant to symbolize. Appeals to the collective diasporic imaginary fuse luxury with dreams. Delhi is represented as a "dream city"; builders are said to be "cashing in on the NRI need to have dream houses and addresses in India" so they can "come home to luxury." In Madras, another company suggests "We don't build apartments ... . We build dreams."

The principal dream, in fact, may simply be the accumulation of capital. These are "Boom Times in Bangalore," Mumbai, or Chenai, announce the developers. In Rosewood City, a "luxurious 115 acre

English township" in south Delhi, you can "watch your money grow by leaps and bounds"; in the nearby Charmwood Village, prices tripled in three years in the mid-1990s. In Bangalore, "investment priorities have shifted from jewelry and stocks to real estate." Throwing the gauntlet to the financial machismo of the NRI, another company challenges, "The true measure of your success lies in how fast you can identify prime real estate opportunities in your homeland." In reality, of course, the prices (and profits) have fluctuated immensely.

These examples may suggest that the way this new architectural culture is being both imaged and imagined for the NRI diaspora is entirely exogenous, exhibiting little of "traditional" indigenous values and denying the identity from which it originates. This is not entirely correct. Occasionally the plan of a residence will reveal a puja room or, in regard to houses in another Bangalore suburb, reference is made to a nearby temple. Other bungalow plots are "developed with Vedic wisdom" according to ancient principles of Vastu Shastra.

Conclusion

If we accept advertising copy in *India Today* at face value, what meanings can we ascribe to the representations and the reality they purport to describe? My first inclination is to return to my comments at the start; to see these phenomena as the outcome of the interrelationship between media, migration, and imagination; between changing subjectivities and actions of the state and private capital. They represent a unique example of how spaces are produced and the very historically, culturally and geographically specific conditions which produce them.

What these materials also tell us is that there is no singular phenomenon that can be categorized as an "international" or "transnational identity" any more than one can speak, in the singular, about a "global culture." International identi*ties*, in the plural, are formed and framed from socially constructed historical, cultural, and spatially specific hybridizations. Nor, for obvious reasons, can there ever be "global" or "international standards," defined independently of the wealth, resources, and power of the richest and most powerful states.

If we consider Breckenridge's (1995) view that it is "the connection between public culture (in India) and global cultural flows that are at the heart of the matter." I believe what we are seeing here is one dimension (though an important, spatial one) of a transnational Indian diasporic culture. A significant determinant of this, on the evidence here, is clearly postcolonial: in the prominence of affluent English-speaking countries in determining the location of a large and influential number of NRIs (United States, United Kingdom, Australia – but also other postcolonial sites such as Singapore, South Africa, Hong Kong, Malaysia) where English is the enabling language and where a level of reciprocity in regard to educational and professional qualifications persists. These, principally "first world," societies also provide the models for emulation and/or cultural translation: when advertisers exhort readers to "Live the Way the World Does" they no more refer to rural Bangladesh than they do to Afghanistan or, indeed, rural India.

The assumption behind the advertisements – of the developers, architects, or potential customers – is to create an equivalence between the residential developments and the wealthiest locations in the world. A similar logic explains the style of architectural and urban design, except that here the distinctive historical connection to England privileges, for affluent NRIs who live there, their English associations. In this sense, not only is the economic, social, and legal situation of the NRI historically and geographically unique but the Indian diaspora it supports is representative of no one but themselves.

When looked at "internationally," and specifically in relation to the NRI community in either Britain or the United States, it is evident that Indian identities (and perhaps of others "displaced" abroad) are apparently dependent on their cultural and spatial context, and formed in a dialectical relation (and reaction) to it. In the cultural space of "the West," the objective is to look, and be, more "Indian," signifying one's own difference in response to the difference of others; in India, on the other hand, the NRI's cultural identity is again signified by showing one's difference to others, though in this case, it is by being more "Western."[12] This spatially split identity is especially evident when leafing through the pages of *India Today*. Cultural performances in the United States – traditional forms of dance, music, theater, as well as the Bombay film – when reported, are typically "Indian." In India, on the other hand, the new domestic architecture of the NRI is typically "international." Identities – social, spatial, and cultural – are being remade from outside.

The relative architectural uniformity which, for four decades of postindependence development, had spread over the built environment of new housing in Indian cities has, in the last decade or so, gradually become diversified. The combination of a state socialist agenda, the relative stranglehold of the Public Works Department, and the government ceiling on urban land holdings, had, until the early 1980s, resulted in a typologically constrained culture of domestic architectural design. In Delhi and elsewhere, hierarchical government quarters, private flats, and PWD bungalows and private houses were the concrete (and pukka) building types which served to marginalize the makeshift dwellings of the poor (*cacha*). From the mid-1980s, however, the suburbs of such cities as Bangalore, Pune, Delhi, and Mumbai have been planted with a whole new array of market-driven space of, and for, domestic consumption – four-bedroom penthouses, luxury villas, garden homes, apartment blocks, duplex apartments, row houses, studio apartments, designer bungalows and, in Bangalore (if the advertisements are to be taken at face value) "100 aristocratic villas specially designed by an American architect." With high-rise towers and luxury villas come designs for ranch houses from the United States, brick-built English homes from Surrey, and Canadian villas. As the habitus of the house and its environs establishes a particular kind of social, spatial, and cultural order (Bourdieu, 1977), the destabilization of old orders and the cultural imaginations of the new now create a totally new set of globally generated social, economic, and political parameters.[13]

These are the complex conditions under which new "local" as well as traveling "global" class identities are being formed. They result from the interactions between the real as well as the imagined lifestyles of a globally dispersed, diasporic NRI, the local middle class, developers, entrepreneurs, and the urban policies of the state. Yet it is also worth noting that where McDonald's has met with substantial cultural and political resistance in India (dietary habits touching more deeply held sacred and bodily taboos), exogenous spatial and architectural images have so far sparked off no riots.

From a more political position, however, we can see that this expanding architectural culture emerges from a hybridization of historic (colonial) times and diasporic spaces, an imagination of exogenous standards and transnational lifestyles. The existence of developers' agencies in the United States, United Kingdom, Australia, Bahrain, United Arab Emirates, Dubai, or Kuwait suggests some of the locations from which ideas, finance, and imaginations may arise. But property is also being sold to NRIs from the Sudan, China, Libya, Hong Kong, South Africa, Singapore, France – each group of potential investors and consumers responsible, if only in theory, for the expectations and standards of the lifestyle cultures.

In India, this internationalization of architectural space (whether in representation or reality) can, of course, be seen from many different viewpoints. The obvious point to recognize here is the etic or external subjectivity which has been given epistemological primacy in this inter-pretive account. From such a position, it can be said, for example, that the Indian city is becoming much more cosmopolitan, international-ized by designs for suburban housing from the United States, Canada, or Britain. It can also be said that these most recent developments are massively adding to the ways in which different forms of housing provi-sion both signal and shelter momentous social and economic divisions between the impossibly rich and the miserably poor, such that the dif-ferences one might see in Manhattan will, by comparison, look like a socialist paradise. From this perspective, New Delhi is fast becoming the most spatially refeudalized city in Asia, with new walled compounds sealing off luxury lifestyles from surrounding seas of poverty.

Notes

1   Acknowledgements: This chapter was given as a paper in the colloquium series "On the Margins Of Globalization" at the Global Affairs Institute, Maxwell School of Citizenship and Public Affairs, Syracuse University, January 29, 1999. It developed from an earlier, and shorter, paper read at the University of Michigan, published in Hemalata Dandekar, ed., *Cities, Space, and Globalization: An International Perspective*, College of Architecture and Urban Planning University of Michigan, Ann Arbor, 1998. I am indebted to various members of the audiences for comments on these occa-sions and, especially, to Abidin Kusno and Lt. Col. C. B. Ramesh (retired) of Bangalore for their suggestions on earlier drafts.
2   By transmigration, Schiller, Basch, and Blanc (1995) refer to the frequent and often regular movement between "home" and destinations "abroad".
3   *India Today* was first published from India in 1975, its circulation rising from an initial 5000 to 400 000 in December 1995. With its regional edi-tions and four international editions its total was estimated in 1995 to reach 1.1 million (*India Today*, December 31, 1995, p. 3). The international edition began in 1981, the US Supplement to this (from which the informa-tion in this paper is derived), in 1992, and the UK supplement, in 1995 (*India Today*, April 15, 1995, p. 1). Since 1998, the magazine, previously biweekly, has appeared weekly.
4   According to Indian government regulations, NRIs can also be citizens of other countries.
5   In 1987, the number of NRIs was put at 12.6 million, of which the seven largest population were in Nepal (3.8m), Malaysia (1.2m), Sri Lanka (1m), South Africa (850 000), the United Kingdom (789 000), Mauritius (701 000), and the United States (500 000) (see *Statistical Outline of India*, 1995). More recent estimates are likely to double the total number and include 1.2 million Indian Americans in the United States, of whom 25 percent were born in the United States (*India Today*, January 15, 1997, p. 56c), and approximately 1 million in the United Kingdom. According to BBC's World Service (July 1998) a Global Organization of Indians Overseas is in the

process of being formed for an estimated 22 million overseas Indians, the object of which will be to develop various services, including an airline and a system to promote contact between members.

6 As far as my own immigrant status is concerned, when in the United States, I have, technically, the same identity – as a British, Anglo-Saxon, white, UK citizen with a "Green Card" – as the Indian Resident Alien

7 I take this phrase, and much of the following paragraph, from Oncu, 1997.

8 While "Western-style" is too coarse a description, and "Euro-American" too geographically specific (because of its existence elsewhere), I resist the use of other descriptors for reason which will become apparent subsequently.

9 For reasons of anonymity, I have changed the original names throughout.

10 Local informants point out that the "design of kitchen and specific areas to meet 'ladies' demands are invariably incorporated," which confirms the point that the ads are addressed to a male readership.

11 I am indebted to Bangalore realty consultant Lt. Col. C. B. Ramesh (retired) for some of the information here.

12 I am grateful to Abidin Kusno and Shery Ryan for this insight.

13 Advertisements for single apartments from 1995 to 1998 might be from $80 000 upward.

References

Abel, Chris (1997). *Architecture and identity: Towards a global eco-culture*. Boston: Boston Architectural Press, for Heinemann-Butterworth.

Anderson, Perry (l998). *The origins of postmodernity*. London and New York: Verso.

Appaduri, Arjun (1996). *Modernity at large. Cultural dimensions of globalization*. Minneapolis: University of Minnesota Press.

———. (1990). "Disjunction and difference in the global cultural economy." In Mike Featherstone (ed.). *Global culture. Nationalism, globalization and modernity* (pp. 295–310). London and Thousand Oaks: Sage.

Barthes, Roland (1972). "Myth today." In A. Lavers (trans.). *Mythologies*. New York: Hill and Wang.

Bourdieu, Pierre (1977). *Outline of a theory at practice*. New York: Cambridge University Press.

Bourdieu, Pierre (1984). *Distinction: a social critique at the judgement of taste*. Cambridge: Harvard University Press.

Breckenridge, Carol (1995). *Consuming modernity: Public culture in South Asia*. Minneapolis: University of Minnesota Press.

Clifford, James (1992). "Traveling cultures." In Lawrence Grossberg, Cary Nelson, Paula Treichler (eds.). *Cultural studies* (pp. 96–116). London and New York: Routledge.

Crinson, Mark (1996). *Empire building. Orientalism and Victorian architecture*. London and New York: Routledge.

Dovey, Kim (1999). *Framing places: Mediating power in built form*. Archi*text* Series. London and New York: Routledge.

Evenson, Norma (1989). *The Indian metropolis: A view towards the West*. New Haven: Yale University Press.

Featherstone, Mike (ed.). (1990). *Global culture. Nationalism, globalization and modernity.* London, Newbury Park, and New Delhi: Sage.

Gupta, Akhil and J. Ferguson, (1992). "Beyond 'culture': Space, identity, and the politics of difference." *Cultural Anthropology,* 7 (1), pp. 6–23.

Hannerz, Ulf (1989). "Notes on the global ecumene." *Public Culture,* 1 (2), pp. 66–75. *India Today.* (1995–96).

Jencks, Charles (1986). *What is post-modernism?* London and New York: Academy Editions/St Martin's Press.

Jameson, Fredic (1992) *Postmodernism, or, the Cultural logic of late Capitalism.* Durhan; N. C.: Duke University Press.

King, Anthony D. (1997). *Culture, globalization and the world-system. Contemporary conditions for the representation of identity.* 2nd edn. (Binghamton: SUNY, 1991). Minneapolis: University of Minnesota Press.

King, Anthony D. (1995). "The times and spaces of modernity (Or 'Who Needs Postmodernism?')." In Mike Featherstone, Scott Lash, Roland Robertson (eds.). *Global Modernities* (pp. 108–23). London, Delhi, and Thousand Oaks, Calif.: Sage.

———. (1976). *Colonial urban development.* London and Boston: Routledge & Kegan Paul.

Kusno, Abidin (2000). *Beyond the postcolonial: Architecture, urban space and political cultures in Indonesia.* Architext Series. London and New York: Routledge.

Leaf, Michael (1994). "The suburbanization of Jakarta: A concurrence of economics and ideology." *Third World Planning Review,* 16 (4), pp. 341–56.

Lefebvre, Henri (1991), *The production of space.* Cambridge: Blackwell.

Metcalf, Thomas R. (1989). *An imperial vision. Indian architecture and Britain's Raj.* Berkeley: University of California Press

Oncu, Ayse (1997). "The myth of the 'ideal home' travels across cultural borders to Istanbul," In A. Oncu and P. Weyland (eds.). *Space, culture and power. New Identities in Globalizing Cities* (pp. 56–72). London and New Jersey: Zed Books.

Robertson, Roland (1992). *Globalization: Social theory and global culture.* London, New Delhi, and Thousand Oaks, Calif.: Sage.

Schiller, Nina Glick, Linda Basch, and Cristina Blanc (1995). "From immigrant to transmigrant: Theorizing transnational migration." *Anthropological Quarterly,* 68 (1), pp. 48–63.

Scriver, Peter (1995). *Rationalisation, standardisation and control in design. A cognitive historical study of architectural design and planning in the Public Works Department of British India, 1855–1901.* The Hague: CIP-Gegevens Koninklijke Biblioteek.

Short, John Rennie and Y. Kim (1999). *Globalization and the city.* New York: Addison Wesley Longmans.

Sklair, Leslie (1989). *Sociology of the global system.* London and New York: Harvester Wheatsheaf.

Statistical Outline of India 1994–95. (1995). Bombay: Tata Services. Ltd.

Sudjic, Deyan (1992) *The hundred mile city.* New York: Harcourt Brace

Thrift, Nigel (1986). "The internationalization of producer services and the intergration of the Pacific Basin property market." In M. J. Taylor and N. J. Thriff (eds.). *Multinationals and the restructuring of the world economy.* London: Croom Helm.

Part III
Globalization in the Margins

7

Globalization and Women: Gender and Resistance in the Informal Sector of Peru[1]

Maureen Hays-Mitchell

Although the term "globalization" became a keyword of the late twentieth century, only recently has scholarly discourse focused in a rigorous and meaningful way on the character and implications of this seemingly inexorable process. Despite its diverse expressions ranging from the economic to the cultural, social, political, and environmental, most observers agree that the central component of late twentieth-century globalization was the economic reorganization of our world. At the global scale, such reorganization has led to unprecedented economic growth as vast amounts of wealth have been generated within the past several decades. Notwithstanding, it is increasingly apparent that the uncritically celebrated benefits of economic globalization have not been shared equally among all regions and populations of the world. Indeed more than ever, troubling inequities mark the production, distribution, and enjoyment of wealth not only between the North and the South but also within each region. The market-driven model of development that characterizes the globalization process has directly contributed to the increasing intensification and sophistication of worldwide economic integration. Institutional measures to liberalize and deregulate trade, together with the Third World debt crisis and related economic reform measures, have required that developing economies restructure and open themselves to a liberalized network of global trade and investment. As a result, services, production, markets, labor, capital and debt have increasingly globalized. This harbors both positive and negative ramifications for developing societies.

It is difficult to tease out the positive from the negative when examining the impact of global economic change in the developing world. Many restructured Latin American economies, for example, are experiencing rapid macroeconomic growth, especially as public sector entities are privatized and foreign investment returns to the region. However, microeconomic indicators suggest that important sectors of society are not included in the economic expansion publicized in official statistics; poverty and social dislocation remain entrenched in the very same settings. Moreover, mounting evidence suggests that the negative effects of globalization disproportionately affect poor women throughout the developing world. Debt-related economic restructuring, for example, has entailed cutbacks in public services and large-scale job losses. Both measures hit poor women especially hard, as they place great strains on their time, energy, resources, and goodwill. The immediate price that women pay is directly attributable to the central, unique, and incomparable role they play in sustaining society. They devote greater time to income-generation, household production, and community management activities. In so doing, they experience deteriorating health, widespread exhaustion, and increasing levels of poverty. Not only does this bode badly for poor women in particular but, due to the critical role that women play in all societies of the world, it bodes especially poorly for societies in their entirety.

Such a state of affairs compels us to ask serious questions about the nature and implications of economic globalization and accompanying development models. Accordingly, in this chapter, I explore the socioeconomic impact of globalization on the most vulnerable sectors of Latin American society by examining the changing status under economic restructuring of poor urban women and their dependent relatives in Peru as well as the responses of this population to their changing circumstances. Although it may be fair to ask whether increased poverty can be attributed directly to economic globalization in the form of debt-related restructuring, widely accepted data are incontrovertible that poverty has increased for the majority of men, women, and children in the world's poorest countries within the era of neoliberal restructuring. Moreover, it has increased disproportionately for poor women in particular. Today in Latin America, as throughout much of the developing world, "women in their vast majority [are] concentrated in the most impoverished and oppressed sectors of societies" (Molyneux, 1992, p. 254). Clearly, economic globalization is occurring on a gendered terrain.

Nuancing the gendered dimensions of global economic change

Much of the poverty and oppression experienced by the majority of Latin American women is the result of complex and interrelated factors, including the ongoing process of global economic restructuring, old and new development paradigms embraced by Latin American governments, and an entrenched system of patriarchy characterizing social relations throughout the region. Although advances are underway in understandings of the differential impact of economic globalization, neoliberal restructuring, and changing development paradigms on diverse populations throughout the region, scant attention is being directed toward the implications of these processes for gender relations in the workplace, household, and society at large. Instead, the bulk of scholarship produced in the past decade has focused on the crises of survival faced by women and the household strategies they have devised to mitigate their deteriorating status. This literature locates women as "victims" of globalization and/or their own patriarchal cultures rather than as agents actively engaged in their economic, social, and/or political environments.

In this analysis, I seek to explore the more subtle and nuanced meanings of global economic change by analyzing the efforts of poor urban women to resist and transform the disempowering and hegemonic ramifications of economic restructuring. I ground this analysis in the experiences of women who participate in microenterprise development programs[2] in the shantytowns surrounding Lima (1) to illustrate that the negative effects of economic globalization and neoliberal restructuring disproportionately affect poor women, and (2) to highlight the empowering dimension of their responses to their changing circumstances. I maintain that making the decision to participate in a microenterprise development program constitutes a strategy of defiance and/or resistance which is rooted in the everyday experience of poor urban working women. The few programs which respond to the needs and aspirations of participating women, by directly incorporating them in the design and operation of the program, help women confront and cope with the negative effects of economic restructuring. They unlock for women the opportunity to acquire the social, technical, and financial skills that are necessary to move beyond the status of "victim" or "survivor." Yet, to reconceptualize poor urban women in an alternative and empowering way, we must understand, first, that such women are active agents of social change who make choices, have critical perspectives on their own situations, and think and organize collectively and, second, that their daily activities represent more than survival strategies. They are conscious efforts to change their economic and social environment, that is, to effect long-term change.

The analysis presented here builds on new feminist scholarship whose methodologies not only provide a more gender-aware economics but reveal broader dimensions of women's resistance to their subordinate status than previously recognized (see, for example, Elson, 1995a; Bakker, 1994; Sparr, 1994; Van Lieshout, 1996; Waring, 1999, 1988; among others). For instance, Aptheker contends that since much resistance is based on the need to survive, the act of survival itself is a form of resistance and "[t]o see women's resistance is to also see the accumulated effects of daily, arduous, creative, sometimes ingenious labors, performed over time, sometimes over generations" (Aptheker, 1989, pp. 173–4). Hence, it is possible to see how the daily "survival" activities of poor urban women – many of whom labor in the informal sector – represent, in the words of Eckstein, "different traditions of protest" to the market and state forces that have made their lives increasingly difficult (Eckstein, 1986, pp. 10–11). This discussion represents one component of an ongoing investigation into the gendered dimensions of the processes of capitalist development and economic restructuring in Latin America. It is based directly on fieldwork conducted in 1993, 1994, and 1997, which itself was the outgrowth of a national-level investigation of women informal traders conducted between 1986 and 1988. Mindful of my position as a woman of the North, I do not presume to represent poor Peruvian women but rather I aim to provide a space for their voices to be heard.

Economic restructuring and women's poverty in Peru

In Peru, economic globalization has assumed the form of economic restructuring imposed in the name of debt relief and development. Austerity measures accompanying the structural adjustment program that was designed and imposed by the international financial community in August 1990 precipitated conditions of economic crisis and political violence. Despite recent improvements in macroeconomic indicators, such as inflation and GDP, adjustment policies have yielded debilitating consequences for low-income and middle-income families in general, and they have affected the lives of women in disproportionate, gender-specific, and multidimensional ways. The majority of the poor in Peru are women and dependent children (Feldman, 1992; FLACSO, 1993; Tanski, 1994; United Nations, 1995). Women, whether single-heads or co-heads of households, have seen their purchasing power as food providers deteriorate as adjustment policies have reduced wages, eliminated food subsidies, and inflated prices. Cutbacks in public expenditures in health care and education have led to diminished care and training for poor women and their families while increasing their burden as the primary health care providers and educators within families. Throughout Peru, women are increasingly forced to balance greater amounts of wage work with higher levels of subsistence, domestic, and community production in meeting household needs, thus intensifying their double – indeed triple – burden.

For many women throughout Peru, the threat to household survival inherent in the difficulties associated with structural adjustment has especially intensified their participation in the paid workforce. Women's participation in the formal sectors increased from 24 percent to 38 percent of the total economically active and employed population between 1981 and 1993. In the informal labor market, their participation increased from 35 percent to 52 percent within the same period and is assumed to be even greater at present (FLACSO, 1993, p. 46, p. 52; Webb and Fernández-Baca, 1994, p. 674, p. 676). Although poor Peruvians in general are at a disadvantage within the urban labor market, women's position is characterized by employment relations and work conditions that place them at the bottom of the occupational hierarchy. That position within the urban labor market is marked by limited and insecure employment opportunities with substandard wages, poor work conditions, unstable hours, and disadvantageous – if any – contracts. Women predominate in low-wage jobs or extremely small-scale, owner-operated ventures both of which shunt them into gender-segregated occupations including streetvending, domestic service, industrial homeworking, food preparation, and repetitious manual production. These occupations offer limited access to productive resources, autonomy, and opportunity for advancement. Women hold few positions of power within labor organizations and are further handicapped by the lack of affordable and adequate child care, escalating rates of spousal abandonment, an increasingly high cost of living, and gender stereotyping which denies them the requisite skills, training and capital to secure more lucrative and/or secure employment.

Newly emerging scholarship suggests that women's gender-specific experience of structural adjustment is the outcome of gender bias inherent in the restructuring process, which fails to consider women's unpaid work (and the resources required to discharge that work) as well as the relationship between women's occupational subordination and gender relations within societies such as Peru. Indeed, it posits that the concept and implementation of structural adjustment programs are premised on women's unpaid labor as well as on the existing unequal division of roles, responsibilities, and rights between men and women within underdeveloped societies. That is to say, not only does structural adjustment perpetuate and exacerbate such conditions, but it presumes that women's unwaged work within the home, community, and workplace will continue (Afshar and Dennis, 1992; Bakker, 1994; Elson, 1991 1992, 1995b, 1995c, 1995d; Emeagwali, 1995; Moser, 1989, 1993; O'Connell, 1996; Sparr 1994).

The marginalization of women informal workers

In the absence of viable employment opportunities, many poor urban women are left with no option but to turn to their own resourcefulness and attempt to produce and/or market goods in the hope of earning enough income to support their families. Most small businesses (that is, microenterprises) operated by women, when compared to those operated by men, are found to be extremely small-scale, based in or out of the home, undercapitalized, and exceptionally insecure. While limited capital assets combined with an ambiguous legal status (for example, "formal" versus "informal") exclude most small-scale operators – male and female alike–from official channels of institutional credit, women find themselves disadvantaged relative to their male counterparts within both formal and informal credit markets. Traditionally, small-scale operators, popularly referred to as *informales* or microentrepreneurs, have been restricted to informal sources of credit (for example, relatives, friends, creditors, suppliers), often paying several times the official interest rate. A national-level study of informal commerce in Peru found that, although women traders profess a need for credit, they are less likely than their male counterparts to secure loans within the informal credit market, and those who do secure loans are typically charged interest rates in excess of the prevailing rate even for the informal market (Hays-Mitchell, field surveys 1986–7).

In recent years, credit-extension programs specially designed to support small-scale production and commerce and sponsored primarily by non-governmental organizations (NGOs) have actively sought out *informales*, or microentrepreneurs, to receive loans at the official financial market rate. Responding to a highly visible and compelling need, such organizations have proliferated as Peru's institutional crisis has intensified. However, in an environment of neoliberal restructuring, characterized by diminishing financial support and heightened demand for accountability on the part of donor organizations, most credit-extension programs are forced to adopt a lending philosophy and methodology consistent with the ideological underpinnings of neoliberal capitalism. They are pressed to target "credit-worthy" clients whose operations are deemed most likely to respond quickly and positively to an infusion of capital in terms of capital accumulation and employment creation. Accordingly, most programs seek out candidates who are in relatively lucrative lines of work (for instance, manufacturing), have previous business experience, employ workers other than the owner and his/her family, and demonstrate the potential to expand and become profitable.

Although women constitute approximately 40 percent of the informal sector in Peru (Webb and Fernández-Baca, 1994, p. 674), these criteria exclude most of them because they predominate in the least capitalized and most poorly remunerated sectors of the economy (for example, informal commerce, food preparation, garment assembly) and are more likely than men to be new entrants into the workforce, to have limited formal work experience, and to work alone or with the assistance of family members. So, unless women *informales* themselves or the economic activities in which they predominate are specifically targeted by microenterprise development programs, they are all but systematically excluded from the benefits of these programs.

Despite the widespread marginalization of women in programs of microenterprise development, the reality persists that women producers play a critical role in the economic and social life of Peru. Their work directly and indirectly provides sustenance to a large proportion of the urban population living in poverty. Women are known to reinvest in their own and their husbands' productive enterprises, using a high proportion of locally produced goods. They are also more likely to hire workers as a growth strategy than their male counterparts, who tend to purchase equipment with any surplus capital. Further, women invest heavily in family welfare – especially in the nutrition, clothing, health care and education of their children – as well as in community welfare through active participation in organizations designed to facilitate collective consumption. In these ways, women producers enhance the human resource base of Peru and contribute to local economic activity (Hays-Mitchell, field surveys 1986–7, 1993–4). This is true also of women small-scale producers elsewhere in Latin America (Berger and Buvinic, 1989; Blumberg, 1995; Lycette and White, 1989) and in general (Baud and de Bruijne, 1993; Weidemann, 1992).

Because the multiple roles of poor urban women in Peru render largely indistinguishable the boundaries that conventionally delimit the productive and reproductive realms of society, many of the activities they perform are irreconcilable with the rigid conceptualization of the notion of work prevalent in social science discourse, development praxis, and neoliberal restructuring. By conceptualizing the multiplicity of activities through which poor urban women in Peru "make a living" as a collection of strategies designed to maintain the household and community in times of crisis, rather than as a composite of occupations bearing economic and social significance, hegemonic notions of "work" deny the productive content of their diverse activities. These notions not only denigrate the work of women in general but disempower women producers themselves. Interviews with randomly selected women informal workers indicate that, although they consider themselves to be producers of goods and providers of services for a large segment of the urban population, like society in general, these women have a low estimation of the value of their own labor (Hays-Mitchell, field surveys, 1986–7, 1993–4). Not only do they commonly neglect to consider the time and effort expended in producing and/or marketing their goods and/or services, but they typically view their efforts to be tangential to processes operating in the national, regional, and/or global economy. The large-scale exclusion of women from mainstream programs of microenterprise assistance serves to reinforce this situation.

It would seem that poor urban women are doubly injured by global economic change. On the one hand, the threat to household survival inherent in the difficulties associated with structural adjustment has increased the work load and diminished the living standards of poor urban women and their dependent relatives. On the other hand, efforts designed to mitigate the negative impact of structural adjustment on the poor – such as microenterprise development programs – bypass and serve to reinforce, if not exacerbate, conditions of poverty and oppression for those most seriously affected by it.

Resistance and empowerment

Cognizant of the vital role women play in the economic and social life of Peru and of data from around the world indicating that women are a highly credit-worthy clientele (see Berger and Buvinic, 1989; Blumberg, 1995; Bornstein, 1996; Clark,1991; Creevey, 1996; Weidemann, 1992), a small group of development agencies have either initiated or redirected programs specifically toward women *informales*. Their programs comprise a cluster of innovative methodologies which provide credit and training specifically for sectors in which women predominate, including commerce and services as well as operations with very few employees (such as home-based and mobile activities). In the course of my fieldwork, I conducted case studies of six microenterprise development programs. Of these, five are gender-focused in that they target women producers in particular and one, though purportedly gender-blind in selection criteria and program methodology, targets small-scale business sectors in which women predominate (for example, commerce and services). Of the five gender-focused programs, three utilize a variation of the "village-banking" methodology pioneered in the early 1980s by FINCA-International and two apply a gendered methodology exclusive to their organizations. The village-banking style programs serve women who have come together to form credit cooperatives which, in turn, serve as a forum for gender consciousness raising. The two other programs involve credit and business training customized for each woman and training of women to manage their businesses. Integral to the five gender-focused programs is the expectation that participating women will contribute directly to the design and implementation of the program. The one gender-blind program in which women predominate as participants utilizes the "solidarity group" methodology, in which credit recipients form a group and guarantee one another's credit worthiness, agreeing to meet any default on the part of any group member. It is devoid of a gendered dimension in that gender is neither a criterion for participation nor a component of methodology.

Without exception, women indicate that participating in a program of microenterprise development has enabled them to confront and cope with the debilitating effects of structural adjustment. Nearly all explain that they have been able to move beyond a preoccupation with survival. They are able to diminish debt, expand savings, improve family nutrition, reduce production and marketing costs, and increase their ability to make short and long-term investments in both their professional and personal lives (for instance, pursue education, build a home, upgrade living and/or work conditions). For many, even experienced producers, these programs provide their first opportunity to access working capital on nonexploitative terms as well as a rare opportunity to come together to achieve something for themselves and independent of their families.

In gaining access to economic resources and greater control over their own labor, women workers are able to enhance the quality of their employment. Many (approximately one-third of new socias [members/associates] in the five gender-focused programs studied) have been empowered – personally, technically and financially – to enter the labor market for the first time:

[The program] has been like bread from heaven. ... For us who didn't know how to do business, it's given us an opportunity to begin on our own. (36-year-old mother of three who had never worked for any sustained period of time outside the home).

And now that I know how to work outside [of the home] I think about how to improve my business, how to sell more. ... I began with just one little kilo of rice and then I bought my little cart ... now I have kerosene, a stove and two stools.

(44-year-old mother who was often involved in preparing food for community fundraisers but lacked the self-confidence and financial means to prepare food for sale).

Some have been empowered to develop their businesses; for example, switching to more lucrative lines of work or making the move, as has this 52-year-old widow, from a *rodante* (transient streetvendor) to a *puestera* (streetvendor selling from a permanently located stand):

The loan is a great help ... with it I bought animals and birds ... I would leave early to sell. ... I sold pretty well. ... With my profit I then bought a kilo of sugar, soap ... and walking I would sell more ... and before long I was able to cancel my debt [to the moneylender]. Next, I will buy undergarments and maybe even shoes to sell ... and I will set up my little stand *allá* [indicating a busy street near the retail market].

Others, such as this 28-year-old knitter who was languishing in a dead-end job, have been empowered to leave unfavorable employment arrangements and start their own businesses:

I wanted to work with alpaca and lamb's wool the way my mother and aunts and uncle taught me. ... But this requires a lot of capital. ... With so little capital I was not able to work for myself but only in a workshop with the owner's wool and machines. ... At the end of the day all I had was a few *intis* and with that I would go to the market to buy a little food and it was gone. ... But now I have a loan and I am able to make some capital. ... I buy first a little lamb's wool and even some alpaca. ... I work with needles and want soon to rent – maybe even buy – a machine for larger pieces. ... Without this loan I wouldn't even have capital to buy wool for one little sweater.

In the process, some generate employment – a tenet of neoliberal reform:

I invest this capital in my business. ... I try to buy more fabric and, whenever possible, a new machine and little by little I'm earning more. ... I began with one machine, now I have three [machines] and two friends who sew with me.
(35-year-old seamstress who employs two neighbors in her home).

Women's comments concerning income expenditure highlight the intimate linkage between their productive and reproductive lives. Of the three village-banking style programs studied, *socias* improved their income-earning capacity by, on average, 300 percent in the first year of participation. Over 80 percent of all *socias* were married or co-heads of household while the remaining were single-heads. The increased income-earning capacity of women co-heads contributed significantly to household incomes and translated immediately into improved nutrition, clothing, and education for children as well as upgraded housing conditions for the family as a whole. The experience of this 34-year-old mother of five is typical:

My husband drives a *colectivo* ... after he pays his cousin for the car and buys his gasoline he sometimes doesn't have even a single sol for us. ... I took in laundry for the women on the other side [more affluent neighborhoods] ... but still only had money to buy what we would eat today. ... Now with this loan I have a sewing machine and repair clothing for those same women and even make clothes for my sister to sell at her stand in the market. ... Now the children always have something warm to eat before going to school. ... If my baby gets sick ... I take her to the clinic. ... We are constructing a house. ... If we need a light bulb, a bucket for water, I buy it.

For single heads of households, the opportunity to increase a women's income-generating capacity has proven critical, as in the case of this 31-year-old single mother of four:

We single mothers always have to think about how we will get ahead enough ... enough for our children to eat, to go to school. ... Thank God for this [money] that lets me work and feed my children. ... My life has changed substantially for me and especially for my children ... this money that I am able to borrow allows us to live ... it allows us to think not only about what we will eat today.

Most *socias* acknowledge that significant changes are underway in their lives – changes that transcend a preoccupation with economic survival. Many *socias*, for example, claim to exert greater control over their lives in decisions concerning fertility and income expenditure and to be better able to bargain and bring pressure to bear both at the workplace and within the household:

I feel more self-confident. ... I feel better organized. ... I have more control in economic decisions in my house and in other matters too. ... Look, I have told my husband that I do not want to have more babies. ... I want us to be able to provide for the pair that we have, to educate them, to help them advance. ... He accompanies me to the family meetings. ... He understands how I feel and he agrees with me.

(27-year-old mother of two who operates a juice stand in a busy
market).

We have become *machas*. ... If we want a refreshment, a new blouse or something for the house, we buy it, and our husbands can't ask us how much it cost. ... We alone keep track of our costs and expenditures. ... We are much happier, much more content.

(48-year-old women who rents cellular phone time in a community without phone service).

Similarly, they indicate that they have acquired a clearer sense of their rights as citizens and that they have gained respect, influence, and authority at home and in the community. Their remarks underscore the complementarity between women's practical and strategic gender interests as they suggest that organizing to meet immediate material needs (that is, practical gender interests) necessitates addressing long-term ideological goals (that is, strategic gender interests):

Our husbands abused us before, now they don't say anything ... they are not able to treat us as before.

(woman, in her early forties, who markets small electronic devices).

Before we refused to speak up, now we have learned to speak out. … The program has taught us that not only men have rights … it has taught us to respect ourselves.

> (48-year-old woman who sells refreshments "office-to-office" in an affluent business district of Lima).

Now we women can be independent because before … we only thought men could get loans and that women couldn't.

> (woman, of unspecified age, who sells women's lingerie in a market stall).

These changes may be a function of the integrative and holistic nature of gender-focused methodologies which proceed beyond the technical aspects of credit dissemination to broach issues relating to self-identity, group consciousness, and gendered social relations. By infusing a human dimension into the credit process, gender-focused programs endeavor to strengthen the creative capacity, initiative, and confidence of participating women while providing critical information, experience, and expertise. Methodologies stress the self-worth (auto-valorización) of individual socias and the need to be active agents influencing their own destinies. Conversations with women microentrepreneurs suggest that questions of consciousness and self-identity are central to defining their engagement with the economic and social environments. Many *socias*, for example, have concluded that, after a lifetime of economic marginalization and political disenfranchisement, if they are to withstand the difficulties associated with structural adjustment, it will be due to their own strength, skills, and determination. This psychological impact is perhaps the most critical change evidenced in individual women who participate in such programs and is summed up in the words of a women microentrepreneur who used her credit and training to begin a shoemaking business with her husband: "I feel valued, and if I am left alone I will be able to support my children."

The experience of organizing collectively seems to open *socias* to an important social space, giving them the opportunity and confidence to advise colleagues, converse with acquaintances, and contribute to community-wide gatherings with greater ease and confidence. It also serves as a mutual support system, providing women the opportunity to establish relationships outside the family, to recognize that their problems extend beyond their households, to vent concerns, and to seek solutions collectively. In describing their experiences at a gathering following a routine community bank meeting, *socias* explained:

> [the program] is like a school for us, something most of us did not have since we were forced to earn our own living since an early age … Because we come together to reflect collectively on the activities we engage in, together we are educating one another and that only happens because we do it together.
>
> Before it was different than it is now, perhaps because before we were inhibited, but not anymore. … We've learned a lot from it because we have friends, we relate our problems and we try to solve our problems together. … We know one another like sisters. … Now we are free because we are able to get out to meet and to work. … We've even formed a volleyball team, we can play … participate in the sport and no one can say anything to us because we are doing it together.

In this way, gender-focused microenterprise development programs provide a space in which *socias* can resist and challenge hegemonic forces as well as envision and negotiate alternative futures.

The space opened by these opportunities is not, however, uncontested. Women encounter opposition both at the workplace and in the household. Male opposition to female "entrepreneurs" is not clear-cut but rather complex and ever-changing. For example, the same men can be both partners/husbands within the household who learn to appreciate the improved income-generating capacity of their wives/partners and microentrepreneurs in the workplace who feel threatened by the perceived competition posed by female counterparts. To maintain their participation in their new space (that is, gender-focused microenterprise development programs) as well as peace at home, women must negotiate away the everyday oppositions generated by their male partners and/or workmates. Accordingly, they represent their participation in the programs as a necessary act – incumbent on them as wives and mothers – to ensure family survival. However, their understanding of themselves is an internally generated and empowering identity and, hence, represents a deliberate act of resistance – the outcome of which enables them to better confront and withstand the difficulties associated with economic restructuring. The degree of success that women experience in negotiating away opposition in large part depends on their ability to convince male partners and co-workers that denying poor urban women their equal share of development resources has far-reaching negative ramifications for them as individuals and for members of Peruvian society in general. The extent to which this is possible hinges on women's ability to persuade them that women's new social space is nonthreatening and mutually beneficial. The imperative to accept this may well be an unanticipated imperative of economic globalization and neoliberal restructuring.

Conclusion

Although processes of economic globalization and neoliberal restructuring have affected poor urban women in multidimensional and gender-specific ways, analyses of their experiences tend to locate them unidimensionally as "victims" or "survivors" of economic change whose everyday efforts and activities are undertaken simply in reaction to these processes and events. Such approaches reflect a gender bias embedded in social science discourse, development praxis, and neoliberal capitalism which diverts attention from issues of women's agency, resistance, and empowerment. In contrast, I have argued that the act of survival itself (that is, the diverse production, reproduction, and community-management activities undertaken on a daily basis by poor women in Peru) is a form of resistance that represents a willful effort by such women to engage their economic, social, and/or political environments. That is to say, it represents a willful effort to resist the disempowering and hegemonic tendencies inherent in their national program of structural adjustment and, by extension, the global process of economic reorganization – tendencies that disproportionately affect poor urban women.

In offering women the opportunity to access economic resources, acquire technical skills, and come together to achieve something for themselves alone and independent of their families, gender-focused microenterprise development programs provide the space for poor urban women to construct and negotiate clearly-defined identities that reflect who they truly are – women who do not simply have problems and needs (passive victims) but who perceive choices and possess the capacity to act on them (active agents). As one woman in the informal sector explained, "I have come to understand that I don't have to suffer the things that happen around me. ... The worst thing is not knowing this ... not knowing that you can do something about your life. ... That is like slavery." Although the experiences of women participating in gender-focused programs of microenterprise assistance suggest that, through them, they are better able to withstand the debilitating effects of neoliberal restructuring as well as acquire a stronger voice within their households, workplaces and communities, this should not necessarily be taken as an unqualified endorsement of all such programs. Instead, we should challenge the very conditions that have made such programs necessary. Indeed, their very existence is testimony to the deeply gendered and troubled nature of the type of global economic change presently underway as well as to the isolated nature of efforts to mitigate the disenfranchising conditions of this change.

Notes

1 Excerpts of this chapter are drawn from a previously published study of the gendered experience of economic restructuring and its relevance to the creation and reproduction of ideologies and identities of gender within Peruvian society and the international development community. They appeared in "From survivor to entrepreneur: Gendered dimensions of microenterprise development in Peru." *Environment and Planning A: International Journal of Urban and Regional Research*, 31: pp. 251–71, and are reproduced with permission from Pion Limited, London.
2 Though definitions vary, it is generally agreed that microenterprise employs one to four workers and has a working capital of US$600 per employee. It is estimated that the number of microenterprises operating in Peru increased from 75 000 in 1988 to over 100 000 in 1994 and is projected to reach approximately 135 000 by 2000. Of these, approximately 40 percent are believed to be owned and operated by women (Webb and Fernández-Baca, 1994, p. 671, p. 674).

References

Afshar, H. and C. Dennis (1992). "Women, recession and adjustment in the third world." In H. Afshar and C. Dennis (eds.). *Women and adjustment policies in the Third World* (pp. 3–12). New York: St. Martin's Press.
Aptheker, B. (1989). *Tapestries of life*. Amherst: University of Massachusets Press.
Bakker, Isabella (ed.). (1994). *The strategic silence: Gender and economic policy*. Ottawa: North–South Institute.
Baud, I. and de G. Bruijne (1993). *Gender, small-scale industry and development policy*. London: Intermediate Technology Publications.
Berger, M. and M. Buvinic (1989). *Women's ventures: Assistance to the informal sector in Latin America*. West Hartford, Conn.: Kumarian Press.
Blumberg, R. (1995). "Gender, microenterprise, performance, and power: Case studies from the Dominican Republic, Ecuador, Guatemala and Swaziland." In

C. Bose and E. Acosta-Belén (eds.). *Women in the Latin American development process* (pp. 194–226). Philadelphia: Temple University Press.

Bornstein, David (1996). *The price of a dream: The story of the Grameen Bank and the idea that it is helping the poor to change their lives.* New York: Simon and Schuster.

Clark, J. (1991). *Democratizing development: The role of voluntary organizations.* West Hartford, Conn.: Kumarian Press.

Creevey, L. (1996). *Changing women's lives and work: An analysis of the impacts of eight microenterprise projects.* Intermediate Technology Publications.

Eckstein, S. (1986). *Power and popular protest: Latin American social movements.* Berkeley: University of California Press.

Elson, D. (ed.). (1995a). *Male bias in the development process.* 2nd ed. Manchester: Manchester University Press.

———. (1995b). "Male bias in the development process: An overview." In D. Elson (ed.). *Male bias in the development process.* 2nd ed. Manchester: Manchester University Press.

———. (1995c). "Male bias in macro-economics: The case of structural adjustment. In D. Elson (ed.). *Male bias in the development process.* 2nd ed. Manchester: Manchester University Press.

———. (1995d). "Household responses to stabilisation and structural adjustment: Male bias at the micro-level." In D. Elson (ed.). *Male bias in the development process.* 2nd ed. Manchester: Manchester University Press.

Elson, D. (1992). "From survival strategies to transformation strategies: Women's needs and structural adjustment." In L. Benería and S. Feldman (eds.). *Unequal burden: Economic crises, persistent poverty, and women's work* (pp. 26–48). Boulder, Colo.: Westview Press.

———. (1991). "Male bias in structural adjustment." In D. Elson (ed.). *Male Bias in the Development Process* (pp. 46–68). Manchester: Manchester University Press.

Emeagwali, G. (ed.). (1995). *Women pay the price: Structural adjustment in Africa and the Caribbean.* Trenton, N.J.: Africa World Press.

Feldman, S. (1992). "Crises, poverty and gender inequality: current themes and issues." In L. Benería and S. Feldman (eds.). *Unequal burden: Economic crises, persistent poverty, and women's work* (pp. 1–25). Boulder, Colo.: Westview Press.

FLACSO. (1993). *Mujeres en Cifras.* Santiago: Ministerio de Asuntos Sociales de España, Madrid and Facultad Latinoamericana de Ciencias Sociales.

Lycette, M. and K. White (1989). "Improving women's access to credit in Latin America and the Caribbean: Policy and project recommendations." In M. Berger and M. Buvinic (eds.). *Women's ventures: Assistance to the informal sector in Latin America* (pp. 19–44). West Hartford, Conn.: Kumarian Press.

Molyneux, M. (1992). "Final declaration ... beyond the debt crisis: Structural transformation." In H. Afshar and C. Dennis (eds.). *Women and adjustment policies in the Third World* (pp. 253–56). New York: St. Martin's Press.

Moser, C. (1993). *Gender planning and development: Theory, practice and training.* New York: Routledge.

———. (1989). *The invisible adjustment: Poor women and economic crisis.* Bogotá: UNICEF.

O'Connell, H. (1996). "Going global: Women and economic globalization" In M. Van Lieshout (ed.). *A woman's world: Beyond the headlines.* Dublin & Oxfam, London: Attic Press.

Sparr, Pamela (ed.). (1994). *Mortgaging women's lives: Feminist critiques of structural adjustment.* London: Zed Books.

Tanski, J. (1994). "The impact of crisis, stabilization and structural adjustment on women in Lima, Peru." *World Development,* 22 (no. 11): pp. 1627–42.

United Nations. (1995). *The world's women: Trends and statistics.* New York: United Nations.

Van Lieshout, M. (ed.). (1996). *A woman's world: Beyond the headlines.* Dublin & Oxfam, London: Attic Press.

Waring, M. (1999). *Counting for nothing: What men value and what women are worth.* Toronto: University of Toronto Press.

———. (1988). *If women counted: A new feminist economics.* San Francisco: Harper and Row.

Webb, R. and Fernández-Baca, G. (1994). *Perú en Números 1994.* Lima: Instituto Cuánto.

Weidemann, C. (1992). *Financial services for women.* Bethesda, Md.: Development Alternatives.

8
Migrant Communities in Accra: Marginalizing the Margins[1]

Deborah Pellow

How can we understand a city in the era of globalization? Globalization researchers typically view the city as an economic system and concentrate on explaining the main circuits of capital. Such an economistic lens focuses attention on the command and control functions of global corporations, the (global) central business district, and specific (global) areas where producer and consumer services concentrate. As a direct result people only think of "slums" when they juxtapose run-down buildings against the glittering architecture of the global financial and services sector.

Much of the globalization debate to date has focused on world cities (London, Paris, Tokyo, New York), major economic success stories (Singapore, Ireland), and globally connected parts of cities such as edge cities, financial districts, cyber districts, and so on. Cities in the less developed world have not received the attention that they deserve and as a result the globalization debate is not nearly as global as it ought to be. Some countries, like Ghana, "the star pupil" of structural adjustment, have received global attention for its successes in implementing liberalization policies that have ushered in globalization. The capital city Accra has emerged as a gateway city that connects that national economy to the global economy (Grant, 2001). However, the dominant representation of Accra as a gateway city does not fully represent the experiences of most of the cities' residents. There is a particular unevenness to the globalization experience in Accra; most places and most people are excluded.

To fully appreciate the variety of globalization experiences, I concentrate on a particular area within the west of the city, called Sabon Zongo. It occupies a community of 75 acres in Accra, just outside the global central business district. For many in Accra, it carries all sorts of

epithets, generally negative, perhaps because it is old and has been for-
gotten by Accra, perhaps because most who live there are poor,
perhaps because its population has been mythologized to fit people's
prejudices. The social, economic and human potential remains
untapped in these *zongos* (stranger settlements). Pejorative labels cut
them off. The reality is that Sabon Zongo is indeed in a state of physical deterioration. It is peripheral. It is a migrant community. It is on
the margins of the margins.

I challenge the notion that all places are being homogenized under
global economic flows. My research illustrates the social and spatial differentiation that characterizes different communities in Accra and I argue
that this differentiation is more a product of historical forces than contemporary global economic patterns. While there was European input
into the creation of the community, much of today's decay and neglect
that I decry are due to indigenous rather than global forces. Even the allocation of so-called global monies from organizations like the World Bank
and the IMF is screened through local authorities. Sabon Zongo's limited
exposure to the global economy is to a large part determined by the government of Ghana and the lack of attention that is given to non-strategic
areas to global capital. Liberalization policies have favored and promoted
export processing zones, central business districts and port and airport
areas to the detriment of all other areas in the country. Liberalization
policies have reinforced the existing patterns of domination.
Historicizing the evolution of Sabon Zongo is important to understanding how the place was created and how pre-existing patterns and level of
economic development affect possibilities under globalization

I have been doing research in Sabon Zongo since 1982 (Pellow, 1985,
1988, 1991, 1999). I chose Sabon Zongo for several reasons. It was one
of the first Accra stranger enclaves. The creation of the area is an early
product of cross-border migration dynamics that predate the globalization era in Ghana (typically equated with the liberalization period post
1983). The son of the man thought to be the first Hausa landlord in
Accra created this community to maintain Hausa institutions without
interference from other "stranger" groups. Nearly one hundred years of
archival materials (in the National Archives of Ghana) survive on the
establishment of the community.

The colonial city

The colonial city was founded by foreigners to promote their own
interests (Rayfield, 1974, p. 173). It consisted of two or three major

areas: the indigenous, often precolonial, settlement; the so-called "Western," "modern," or "European" sector, which King refers to as "the colonial urban settlement"; and in some colonial territories, there was a "stranger" sector, occupied by migrants (King, 1976, p. 33). In West Africa, the colonial city was intended for a principally African population and served as a nodal point within the export-based colonial spatial economy (Mabogunje, 1970, p. 346). Urban hierarchies were organized, and political, administrative, and military centers established (King, 1990). The social organization of the colonial city reflected the spatial organization of the colonial society.

Accra exemplifies the spatial impact of the colonial system of organization on the urban landscape, with regional inequalities complemented by sociospatial inequalities of density, modernization, and residential exclusion in the capital city.

After the fifteenth century, great migrations brought new African populations and early European explorers to the Gold Coast. The Africans established territorial rights and hierarchies and competed over trading links with the Europeans. By 1600, the Ga people had settled in, with Accra on the way to becoming the capital of their federation. The European forts, including the three built in Accra, became centers of economic and political power.

The British prevailed over other European powers with imperial interests in the Gold Coast. And as Arn (1996, p. 429) observes, the critical event that favored Accra's future was the decision of the colonial administration to transfer its headquarters from Cape Coast to Accra in 1877. As Accra's population grew through migration, so did residential and commercial space. With expansion came the growth of new neighborhoods, similar to the old Ga towns, with distinct names and locations. In the 1890s, the British built up Victoriaborg as a European quarter and, being aware of subtle and not-so-subtle differences among the indigenous people, cordoned off other sections for various groups. This created a de facto social and spatial compartmentalization of the town (Brand, 1972), including the establishment of zongos. The marginal zoning of the zongos reflected the separateness and powerlessness of the component populations, "accounted for not simply in terms of cultural differences but in terms of the distribution of power" (King, 1976, p. 40).

After independence, the barriers of segregation implicit in the colonial pattern were removed, "the fundamental principles, laws and procedures of planning remained the same... . In the main, planning was concentrated on state land to the neglect of customary lands" (Larbi, 1996, p. 198). In 1983, Ghana became one of the first African countries to implement a structural adjustment program, known as the Economic Recovery Program (ERP). Urban planning was tackled as part of ERP because of the state of spatial planning. Based on social and cultural identification processes, primary loyalties go to extended families and hometown kin. This has led to rules and regulations being based on favoritism (Larbi, 1996).

In 1988, under the Local Government Law, the British-created Accra Municipal Council was restructured into the Accra Metropolitan Assembly (AMA). One of 110 district assemblies, the AMA oversees the public toilets, waste management, and the city's markets (cleaning, maintenance, provision of electricity and water, patrolling). "It functions as a single-tier local government authority responsible for the development of the city" (Larbi, 1996, p. 199). It is true that the AMA is battling a deteriorating and insufficient infrastructure, with inadequate public transportation, roads that cannot contain the number of automobiles, and ambulatory hawkers and traders who illegally claim the sidewalk as their stalls. But it is also true that the AMA is heir to the legacy of favoritism carried over from the British to the African elite, and the usual twin scourges of mismanagement and corruption, which have made some areas "better" than others, have led to the differential provision of facilities and their upkeep in communities throughout the city.

In Accra, as in much of the third world, it was simplest for the postcolonial government to turn a blind eye to the problems and misery in places like Jamestown and Sabon Zongo. The stated ideal throughout the colonial and postcolonial world is to rehouse the poor. "Yet few states have been able to build more than a minute fraction of the houses needed – and those which they do build are occupied by those with high regular wages, as they are beyond the means of the poor" (Lloyd, 1979, p. 50f.). In Ghana, the first housing estates were built in Accra in 1949 for those left homeless by the June 22, 1939 earthquake. While estates were to be built at Sabon Zongo, along with five other areas, Blankson (1988) indicates that by 1970, they had been constructed only in Kaneshie, East Christianborg, and South Labadi. The housing estates were seen as slums, due to residents' construction of makeshift structures to make up for inappropriate spatial layout, lack of maintenance by the corporation, problems of sewage and refusal disposal. The local population, however, has not perceived these estates as slums.

The creation of zongos

Accra is a plural society made up of diverse collectivities, one of which is the Muslim community (see Pellow, 1985). The latter, in turn, was established, and is currently dominated, by migrant ethnic groups – primarily from Nigeria, as well as parts of French West Africa – although in the last forty or so years, Islam has claimed many converts among southern Ghanaian ethnic groups, including Akan and Ga. The dominant group, referred to as "Northerners" or "strangers," are bound by language (Hausa), cultural orientation (maintenance of traditional chieftaincies, observance of the law as set down by *shari'a*, wearing traditional robes, eating traditional foods), and education (sending children to Koranic school) (Peil, 1979). They also live separately in zongos that have a distinctly Muslim flavor, complete with mosques. The indigenous Muslims are rather different. Referred to as "southerners," Hausa is not their lingua franca, most dress and eat like other southern Ghanaians (with the exception of pork and alcohol), their children have always attended secular Western schools as well as the conservative Koranic ones, and many do not live within the zongos – the sociospatial referent for northern identity. Indeed, they are careful to separate themselves – culturally, socially, economically, politically, spatially – from the "alien" segment, as they have sought active leadership in the Islamic community of Accra.

In 1908, the ethnic composition of Accra's Muslim community was primarily Yoruba and Hausa, supplemented by Kanuri, Fulani, Nupe, and Wangara (Pellow, 1985). The collectivity looked and dressed alike, and they lived together in the old Ga area at Zongo Lane, Okanshie, and Horse Road (Post Office Square). They prayed en masse at the main mosque. There were interethnic quarrels over the Muslim headmanship and imamship, which resulted in religious disturbances, as the Hausa perceived themselves to be superior to all other Muslim ethnic groups and held a disproportionate influence on the others in dress, language, roles, and offices.

While the British regarded the Muslims as one community, they were aware of differences and hostilities (they closed down the main mosque from 1915 to 1922 because of ethnic disturbances). Their awareness had some impact on their urban neighborhood plans for Accra. In 1908, an epidemic of bubonic plague broke out in downtown Accra. The government concluded that sanitary improvements were essential and subsequently made plans for new settlements. One was Adabraka, which was established on April 24, 1910. The idea was to relocate "two Hausa tribes viz: – the Fulanis and the Yorubas and also

dispossessed Ussher Town (Ga) people."[2] What was the space like?
According to an old-time resident of Adabraka,

> Round about 1914, 1916, there were wolves after 6 o'clock round
> about this side. I actually heard them… . The doors shut and you
> heard the wolves. Everybody is frightened. Gradually the road was
> repaired and people travelling on it to Nsawam, and the animals
> were frightened away. This was in '16 and '18. And during that
> time, water was scarce in Accra. And people came all the way down
> to this side of Adabraka, called Anetaibu. There they collected
> water… . At that time there were not so many people living here.
> The whole of this side was bush.
>
> (Pellow, 1977, p. 89).

Through the efforts of A. K. W. (Kojo) Thompson, Adabraka Market
was built in 1926–7. When the British began to divide up the land,
some civil servants built houses. The government built a few sample
dwellings as models for others. In the 1930s, architects came in with
different blueprints, and well-constructed multistory buildings were
introduced. As time went on, Adabraka became a mixed community,
attracting a diverse population, and a central residential area. Land
values rose in Adabraka, due to residential development in the city.
Thus a plot of land with no road frontage sold in 1947 at the rate of
£418 sterling per acre. The same plot was resold in 1951 at the rate of
£1500 sterling per acre. Adabraka became inhabited by persons of
higher income groups, mostly members of the African intelligentsia,
executives of African and non-African trading, well-known families like
the Bossmans, Amartefios, and Foulkes-Crabbes. Today Adabraka bears
little resemblance to the zongo planned eighty-odd years ago.

Africans also chose to establish their own new community areas.
Malam Bako, an important Hausa *mai gida* (patron) at Zongo Lane,
wanted a new site for his followers, who had outgrown the space allotted
them by the Ga Manche. In 1907 he began to approach the other Ga
chiefs for a piece of land for a Hausa settlement. Subsequently, in the
wake of the plague epidemic, the British met with representatives of the
Hausa, Fulani, and Yoruba populations in Accra to discuss the creation of
a new zongo, "so that all the Mohammedans can have a place to live
together" (Pellow, 1985, p. 432). Malam Bako received land from Sempe,
Alata, and Akumaje,[3] which was supported by the British, and by 1912
he and his family and his followers had established themselves at Sabor
Zongo, where Bako informally played the role of headman.

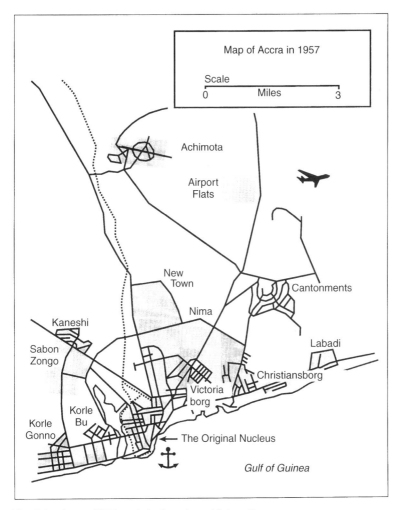

Map 8.1   Accra, 1957, and the location of Sabon Zongo

Although it lies only two miles northwest of Zongo Lane (Map 8.1), Sabon Zongo was at first a town apart, outside Accra's city limits. Like Adabraka, Braimah, former Yoruba chief, described it to me as "bush": "They had animals, bad animals even … wolves. At that time, if you were going to Sabon Zongo, you came to a river – they called it Korle. You paid a penny before you could cross. At that time, there was no street" (Pellow, 1991, p. 427).

Most Ga families living on the land, where they cultivated cassava, cashew, and mango, relinquished their farms. Malam Bako demarcated living space for his people, subdividing the 75 acres into 32 portions, varying somewhat in size and greatly in the number and dimensions of the compounds erected (Map 8.2). According to the current chief and his elders, the ethnic variability of houseowners was minimal, the Hausa constituting almost 85 percent. Seventeen parcels had no non-Hausa owners; another ten contained only one each. In 1933, Malam Bako stated that there were 600 residents in Sabon Zongo.

The community expanded over the years, but unlike Adabraka, remained a zongo and marginal, attractive to newly migrant "strangers," Muslim and non-Muslim alike. Sabon Zongo has retained a village flavor. The community's sociopolitical institutional structure has remained kin-based, with a Bako as zongo chief.

Compare this with Nima, which has no overall zongo chief (every tribe has its own)[4] and, given the contemporary layout of Accra, is quite centrally located. Although Nima-Maamobi became important after World War II with rapid rural–urban migration, in fact its history began years earlier. Like the space that became Sabon Zongo, Nima's land was Ga owned (see Arn, 1996, pp. 436–9). Then, in 1931, one Alhaji Futa, a Muslim cattle trader resident at Cow Lane, was allowed to settle the area of Nima, where he had been grazing his cattle. Nima at that time, like Sabon Zongo, was outside the city. Futa, like Malam Bako, became a patron, providing accommodation to migrant clients. Thus Nima began as a typical zongo. Situated between a military base and a European residential area, it was attractive to those who worked in the two adjacent neighborhoods (cooks, stewards, laborers, and prostitutes). It also attracted migrants, primarily Muslims and northern Ghanaians. By the time of the Second World War, there were over 21 tribal heads in Nima.

Many soldiers in the Gold Coast military were notably of Muslim and/or northern Ghanaian extraction, and after the war many settled in Nima, expanding the population. The cocoa boom and new economic programs in the 1950s boosted the economy and contributed to another wave of immigration to Nima, but many of these skilled and unskilled laborers were from southern Ghana.

Nima was incorporated into the municipality in 1951, yet "the Municipal Council did not ameliorate the established squalor, in practice only managing to install some public latrines and several standpipes in 1954. From this date onwards infrastructural improvements in Nima were effectively 'frozen' while population continued to rise"

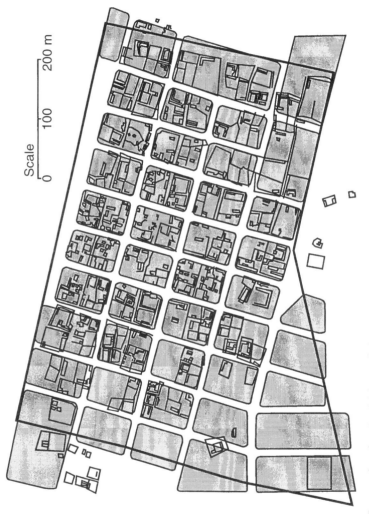

Map 8.2 Zongo: plan showing Malam Bako's area

Scale

0   100   200 m

(Arn, 1996, p. 438). By 1980, Nima became a geographically distinct squatter area with a high concentration of "sub-proletarians" and of varied ethnicity. Nima, like Sabon Zongo was, and is, a zongo.

The big difference between the two, as far as the municipal power structure is concerned, is that Nima is centrally located and adjacent to, indeed en route to, first-class residential areas (Airport and Roman Ridge). Moreover, Nima has Alhaji Yahaya, a highly effective leader (albeit illiterate in English), who as assemblyman was able to get development started in Nima, and as MP for Central Ayawaso helped secure World Bank resources for further rehabilitation. As far as their respective social organization is concerned, the differences are vast. Nima is composed of many ethnic groups, with no overall customary leader or structuring and thus no real moral center. It is reputed to be a haven for gamblers and criminals. Alhaji Yahaya carries legitimacy as a political head whose successes have involved pulling together a coalition of elders to bring in physical improvement. For example, according to Elliot Barbour-Sackey, at Technical Services Centre, when the World Bank came back to Ghana in 1983,

> we got the community to form their own Welfare Organization. The then-Assemblyman (current MP) Yahaya, was in fact dynamic, and he worked with very dedicated people. We got them to organize and to educate the people. Then when we had the preliminary engineering design, we took it to the community – to have a look at it and tell us whether they liked the scheme (6/17/96).

Unlike Nima, Sabon Zongo continues to be kin-based, which is to say that the zongo chieftaincy follows a traditional Hausa line of descent, the Bako family maintains the trappings of leadership, and compound ownership is still largely tied to the original settlers. On the positive side, kinship ties, genealogical loyalty, provide an implicit overarching morality and a sense of belongingness. On the negative side, renters desirous of community involvement feel themselves deprived of any say in community affairs, such as development efforts. Some residents (even some of the Bako family), resentful of the Bako family, are believed to thwart attempts at community rehabilitation to prevent the chief from gaining credit.

The Final Report for the World Bank–funded Urban Environmental Sanitation Project (Government of Ghana, 1995, p. 54) indicates that in Sabon Zongo, "there is a high level of community participation. Communal labour is organized once every month, takes the form of drain cleaning and sweeping. Mobilizing is thus not difficult." Yet Sabon Zongo did not make it into the current Project Urban IV World Bank venture, because it did not meet some of the proposed criteria: proof of communal organization, an NGO (nongovernmental organization) already working there, and the ability to contribute monetarily toward the work (because they were going to pay part of the costs of the facilities being provided). In other words, even if poor, the people must show that they have done as much as possible to get things done.

Yet how does a community counteract perceptions of residents as backward, ignorant, disorganized? What are the politics behind one community (for example, Nima) rather than another (such as Sabon Zongo) succeeding in attracting an NGO? If development is tied to location and a community is not located centrally or along an important feeder road, what is to convince a government agency to come in? How do residents learn new habits of sanitation if they are not taught? Why would they gather their garbage if there is no collection?

My concern is not the World Bank and its conditionalities, although I do think these are generally off-base in the non-Western world, rarely shedding its ethnocentric understandings of problems and how to fix them. The World Bank is, after all, just another example of foreign penetration into Ghana. Rather, my concern lies with local governments or ministries or agencies that have chosen not to know their communities and have deprived them of a fair shot at a comfortable existence.

The development of development: Sabon Zongo today

Spatially and socially, Sabon Zongo has changed considerably from its early days. The estimated population in 1991 was 14 622 (Government of Ghana, 1992, p. 9), although this does not include squatters and permanent guests. It is no longer "bush": there is now a road bridge over the lagoon, and no toll is exacted from the masses who travel it daily in buses, trucks, taxis, private cars, or on foot. Not many trees remain. In place of the maze of alleys characterizing the downtown zongo, there is a gridlike patterns of roads, some suitable for motorized traffic. The original compounds still stand, joined by additional buildings – houses, mosques, schools, shops, and a movie theatre.

Sabon Zongo is part of the larger urban landscape (Map 8.1): it is bounded to the north by Oblogo Road and to the east by Mortuary Road (the continuation of Ring Road), both main thoroughfares that connect areas of the city; homeowners pay property taxes to the AMA;

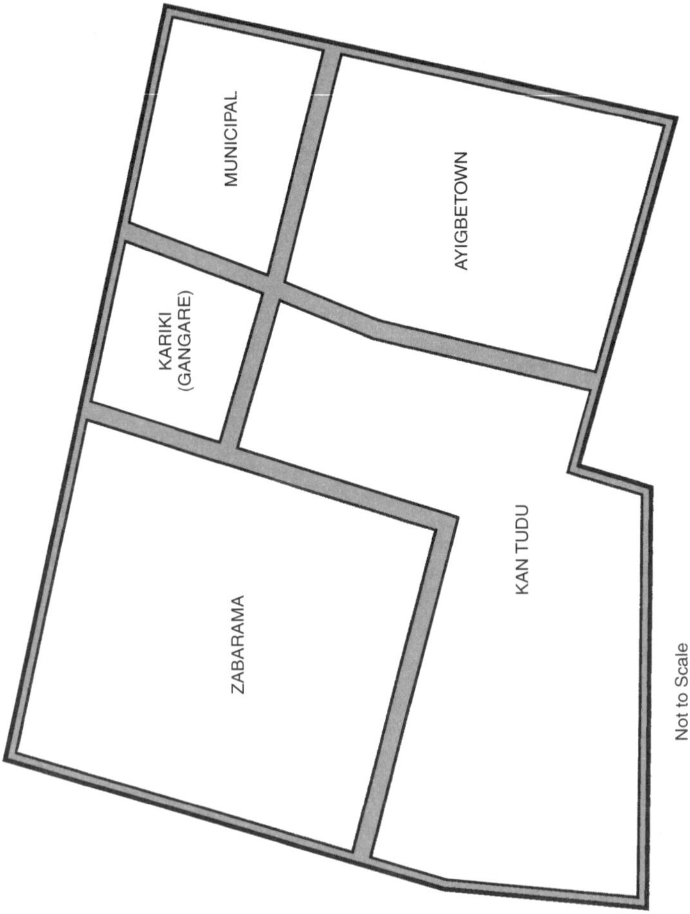

122

MUNICIPAL

KARIKI
(GANGARE)

AYIGBETOWN

ZABARAMA

KAN TUDU

Not to Scale

Map 8.3 Inside Sabon Zongo

and the AMA oversees waste disposal, public toilets, and construction of street gutters (in Sabon Zongo as elsewhere in Accra). Electricity is provided here as everywhere by the Electric Corporation. Telephone service, provided by Ghana Telecom, is currently nonexistent in private homes in Sabon Zongo; only the four communication centers in the community have telephones. Two of them utilize radio waves, one paid dearly to bring in phone lines from neighboring Abossey Okai, and the fourth is located on Oblogo Road. Indeed, the closer one gets to Oblogo Road, the main east–west thoroughfare on this side of Accra which marks Sabon Zongo's northern perimeter, the more likely the presence of "modern" amenities. There are, for example, storied buildings, similar to those elsewhere in the city, with modern kitchens and flush toilets.

Sabon Zongo is also culturally distinct: Islam is the centripetal force for community identification and continuity. There are twenty-seven roofed and two unroofed mosques; while there are Christians resident, there are no churches. On Fridays, most of the men go to the main Accra mosque (constructed in 1982) that is walking distance from Sabon Zongo. Chief Sha'aibu Bako has strong political ties to the other Muslim chiefs and belongs to the Council of Muslim Chiefs. He also has strong ties to a select group, descendants of the "first families of Islam" in Accra (including Yoruba, Wangara and Nupe), and unlike his grandfather, Malam Bako, involves himself in parochial Muslim affairs external to Sabon Zongo. Northern Nigerian specialties, such as the staple tuwo (in Accra made from flour of rice or cassava) are sold daily on the street. In addition to the Hausa, other Muslim groups include Yoruba, Fulani, and Zabrama. And despite popular perception, Sabon Zongo also houses many non-Muslims, most of whom are from southern Ghana (for instance, Akan, Ga, Ewe).

Sabon Zongo is informally divided into neighborhoods (not bounded but known to all residents), which encompass distinct social and physical differences and are aligned with the up/down axis (Map 8.3). From the beginning, subchiefs and their subjects were allocated space. Spatial and sociological subdivisions (aside from ethnicity) were built in, including subchiefs (Mossi, Wangara, Chamba, and Ewe). One area in Ayigbetown is called ungowan katifa (mattress area), due to its occupational specialty; another, in Kan Tudu near the chief's house, is makwala (tureen), because it is an area of much food-selling activity.

All Muslim parents send their children to makaranta, Koranic school. There are currently eight operating in Sabon Zongo, three of which offer a combined English/Arabic curriculum, on top of the regular Western primary-plus schooling that many children acquire elsewhere.

Among the adult population, many of whom have had minimal secular education, professional expertise is low, there has been severe unemployment among men, and there are fewer women than in the wider society in the wage-earning labor force (Brand, 1972, p. 288). Alhaji Sule Bako, a college graduate and son of the current chief, observed to me that "if the children of our fathers had gone to school, there would be many, many Hausa in educated positions." According to the insider stereotype, all the men in Kan Tudu (the core) are Koranic teachers, while the men in gangari are tailors and mechanics. In fact, among the 302 men of mixed ethnicities I interviewed, 19 percent are tailors, 30 percent are in commerce, and 17 percent are in transport. Commercial enterprises span mobile traders in watches and used cloth to wholesalers and large-scale merchants. At Sabon Zongo's Freedom Market, there is not a single Hausa woman trader; 38 percent of the traders are non-Muslim Ga, 26 percent Ewe, and the balance primarily Akan – all southern Ghanaian. Traditional service roles for residents who are not literate, such as carriers, watchmen and messengers, have been transposed to the modern sector, to government and private business. And all of them are sending their children to school, so that literacy among the younger generation is far higher than in the past. Carpentry is, following the ethnic stereotype, still overwhelmingly Ewe, charcoal sellers are Sisala or Grunshie, corn sellers Zabrama, butchers and Koranic teachers Hausa. But men are also white-collar workers and businessmen in greater Accra – all indications of slowly penetrating change as the social and spatial boundedness of the community has eased.

Compounds are primarily owned by descendants of the original Hausa families. Yet my census of eighteen compounds produced 700 adults, most of whom are tenants and only 289 (or 41 percent) of whom are Hausa. What about the compounds themselves? Here we see a unique adaptation to city life. The house is a social space. The courtyard house predominates, albeit in an evolved form. Most of the compounds have changed, taking on characteristics unlike either northern Nigerian or indigenous Ghanaian physical structures but socially conforming to a growing, urban spatial milieu. They are built in mud/wattle, cement block, wood, zinc, asbestos; even kiosks have been adapted as housing! The compounds are family-owned, families have expanded, and tenanting has also come in. Residents cannot build up and cannot easily build out (though some do with individual rooms, so they have built in, which has led to the loss of the courtyard. The house embodies tensions between lineage culture and urban culture: the alienation of property by selling it to make money and the destruction of the core family by introducing tenants.

I believe that over the last eighty years residents have developed a zongo culture, what I call *zongwanci,* the markings of zongo-ness socially produced and reproduced there in time and space. It is a melding of the "northern" ethos, informed by Islam and its values and institutions, with what Rotenberg calls "metropolitan knowledge," the meanings shared by city dwellers, "because they live within the densest and most specialized concentrations of people, information, built form, and economic activity" (1993, p. xii). It is born of social relationships and work relationships, knit into social networks, played out in daily work life and cycles of observances and activities, which are associated with the neighborhood and anchored in the material environment.

Thus, there are two inherently contradictory conditions to Sabon Zongo's marginalization: on the one hand, the community is badly underdeveloped. There are no proper roads (that is currently changing for one north–south and one east–west street), no phone lines (one new communication office has just brought in two telephone lines), no street lights, few proper gutters, perhaps five houses with indoor plumbing, indeed shameful toilet facilities (overseen by the AMA), no post office, no police station – in other words, a lousy infrastructure. Yet, this community is like a village in the city, with many of the positives: the streets are an extension of the compound and are safe for children, life-cycle celebrations envelop all, residents (including non-Muslims) speak of being able to live in peace, there is a local native court (the chief's) to settle local disputes, organizations crosscut and integrate the community.

This is not a disorganized space. A space that has been marginalized for generations by the power structure is, in fact, vibrant, alive, real. The key value that I think holds it all together is exchange – of tangible goods and of intangible services. Sabon Zongo carries a siege mentality – the community was established to flee conflict with others, and currently it is perceived by many who do not live there as somehow disreputable, which I think intensifies exchange within the community. This, I believe, has also cut it and its populace off from the benefits of Accra.

Conclusion

While globalization, by telescoping connections, has made the world smaller for many places and the people who live in them, it has homogenized neither people and places nor are all places and their residents part of the global equation. Sabon Zongo is exposed to much of what the global world has to offer through television and film, for example, but that does not make the community similar to like-sized neighborhoods in capital cities of the United States, Europe, South or East Asia, or middle or upper income areas in Accra. While Sabon Zongo is part of the larger urban landscape, it is also culturally and spatially separate. It began as a node in the Hausa diaspora, and Hausa structures, customs, and institutions are highly influential, but through immigration, it has evolved into a very diverse "stranger" community, an enclave of sorts. Through immigration, a variation of a local culture has emerged that transcends the local Ga culture of Accra and diverges from the new global consumer culture of some elites in Ghana. The main languages spoken are Hausa, Ga, and Twi (and English), but the extraordinary array also includes Fulani, Yoruba, Kanuri, Zabrama, Wangara, Buzu, Kotokoli, Mossi, Ewe, Dagomba, and Dagati. It is also by no means a bounded community cut off from "global flows" (Geschiere and Meyer, 1998, p. 605). Televisions abound, and CNN is carried every morning by Ghana Broadcasting. Individual homes may lack telephones, but there are telephone services throughout Accra and several even in Sabon Zongo. As in communities throughout sub-Saharan Africa, the local movie house shows Chinese and Indian movies weekly, which generate what Larkin calls "parallel modernities" (1997). Every year, a handful of residents is privileged to go on hajj to Mecca, where they are confronted by a host of "glocal" traditions and dazzled by the cheap prices of gold jewelry. None of this has homogenized the population; there is still internal cultural differentiation.

Indeed, uneven development has not only exacerbated the differences between this Accra community and places elsewhere in the Western world, but even between Sabon Zongo and the suburbs of Accra. Airport Residential Estates and Cantonments, for example, are elite gated communities, with grand walled houses, cared for by gardeners and stewards and protected by night watchmen. The houses have all of the global amenities and are inhabited by more cosmopolitan Ghanaians and by foreigners. There is no public transportation in these areas, but all of the residents have imported luxury cars. The residents here are very much in contact with the global community by phone, email, travel and film rentals, and satellite television. Residents in these worlds live in time. Space matters little since spanning many distances is possible. In contrast, residents of slum areas are prisoners of place.

The disparity between Sabon Zongo and Accra's suburbs is in part economic, but it is also largely due to histories based on cultural differences.

I initially posed the question, how do globalization processes affect the city? My answer is that there is globalization for some but localization for most others.

From the start, Sabon Zongo was a community of kin who sought refuge from dissent and discord. It began as an insular community and its intertwining attachments have helped keep it so.

The globalization agenda of the government and business community in Ghana has not yet addressed the issue of non-participation and exclusion from the spoils of the global economy. The documenting of the experience of slum areas in the globalization era is important. Only by acknowledging that geographic and social mobility are dichotomized can we appreciate the diverging experiences. We can only begin to bridge the gap between global and non-global spaces in the less developed world by education and negotiation. This is where government must come in: good schools with highly motivating teachers for the children; adult education, including literacy training; classes of a less formal sort in civic education; and, not least, education in areas of health and sanitation, accompanied by government programs for inoculation against disease. All of these interventions are not the role of outside aid agencies, who do not know the population and its lifeways, who create unhealthy dependencies, and who are not around for the duration. Interventions are up to agencies of the state. Government representatives and agencies must come to an understanding of what the cultural and social imperatives of the local population are; they must also relinquish cultural judgements. Only then can the marginalized be brought along, to comply and participate in the global economy and possibly benefit. And finally, what is needed is a better funded and less corrupt municipal authority that properly oversees its constituencies to dispel the cynicism of the less fortunate and give them reason to want and expect more for themselves and their children. Until this takes place, some will inhabit the globe while most others will be chained to place.

Notes

1 An earlier draft of this chapter was presented at an international seminar in commemoration of Accra's centenary anniversary, "Migration and

Urbanization – Effects on the Planned City and Its Environment," October 14, 1998. The conference was co-sponsored by the Ghana Institute of Architects and the Goethe Institute. I subsequently presented this paper in the Globalization at the Margins series, organized by John Rennie Short and Richard grant, under the auspices of the Global Affairs Institute in Maxwell School, Syracuse University, on April 9, 1999. I am grateful to the comments of Joseph Hayford, Don Mitchell, and Richard Grant.

2 Secretary of Native Affairs 1348/12: Sanitary Engineer L. C. S. Wellacot's remarks; December 4, 1912.

3 In fact, Akumanje reneged at the last minute, setting the stage for eighty-odd years of land litigation and the consequent question of chiefly legitimacy (see Pellow, 1991).

4 For about twenty years Ali Kado was chosen to represent all the chiefs in Nima (from the 1960s until he died in the 1980s).

References

Appaduri, Arjun (1996). *Modernity at large: Cultural dimensions of globalization.* Minneapolis: University of Minnesota Press.

Arn, Jack (1996). "Creation of a relative surplus population: A history of Accra, Ghana to 1980." *Review,* 19, pp. 413–44.

Blair, Thomas L. (1971). "Shelter in urbanising and industrialising Africa." In Paul Oliver (ed.). *Shelter in Africa.* (pp. 226–39). London: Barrie & Jenkins.

Blankson, Charles (1988). "Housing estates in Ghana: A case study of middle- and low-income residential areas in Accra and Kumasi." In R. A. Obudho and C. C. Mhlanga (eds.). *Slum and squatter settlements in sub-Saharan Africa: Toward a planning strategy* (pp. 53–70). New York: Praeger.

Brand, Richard. (1972). "The spatial organization of residential areas in Accra, Ghana, with particular reference to aspects of modernization." *Economic Geography,* 48, pp. 284–98.

Castells, Manuel (1979). *The urban question: A Marxist approach.* Cambridge, Mass.: MIT Press.

Geschiere, Peter and Birgit Meyer (1998). "Globalization and identity: Dialectics of flow and closure." *Development and Change,* 29, pp. 601–15.

Government of Ghana (1995). *Urban environmental sanitation project (Identification of urban communities suitable for upgrading projects): Final report.* Prepared by The Consortium, Accra-North. Accra: Ministry of Local Government.

———. (1992). "Urban II preparatory studies: Accra residential and market upgrading study: Final report." Accra: Ministry of Works and Housing, Technical Services Centre. Bidex Consult, Accra-North.

Grant, Richard (2001). Liberalization policies and foreign companies in Accra, Ghana. *Environment and Planning* A, 33, 997–1014.

Hart, Keith (1982). *The political economy of West African agriculture.* Cambridge: Cambridge University Press.

Harvey, William B. (1966). *Law and social change in Ghana.* Princeton, N.J.: Princeton University Press.

Jacobs, Jane (1961). *The death and life of great American cities.* New York: Vintage.

Kaniki, M. H. Y. (1985). "The colonial economy: The former British zones." In Adu Boahen (ed.). *General history of Africa, Vol. VII: Africa under colonial domination 1880–1935* (pp. 382–419). Berkeley: University of California Press.

King, Anthony D. (1990). *Urbanism, colonialism, and the world economy*. London: Routledge.

———. (1976). *Colonial urban development: Culture, social power and environment*. London: Routledge and Kegan Paul.

Larbi, Wordsworth Odame (1996). "Spatial planning and urban fragmentation in Accra." *Third World Planning Review,* 18 (2), pp. 193–214.

Larkin, Brian. (1997). "Indian films and Nigerian lovers: Media and the creation of parallel modernities." *Africa,* 67 (3), pp. 406–40.

Lloyd, Peter (1979). *Slums of hope? Shanty towns of the Third World.* Harmondsworth, UK: Penguin.

Mabogunje, Akin L. (1970). "Urbanization and change." In John N. Paden and Edward W. Soja (eds.). *The African experience, Vol. 1: Essays* (pp. 331–58). Evanston, Ill.: Northwestern University Press.

Obudho, R.A. and Constance C. Mhlanga. (1988). "The development of slum and squatter settlements as a manifestation of rapid urbanization in sub-Saharan Africa." In R. A. Obudho and C. C. Mhlanga (eds.). *Slum and squatter settlements in sub-Saharan Africa: Toward a planning strategy* (pp. 3–30). New York: Praeger.

Peil, Margaret (1979). "Host reactions: Aliens in Ghana." In Shack and Skinner (eds.). *Strangers in African societies* (pp. 123–40). Berkeley: University of California Press.

Pellow, Deborah (1999). "The power of space in the evolution of an Accra zongo." In S. Low (ed.). *Theorizing the city: The new urban anthropology reader* (pp. 277–314). New Brunswick: Rutgers University Press.

———. (1991). "From Accra to Kano: One woman's experience." In C. Coles and B. Mack (eds.). *Women and gender in Hausa society* (pp. 50–68). Madison: University of Wisconsin Press.

———. (1988). "What housing does: Change in a community in Accra." *Architecture and Behaviour,* 4 (3), 213–28.

———. (1985). "Muslim segmentation: Cohesion and divisiveness in Accra." *Journal of Modern African Studies,* 23, pp. 419–44.

———. (1977). *Women in Accra: Options for autonomy.* Algonac, Mich.: Reference Publications.

Rakodi, Carole (ed.). (1993). *The urban challenge in Africa: Growth and management of its large cities.* Tokyo: UN University Press.

Rayfield, J. R. (1974). "Theories of urbanization and the colonial city in West Africa." *Africa,* 44 (2), pp. 163–85.

Rotenberg, Robert (1993). Introduction. In R. Rotenberg and G. McDonough (eds.). *The cultural meaning of urban space* (pp. xi–xix). Westport Conn.: Bergin & Garvey.

Shatkin, Gavin (1998). "'Fourth World' cities in the global economy: The case of Phnom Penh, Cambodia."*International Journal of Urban and Regional Research,* 22 (3), 378–93.

9
Foreign Companies and Glocalizations: Evidence from Accra, Ghana[1]

Richard Grant

There are three prevalent economic narratives in the social sciences literature on Accra, Ghana. The first and most common is the placement of Accra in a category of major urban centers marginalized from global capital flows. Commentators of this perspective concentrate on region-wide indicators and extrapolate to what is happening across urban areas of the region. Accra, as part of Africa, has acquired the unwanted status of belonging to the outer periphery of the world economy. Based on data from the North on the relative exclusion from participation in global trade and industry-led development commentators have written about the phenomenon of "marginalization" of the entire Africa region. For instance, Hirst and Thompson (1996) note that Africa is "off the multinational map and the tables of worldwide foreign direct investment," based on their study of the top 500 MNCs (multinational corporations) from Canada, Germany, Japan, the United States, the United Kingdom, and their affiliates abroad. Dunning (1993, p. 23) also concludes that the entire region of Africa accounted for 4.9 percent of the total activity among foreign affiliates of multinational companies in 1980. Some researchers (for instance, Terlouw, 1992) even go as far as to speak about the "excorporation" of Africa from the global economy in the 1980s. And, as a final example, Simon (1992) notes that none of the world cities are in the region and that African cities are weakly connected to circuits of global capital.

The second narrative is more optimistic and is common to both the neoclassical macrodevelopment literature and the government of Ghana. This perspective emphasizes increasing levels of global economic engagement since the introduction of marketization policies in 1983. Researchers have used cross-national comparisons and selected national time-series data to show that Ghana is "the star pupil of structural adjustment" in the margins (World Bank, 1994). The international development community has mostly endorsed Ghana's recent economic performance in positive ways. For instance, on a six-state African tour in March 1998, President Clinton's, first stop was Accra, where he praised Ghana for its economic and political achievements by emphasizing that it "again lights the way for Africa in that business is growing and trade and investment is rising" (Clinton, 1998). Similarly, the Ghanaian government has strongly promoted Ghana's economic successes. The Ghana Investment Promotion Center (GIPC) (1999) stresses the favorable investment climate and the local opportunities for foreign companies. The former president of Ghana, Jerry Rawlings, used every opportunity to place-promote Accra by noting that the return on US investments is 26 percent, more than double the rate of return on US investments in Europe and other world regions (C-SPAN Archives, 1999).

The third narrative argues that globalization has largely negative consequences, particularly at the local level. Many voices (especially NGOs [nongovernmental organizations], some academics, and some opposition political parties in Ghana) emphasize the painful and sometimes crippling effects of the transition to a market economy (Rakodi, 1997; Simon, 1997). These critics dispute the reliance on macroeconomic indicators to assess the condition of the Ghanaian economy. They provide their own facts and highlight worsening conditions, including increasing poverty, growing inequalities, social and spatial polarization, increasing real estate speculation, infrastructure and environmental deterioration, and declining quality of life (Rakodi, 1997; Rogerson, 1997). Globalization critics in Accra differ greatly in their solutions to these problems. Most call for stemming the tide of economic globalization. Some surprisingly call for more globalization; for instance, the head of the Ghanaian Women's Entrepreneurs Association notes, "It is not that we have been left behind by globalization, it is more that we haven't started yet" (interview, July 5, 1998, Accra).

Each of these narratives has supporting facts. The major difference among them is largely a function of the attention given to specific units of analysis. For instance, the marginalization thesis and the macrodevelopment perspective are derived mainly from evidence of engagement with an external arena. By contrast, research emanating from Ghana and antiglobalization perspectives focus on indigenous changes in the economic and social systems. There have been few attempts to link the various scales of analysis, which undermines the objective of understanding how processes of global change and global-ization are constituted in particular places.

A more sophisticated analysis of economic globalization is required. Economic globalization is a much more complex than most policy makers, journalists, and researchers would lead us to believe. All too often there has been a widespread tendency to view the global–local in dualistic terms. I contend that the local needs to be conceptualized in a way that it is clearly embedded in discussions of the global. The compression of the world under economic globalization involves the creation and the incor-poration of locality, processes which themselves largely shape, in turn, the compression of the world as a whole. The concept of *glocalization* is an important effort to capture the complexity in the relationship. At the most basic level it refers to "the processes that telescope the global and the local to make a blend" (Robertson, 1995, p. 28). Glocalization as a process in the urban periphery requires elaboration and examination to prevent the narrative on globalization from becoming a hegemonic history that is imposed on cities in the margins without giving a voice and a role for individuals in the periphery to shape globalization. There are theories about the processes through which glocalization occurs (Robertson, 1995), and studies examining its development have focused on the local interfacing with the global (Swyngedouw, 1992, 1996); fewer have exam-ined the global–local interface (an exception is de Mooij, 1998).

My aim in this chapter is to examine the role of foreign companies in the margins; specifically, how they embed themselves in the local economy via the process of glocalization. For a more accurate reading of globalization I argue for a reconceptualization of economic global-ization in the margins. Economic globalization is defined here as the nature of and the extent to which the urban economy is tied to global economic activities. The notion of globalization that has dominated the debate is based solely on evidence from the North, which results in the widespread use of the term "exclusion" to characterize the global linkages of cities in the margins. To lend some balance to the debate, this chapter is based on data collected during extensive fieldwork in Accra and on a number of interviews with representatives of foreign companies in the metropolitan area.

Reconceptualizing economic globalization in the margins

The present processes of economic globalization are leading to a pro-found geographical reorganization of capitalism and of the role that particular geographic units, such as cities and states, play within the system. In the considerable ongoing debate about the extent and nature of contemporary globalization a major problem is the abstract and general nature of the discussion. Writings on globalization are based more often on opinion and nonempirical generalizations than on evidence. Research in the center on globalization does not connect its findings to what is happening on the ground in the margins. All too often a kind of totalizing or universalizing, unidirectional construct is assembled that makes little sense when it comes to looking at the experiences of the margins. Some observers even speculate at the general theoretical level about the convergence of the development paths of cities in the center and those in the margins due to globalization. Cohen (1996, p. 25), for example, argues that cities from the margins are following a similar trajectory of cities in the center and "a common set of critical economic, social, infrastructural, environmental and institutional problems beset urban areas regardless of levels of national development."

This biased research focus on the economic globalization experiences in the center is leading to widespread use of the term "exclusion" to characterize the experiences in the margins. Misleading conclusions of "marginalization" and "exclusion" result specifically from four main weaknesses in the globalization literature. First, a focus on macroeconomic indicators, such as shares of global trade and global foreign investment flows, hides the many important ways in which emerging markets interact and become and remain integrated into the global economy. For instance, joint venture agreements and joint production arrangements are not revealed in conventional trade and foreign direct investment (FDI) statistics.

Second, the data used to measure global flows is incomplete. The typical focus in economic globalization research on the top 500 MNCs in the world and their affiliates overseas overlooks the activities of thousands of other foreign companies that participate in the global economy and that also make specific business locational decisions (not necessarily on the same basis).[2] MNC data used to investigate globalization is typically collected in the center (from companies from a handful of countries) and is not appropriate for making global claims. For instance, a directory of the top 500 MNCs in the world for 1997 lists four in operation in Ghana (Dun & Bradstreet, 1997), leading to the conclusion that Accra is "excluded" from the flows of foreign direct investment and multinational activity. This data source, however, proves incomplete when compared to data collected by local trade and investment promotion agencies.

Third, the comparative measurement yardstick has always been the US, European, and Japanese economies. Comparing the performance of emerging markets to the experiences of the triad economies may be useful for making arguments about the structural linkages of world economy, but it tells us little about how the processes of globalization are unfolding. This is partly because globalization is itself a global industry, and selling globalization is now a business. Globalization as viewed from the center has become a necessary myth (Veseth, 1998). Comparing completely dissimilar geographic areas also creates a level of generalization about African economies that is misleading and that would not be tolerated in North American or European globalization studies. Universal statements should not take the place of detailed local studies. For instance, the world city literature (based on analyses of the linkages of cities to the global economy) describes Africa as "marginalized": none of the world cities are located in the region, nor is the region part of the semiperiphery or of the functional city systems linked across national borders that have emerged in other world regions (Simon, 1992).

Fourth, the entire set of economic processes is treated in the globalization debate in particularly troubling ways. Theorists unquestionably use combinations of economic events and occurrences (financial integration, internationalization of production, openness in trade, opportunities for foreign direct investment, and the role of foreign companies) to explain globalization without adequately addressing any one aspect in detail. This is made even more problematic when they link explanations of economic phenomena to political or cultural globalization. It has become commonplace for some researchers to claim overattention to economic globalization at the expense of cultural and political globalization. What is most galling is that these same cultural and political globalization researchers use the same poorly understood economic processes to support their claims about cultural globalization.

From this discussion we see obvious, large gaps in the literature on globalization, especially in the linkages between global flows and the local mediation and interpretation of these flows. Anecdotal evidence rather than case studies has become the norm. Particular (Northern) global companies and commodities are used to profile worldwide flows and show evidence for economic globalization. For instance, many journalists and researchers talk about a Coca-Colaization or a McDonaldization or a CNNization of the global economy. We are often told that the global economy is converging in a unidirectional, linear way with a predetermined outcome. However, area studies specialists argue that the relationship between the global economy and global consumers is much more complex. Simply consuming Coca-Cola does not make Ghanaians "Americans" in the same way that wearing kente cloth does not make African–Americans "Ghanaians." A large part of the inadequate conceptualization of economic globalization in the margins lies in the general disregard of local evidence.

Glocalization

The processes of economic globalization have introduced a profound shake-up of geographical scales, their content, and their interrelations. In particular, in the economic arena, regulatory codes and norms are jumping from one scale to another. Foreign companies and foreign direct investment play significant roles in structuring daily life, and the mediation of economic globalization is more critical than ever before. The processes of rescaling the national and urban economies and the opportunities entailed for both global and local players have been theorized (Cooke *et al*. 1992, Robertson, 1995; Swyngedouw, 1992). The coexistence of opportunities for both globalization and localization is a distinguishing feature of the contemporary globalization period.

The ways that "global" and "local" scales are usually studied is problematic. In much of the globalization literature the global is seen as a towering homogenous force sweeping away local particularity. Conceptualizing globalization as if the global excludes the local suggests that the global lies beyond all localities and entails properties over and beyond the attributes of the constituent units. There is a widespread tendency to view the global and the local as a straightforward polarity (Robertson, 1995, p. 29) and to cast locality as a form of opposition and resistance to the hegemonic global (ibid., 1995). There is an increasingly globalwide discourse of locality – as community, home, work, and so on – which in itself is a construction based on the "other."

A more relevant way to investigate the global–local connection may be through the lens of locality studies, where locality is positioned relationally to the global (Cooke, 1989; Dunford and Kafkalas, 1992). In locality studies, however, the emphasis is on the local restructuring in the face of global processes, rather than on global–local interactive processes and results (except in the critical sense of identifying transborder capital alliances).

Glocalization is an appropriate concept for uncovering the global–local nexus. Glocalization, like the term globalization, has many different meanings and uses. The *Oxford Dictionary of New Words* (1991, p. 134) defines glocalization as "modeled on Japanese *dochakuku* (deriving from *dochaku* 'living on one's land'), originally the agricultural principle of adapting one's farming techniques to local conditions, but also adapted to Japanese business for global localization, a global outlook adjusted to local conditions." It goes on to note that glocalization was one of the main marketing buzzwords at the beginning of the nineties. Glocalization is not a condition, as some suggest. For instance, Friedmann (1999, p. 236) interprets glocalizing cultures as "cultures that can filter and assimilate aspects of globalization," "adding to the diversity" without overwhelming their cultures. He, along with a cadre of other global commentators, focuses primarily on the cultural homogenization thesis rather than on the fragmentation debate in globalization literature. While Friedman is entitled to define glocalization in his own way, his conceptualization does not add to the more important theoretical debate about scale.

Importantly, some of the theoretical literature on globalization has persuasively argued that the local is not a counterpoint to the global. It can be regarded, instead, as Robertson (1995) notes – subject to some qualification – as an aspect of globalization. Sassen (1996) similarly observes that the "foreign" is already deeply embedded in the local. She emphasizes that most global processes materialize within national territories and to a large extent through national institutional arrangements like trade policies and through the operations of domestic and foreign firms; they thereby are not necessarily counted as "foreign" (Sassen, 1996, p. 2). The imbrication of global and national actors is thus far more complex than is commonly conceptualized. The scales do not relate to each other in a simple zero-sum situation as antiglobalizationists (Mander and Goldsmith, 1996) proclaim.

There are three main theoretical conceptualizations of glocalization. The first looks at the contested restructuring of the institutional regulatory environment across all scales – from the national scale to both the global and the local (including urban) scales. The second examines strategies of global localization of key forms of industrial, service, and financial capital. The business literature, for example, focuses on micromarketing and on tailoring the advertisement of goods and services on a near global basis to increasingly differentiated and local markets (de Mooij, 1998). Global localization runs fundamentally deeper than mere adaptation of global products to local, ethnic, gender, and lifestyle particularities and to types of differentiated consumers. Heterogeneity does not exist in, of, or by itself; part of it is constructed. Glocalization in marketing research terms involves the construction of consumer traditions. The third conceptualization of glocalization revolves around the subjective and personal spheres that interpret and structure global flows (Eade, 1997). Researchers working in the margins have continually debated about local interpretations of economic globalization. According to Robertson (1995) global commodities are interpreted with great variety around the world. De Mooij (1998) argues that the flow of global commodities results in global customers, global channels, and a global marketplace. Appaduri (1995) observes that a "transnationalism" of global commodities occurs in cross-border flows whereby consumers do not identify products with a single place of origin.

Studying glocalization: assessing the activities of foreign companies

Foreign companies are widely regarded as the major agent of economic globalization. According to a conservative estimate, by the early 1990s there were more than 37 000 foreign companies controlling 170 000 affiliated organizations abroad (Hirst and Thompson, 1996, p. 53), with global assets of $10 trillion, worldwide sales of $13.5 trillion, and employment figures in foreign affiliates of 15 million (Dunning, 1993, p. 17). Although estimates of the numbers of foreign companies from the margins are hard to come by, it is widely believed that the number of new MNCs is currently increasing at a rapid rate, particularly from developing countries. In this chapter I have no intention of getting into the debate over whether hosting MNCs is a good or bad strategy. My purpose is more modest. It is simply to connect a study of foreign companies to the theory of economic globalization. Generally, however, in the context of economic globalization, foreign companies are important to host countries because they facilitate local engagement with the global economy and they connect foreign and local agents in a web of relationships.

There is a tendency in the literature on globalization to use the terms "foreign company" and "MNCs" interchangeably, which is part of the precision problem that characterizes much of the globalization discussion. The first step to clarifying the role of the "foreign" is to define precisely the unit of consideration. Although there is no single agreed-upon definition of multinational or foreign companies (Dicken, 1992), two factors are common: ownership criteria and geographical scope of operations. For MNCs specifically, a firm is multinational when nationals of two or more countries effectively own the headquarters or the parent company. Geographical scope relates to the existence of operations beyond the home country. The MNC definition is problematic because it is typically taken to represent only companies from the OECD (Organisation for Economic Cooperation and Development) based on asset size, it is often expressed as the largest 500 companies in the world, and it usually emphasizes control of operations (that is, a branch and head office arrangements) rather than globa–local organizational arrangements.

We are at ground zero in terms of collecting data on foreign companies in the margins so the most basic information on equity shares in foreign companies is a starting point. The more generic term "foreign company," which covers many types of companies with FDI over $10 000 and foreign country levels up to 100 percent, is more useful for studying African urban economies. Its definition needs to accommodate a wider spectrum of foreign investments, ranging from a large global company (such as Guinness) to an individual investment from abroad in a local company, even if that company's only operations are in the local economy. For example, if a Liberian factory were transplanted to Accra where the owner remained Liberian but where there were no operations in additional countries, it would be classified as a foreign company. This broader conception of foreign company is more relevant for studying regions where business can be disrupted by such factors as major changes in policy, civil unrest, and so on, and where geographical locational decision-making is highly complex. In addition, the notion of foreign company needs to accommodate local and global joint venture arrangements. In Ghana, for example, a wide array of formerly state-owned businesses (including hotels, factories and mines) are for sale to foreign and/or domestic investors as part of the state's divestiture from the national economy.

Collecting primary data in emerging markets is a very time-consuming endeavor. There are no comprehensive and reliable data on foreign companies in the margins. As previously mentioned, relevant publications and directories (for example, Dun & Bradstreet, 1997; United Nations Center on Transnational Corporations, 1988) have very few entries on foreign companies' activities in Ghana. Anyone who is familiar with the business environment in Accra knows that these external data sources greatly underestimate the number of foreign companies; in fact, they miss so much that they cannot be used to assess globalization. Internal sources also present no single published source that provides comprehensive data on the names, activities and locations of foreign companies in

Ghana. The Ghana telephone directory is published infrequently (1984 and 1998) and is very incomplete in its listing of foreign companies. The *FIT Business Directory,* published annually, is also highly selective as companies have to pay to be listed and many choose not to. Even the government of Ghana acknowledges that its information on foreign companies is far from complete. The best source of information on foreign companies in Ghana is provided by the GIPC (GIPC, 1999), which considers US$10 000 of foreign equity a minimum sum for recording information on foreign companies. By law each foreign company is required to register with the GIPC; in practice, though, many do not. The GIPC provided me with a listing of 630 new companies that had registered at its office between 1994 and 1998. A senior GIPC official noted that 26 percent of the companies registered were not functionally operating as of December 1998. Accordingly, the GIPC listing could not be taken to represent fully the population of foreign companies in Accra.

To supplement the GIPC listing I contacted all governmental organizations that work closely with foreign companies for information. Organizations besides the GIPC that provided detailed information include the Divestiture Implementation Committee, the Minerals Commission, and the Ghana Free Zone Board. All made available their listing of foreign companies they worked with. In addition, to check the reliability of this information, I asked all foreign embassies that have economic offices in Accra (ten in total) to provide a comprehensive listing of companies from their home states that were active in Ghana. Most embassies periodically survey companies from their home states to update their listings for their own purposes. In addition, I used the telephone and FIT directories to check information.[3]

There was a considerable overlap among the different foreign company data sources, but no one source was complete. Eventually I constructed a comprehensive listing on foreign companies and their activities for Accra. Fieldworkers then checked and verified that 655 foreign companies were still active in the Accra metropolitan area. I organized the foreign company data to indicate ownership patterns and to identify established companies to study the process of glocalization.

Global business linkages and Accra: the setting for glocalization

The development of international business in Ghana started long before the colonial period, when many business people commuted between West Africa and Europe through the Sahara Desert, trading in Moroccan leather, beads, spices, gold, and other merchandise. Ghana continued to be enmeshed in global business networks via the slave trade. It was the latter part of the colonial period that tied Ghana most closely into the world economy by its provision of raw materials for UK businesses. Consequently, Ghana became part of the metropolitan economy, sucked into the market economy as an adjunct to the British industrial capitalist system. Accra as a city did not engage global business until the colonial headquarters was moved from Cape Coast to Accra in 1877, whereby the city became integrated by a periphery–core relationship (Acquah, 1957).

Low levels of global engagement characterized the post-independence period prior to market reforms (1957–82). During this time few foreign companies established offices or plants in Ghana (Cadbury [1914], Coca Cola [1950], and Guinness [1960] were notable exceptions). Legislation permitted foreign companies to enter the beverage and food sectors. Prior to marketization, the typical economic profile of Ghana, like many African states, was as follows: a miniscule manufacturing base protected by import substitution, a huge mining sector, and a sizable export agricultural sector controlled by the government. The government pursued a policy of import substitution, and foreign companies located both in Kumasi and the Greater Accra region.

The market reform policies introduced by the government after 1983, as part of structural adjustment policies (SAPs), ushered in a period of increased engagement with the global economy. These policy changes were associated with FDI increasing by 700 percent between 1982 and 1998, which translated into more foreign companies entering Ghana. The Ghanaian government adopted the rhetoric of economic globalization and place-marketed Accra as a friendly, safe, cheap, gateway location for doing global business. According to the GIPC (1999) 95 percent of companies entering the market have located their headquarters in Greater Accra. This trend is in accordance with the global restructuring of national economies and the increasing importance of the urban scale in terms of accumulation under the period of intensified globalization.

Among the 655 foreign companies presently in the Accra economy, some are economic giants. For example, Ashanti Goldfields and its subsidiaries employ 11 500 workers and have net assets of over $364 million. Unilever is the second largest foreign company in terms of employment, with 1000 workers. The vast majority of foreign companies, however, are small-scale, employing fewer than 20 workers, but they nonetheless represent a hive of economic activity and a web of glocal connections.

The distinguishing feature of the contemporary period of economic globalization in Accra is the many opportunities for local–foreign collaboration. Foreign companies, for instance, have a variety of entry options into the Ghanaian economy. They can (1) establish a new foreign company; (2) form a joint venture arrangement with local a firm/investor(s); or (3) set up a liaison arrangement (either as a full liaison office or by a lesser liaison commitment, such as securing a mining license). These options serve as counterpoints to generalizations by globalization theorists when they bring attention to a new "greenfield" operation or a foreign company branch, which are not entirely representative of what happens in fact.

The most preferred mode of entry and ownership arrangement in Accra is through an equity joint venture. As of January 1, 1999, 327 foreign and local companies maintained this relationship. These arrangements highlight local and global collaborations and represent an important interface in the processes of glocalization. A smaller but significant number of companies (244) functioned as branches of foreign companies; 84 companies operated as liaisons. Sixty-four companies maintained a representative in Accra, which can be taken to indicate that they are strongly interested in researching the marketplace for investment opportunities. The smallest category of foreign companies (20 in total) held mining licenses authorizing them to explore mining possibilities and to undertake initial research on establishing a regional mining operation.

In terms of the activities of foreign companies, the scope of international business has no limits, encompassing all sectors of economic activity: trading, manufacturing, primary activities (such as agriculture and mining), transportation, and especially services. The diversified profile of foreign companies illustrates that the conventional image of foreign companies as primarily engaging in extractive industries is not representative of the geography of foreign companies' activities. Although the largest foreign company (Ashanti Goldfields) is in the extractive sector it is not representative of the activities of all foreign companies.

The global dimension of foreign company involvement is further expressed by the number of countries represented in Accra. Foreign companies from 80 countries participate in businesses in Accra. The top ten most active countries in terms of the number of foreign companies are, in descending order, the United Kingdom, Germany, the

United States, China, India, Lebanon, Switzerland, Italy, Netherlands, and South Korea. Most of the 80 companies come from Western Europe, followed by Asia and Africa, suggesting that globalization is not necessarily of North American or Western European origins. Some small countries' tally is as small as one entry in the marketplace (for example, Bosnia or Liechtenstein). Nonetheless they represent a global dimension that does not appear in secondary data sources.

Another dimension of the global nature of foreign company activity is that 60 companies are multilaterals, whereby equity shares originate from at least three different countries. Good examples here are Volta Garments, a clothing manufacturer that has equity shares from investors in the United Kingdom, China, Switzerland, and the United States, and Ghana Apshalt, a manufacturer of bitumen (a key ingredient in asphalt), which has equity shares from Ghana, Mauritius, Germany, and the United States. These preferences for joint venture arrangements indicate that foreign companies adapt to local circumstances and that local business interests amend to global circumstances. The great heterogeneity of entry mode and equity share arrangements shows that there is no single model for capturing the dynamics of the global–local interface.

Another distinguishing feature of contemporary economic globalization is how foreign companies pursue global localization once they enter the market. There are at least four prominent vehicles by which foreign companies embed themselves in the local economy. As already noted, the primary means of glocalization is to form a joint venture and merge local capital and experience with foreign capital and expertise. The advantage of a joint venture is that foreign investors can profit from local knowledge of the business, political, and labor environments.

A second vehicle of glocalization occurs when foreign companies develop new products for the local market. Several foreign companies, such as Guinness, Cadbury, and Nestlé, develop specific products for the local marketplace. Nestlé, for example, set up an office and a manufacturing plant in Accra in 1971 and now has six additional factories in West Africa. Despite the company receiving a lot of negative international publicity over its marketing and selling strategies for baby milk, it has been careful to produce and market products that respond to local tastes and backgrounds, and it has nurtured local relationships around the world. Nestlé could not carry out this type of global business by exporting. Nestlé has developed a range of Milo and Cerelac products especially for the West African market. Along with taking great care to market itself in Ghana as a local company, it has taken glocalization further by running advertising campaigns that highlight "the value-added activities in Ghana, including more jobs in design, management, marketing" (GIPC, 1998). Its advertisements convey the fact that the company is not simply exporting unprocessed foods, but is actually processing food in the local economy.

A third vehicle of glocalization expands on the joint venture collaboration arrangement by formally listing companies on the national stock market that was established in 1991. Fifteen of the twenty-one foreign companies listed on the Ghanaian Stock Exchange are joint ventures that involve foreign and Ghanaian shareholders, some of which are familiar names to US and European consumers (such as, Ashanti Goldfields, Aluuworks, Enterprise Insurance, Fan Milk, Mobil Oil Ghana, Guinness Ghana, Kumasi Brewery [subsidiary of Heineken], Pioneer Tobacco, Paterson Zochonis, Standard Chartered Bank, Super Paper Products, Social Security Bank, Unilever Ghana, and UTC Estates of Ghana). Listing on the national stock market is one of the most sophisticated ways to embed companies deeply in the local economy, where they can connect to local stockholders, investors, and business media. Moreover, it engages consumers in the interpretative sphere. For instance, when Ghanaians read and hear about the performance of these companies on the Accra stock market they are more likely to think of them as local and not foreign implants. In this regard, these companies become closely intertwined with both local and global economies.

The fourth and most encompassing vehicle of glocalization occurs when a foreign company historicizes its presence in the market and constructs a consumer tradition. Guinness Ghana, a good example, is a joint venture (30 percent owned by Ghanaian interests) that makes particular products for the African market, such as Malta Guinness and Maxi-Malt, as well as its traditional product range. In its advertisements it uses both local and global images to sell its products. Also, it is listed on the Ghanaian Stock Market. Since its local establishment in 1960, Guinness Ghana has sponsored cultural festivals, "Miss Ghana" competitions, national holiday celebrations, among other events. In 1998 it ran a media campaign to launch a new label in celebration of the one hundred and fiftieth anniversary of the introduction of Guinness into Ghana. The story goes that Guinness Ghana recently discovered shipping records indicating that stout arrived in 1848 on a trading ship captained by McGregor Laird, one of the early explorers of the Niger Delta. The story glorifies Ghanaian dockers, who stole the captain's personal supplies and developed an early taste for stout. According to news reports, the dockers saved the stout for special occasions and warned others not to drink their newly acquired supplies by referring to Guinness as the "the dark medicine" (*Daily Graphic,* 1998, p. 17). Recent company billboard advertisements have both reflected as well as produced global and local images to market its products. For instance, a 1999 advertisement campaign depicted five people from across the world, dressed according to local fashions, to represent the global and local image of the product and to identify with both locals and cosmopolitans in Ghana, the latter perhaps identifying with the New York Yankee (baseball team) character. Arguably, glocalization is extensively developed when foreign companies both reflect and produce it through the images they use to represent themselves to consumers.

The interpretative sphere of economic globalization

The presence of 655 foreign companies in Ghana's urban economy can be interpreted locally through the lens of globalization rather than that of marginalization. Furthermore the strategies of foreign firms to glocalize suggests that locality is in the process of transformation and cannot be taken as fixed in the globalization era. Localities are shaped by foreign companies in conjunction with local business interests shape locality. The artificial distinction of global and local misses the very important ways that the local–global are combined to make a blend. Strategies of glocalization imbricate the global and the local scales and are orchestrated to enhance business success, to depart from the practice of "foreign" impositions under colonialism, and to temper the largely negative experiences with foreign companies in Africa in the 1960s and 1970s. The complexities involved in glocalization mean that the subjective sphere of the interpretation of foreign companies and their activities is much more multifaceted. The enmeshment of a whole variety of locals – from advertising firms, to stockholders, to employees (directly employed or in related businesses that provide services to foreign companies) – creates a mosaic of connections between the global and local economies. The advantage of glocalization for foreign firms is that local residents do not perceive their activities as alien, and as a direct result the latter are more likely to be receptive to the commodities that the former produce.

By contrast, the interpretation of global commodities, when they are viewed as external, can be based on a construction of the global as "foreign." Let me illustrate this with a short story from fieldnotes:

> On a recent research trip to Accra I encountered a Pentecostalist preacher who cautioned me about the dangers of globalization and "foreign" commodities. He recounted the following global dream, which he has told to his congregation on numerous occasions and it is a well-known local story. (See account by Meyer 1998 also.) One day he bought a pair of underpants at the local (Makola) market. Beginning with the day he started wearing them, he had been harassed by sexual dreams in which he made love with beautiful women. But in reality he was alone. Some time later he realized that the underpants were the cause of his dreams. Subsequently, he decided to cast away his "foreign" underpants and he slept undisturbed by seductive women. After his experiences he warned his congregation about the dangers encapsulated in commodities and he suggests a remedy: prayer to defetishize the "foreign" imbued in the imported goods. (December 19, 1998)

Although Pentecostalists are by no means representative of the entire population of Accra, they provide an interesting insight into the complex ways that global commodities and the global market are apprehended locally. Pentecostalists represent a group of affluent middle-class consumers in Accra, but without reliable or even contemporary census data it is difficult to identify this cross-section of affluent urban consumers. Pentecostal churches are particularly attractive to young educated people, middle-aged women, and others who are attempting to move upward economically, mainly by business and trade (Meyer, 1998). Pentecostalists adopt a particular remedy to neutralize the danger imbued in commodities: prayer. All church members are called upon to say a brief, silent prayer over every purchased commodity before entering their homes. Pentecostalism's creation of modern consumers through a ritual of prayer helps them handle globalization and control "foreign" or "transnational" in a way that they can be consumed without danger.

The Pentecostalist illustration underscores the importance of conducting local fieldwork. Studying the many ways that global commodities are consumed is an extremely difficult task and one that the globalization thesis has been particularly resistant to. Each commodity encapsulates its own biography and can be read very differently by individuals, groups, and institutions. It is important to realize that under economic globalization individuals have only a very partial view of the process by which commodities are produced, marketed, and consumed and that they have little control over that process. This is especially true in a place like Accra, where the quantity of imported consumer goods greatly exceeds the number of exported raw materials. All commodities (except locally produced foodstuffs and commodities produced by resident foreign companies) are encountered in the consumer phase and not in the production phase. Thus, religion (and other identities and affiliations) in particular instances can occupy a new space between the known and the unknown in the global economy. Glocalization as a strategy is particularly important.

Conclusions

The major differences between economic globalization in the center and in the margins are not fully and truly captured by studying the size of flows unless one studies the scope, number, and complexity of the economic ties. Many foreign companies engaged in joint venture arrangements, with small investments and opportunities for employment, more accurately characterize the global–local nexus in Accra. Without extensive field research it is too easy to overlook the particular ways that Accra is connected to the global economy.

Economic globalization in Accra is more deeply embedded than most globalization theorists would lead us to believe. The process of glocalization is very layered; I have suggested sets of processes. Guinness Ghana illustrates several strategies of glocalization whereby the boundary between foreign and local firm is virtually impossible to detect. The complex and different ways that foreign companies interact with local agents suggest that it is more accurate to discuss glocalizations and geographies of globalizations in the plural sense. A great heterogeneity of experiences with globalization and glocalization is evident in the margins. (See Scott's 2002 discussion of global–local ties in Kumasi, Ghana.)

Assessing local interpretations of global commodities in the margins is much more complex than theorized in the center. Local consumers of commodities like those produced by Guinness and Nestlé view these products as local, not as Appaduri's (1995) notion of "transnationalism" or as foreign impositions. By contrast, Pentecostalists' attitudes toward the consumption of global products illustrated a particular local variety of interpretation. There are obviously major differences between cosmopolitans and locals in how they interpret global commodities, and much more research is needed to clarify consumption in the margins.

The interface between economic globalization and glocalization in Accra is likely to become even more complex in the future. For example, in February 1999, President Rawlings announced a dual citizenship initiative for African–Americans who relocate and invest in Ghana. This policy could open up even newer possibilities for transnational globalizations of economy and culture. This path-breaking initiative goes against the historical experiences of Africa as a source of out-migrations (with the notable exception of Liberia).

This study clearly shows that foreign companies do not accord with the dominant views of foreign companies as excluded from the margins. Moreover, the apparent reduction in the tension between foreign investors and their host developing countries is also noteworthy. Under marketization policies, there is clearly a more symbiotic relationship between governmental agencies and foreign companies than what existed before. The role of foreign companies in the margins has too easily been written off as an already-understood, out-of-fashion subject rather than as a state-of-the art topic to be investigated. There are now major gaps in knowledge in theorizing, collecting data, and translating this knowledge into policy recommendations.

Globalization presents opportunities for Ghanaian firms to engage in global business. For instance, several Ghanaian companies that produce and sell decorative fantasy coffins (hand-made coffins that are replicas of commercial airplanes, Mercedez Benz motor cars, boats, and so on) now use the internet and other sales opportunities in the United States to market and sell their products. Neiman Marcus' Christmas catalog, for example, displayed fantasy coffins from Accra at $3000 per coffin (Neiman Marcus, 1995), and an organization known as the Canadian Organization for Development through Education (CODE) maintains a website to sell fantasy coffins from Accra. What makes the sale of these coffins in globalwide locations even more profound is that they belong to a Ga tradition (the original settlers of Accra) and represent a very local expression of culture (limited to the western part of the city and to an area called Teshi) not found elsewhere in Ghana (Secretan, 1995). Globalization in the margins can be understood only when we capture the complex reality that the global and the local are imbricated.

Notes

1   This research was funded by the National Science Foundation (grant BCS 0096078).

2   Southern MNCs, for example, are less concerned with shareholder interests. In addition to the common reasons for locating companies abroad (sourcing, market opportunities, tax avoidance, and so on) they may value multinationality for reasons of security, currency conversion, and so forth.
3   It is worth noting that only 10 percent of the assembled foreign company list was found in the 1998 Ghana telephone directory. The locally well-known *FIT Business Directory* was even less complete.

References

Acquah, I. (1957). *Accra survey*. London: University of London Press.
Appaduri, A. (1995). "The Production of locality." In R. Fardon (ed.). *Counterworks: Managing the diversity of knowledge* (pp. 204–25). ASA decennial conference series, The Uses of Knowledge: Global and Local Relations. New York: Routledge.
Clinton, W. (1998). Speech delivered in Accra, Ghana. March 23, 1998. http://www.africanews.org/usaf/clinton98.html
CODE Inc. (1999) http://www.codeinc.com/supplyline/spring96/fund.html
Cohen, M. (1996). "The hypothesis of urban convergence: Are cities in the North and South becoming more alike in the age of globalization?" In M. Cohen *et al.* (eds.). *Preparing for the urban future: Global pressures and local forces* (pp. 25–38). Washington, DC: Woodrow Wilson Center.
Cooke, P. (ed.). (1989). *Localities*. London: Unwin Hyman.
Cooke, P., F., Moulaert E. Swyngedouw and O. Weinstein. (1992). *Towards global localization: The computing and communications industries in Britain and France*. London: University College Press.
C-SPAN Archives (1999). U.S.–Ghana News Conference. White House East Conference Room, Washington, DC, February 24 1999. ID: 120778. Lafayette: Purdue Research Foundation.
Daily Graphic, (1998). Guinness' 150th anniversary in Ghana, p. 15.
de Mooij, M. (1998). *Global marketing and advertising. Understanding cultural paradoxes*. Thousand Oaks, Calif.: Sage.
Dicken. P. (1992). *Global shift. The internationalization of economic activity*. New York: Guildford Press.
Dun and Bradstreet (1997). *Principal international businesses: The world marketing directory*. New York: Dun & Bradstreet.
Dunford M. and G. Kafkalas. (1992). "The global–local interplay, corporate geographies and spatial development strategies in Europe." In M. Dunford and G. Kafalas (eds.). *Cities and Regions in Europe* (pp. 3–38). London: Belhaven Press.
Dunning, J. (1993). *Multinational enterprises and the global economy*. Wokingham: Addison Wesley.
Eade, J. (1997). *Living the global city: Globalization as a local process*. New York: Routledge.
FIT. (1999). *FIT Business Directory*. Accra: Ghana.
Friedmann, T. L. (1999). *The lexus and the olive tree. Understanding globalization*. New York: Farrar, Straus, Giroux.
Ghana Investment Promotion Center. (1999). *Foreign companies in Ghana*. Accra: GIPC.

———. (1998). *Ghana Club 100*. Accra: GIPC.

Hirst, P. and G. Thompson. (1996). *Globalization in question*. Cambridge: Polity Press.

Mander, J. and E. Goldsmith. (1996). *The case against the global economy. And a turn toward the local*. San Francisco: Sierra Club.

Meyer, B. (1998). "Commodities and the power of prayer. Pentecostalist attitudes towards consumption in contemporary Ghana." *Development and Change,* 29: pp. 751–71.

Neiman Marcus (1995). *Christmas catalog*. Dallas: Neiman Marcus.

Oxford Dictionary of New Words. (1991). Compiled by Sara Tulloch. Oxford: Oxford University Press.

Rakodi, C. (ed.). (1997). *The urban challenge in Africa. Growth and management of its large cities*. New York: United Nations Press.

Robertson, R. (1995). "Glocalization: Time–space and homogeneity–heterogeneity." In M. Featherstone, S. Lash, and R. Robertson (eds.). *Global modernities,* (pp. 25–44). California: Sage Publications.

Rogerson, C. (1997). "Globalization or informalization? African urban economies in the 1990s." In C. Rakodi (ed.). *The urban challenge in Africa. Growth and management of its large cities* (pp. 337–90). New York: United Nations Press.

Sassen, S. (1996). *Losing control? Sovereignty in an age of globalization*. New York: Columbia University Press.

Secretan, T. (1995). *Going into darkness. Fantastic coffins from Africa*. New York: Thames and Hudson.

Scott A. (2002) "Regional push: towards a geography of development and growth in low and middle income countries." *Third World Quarterly,* 23: pp. 137–61.

Simon, D. (1992). *Cities, capital and development: African cities in the world-economy*. London: Belhaven.

———. (1997). "Urbanization, globalization and economic crisis in Africa." In C. Rakodi (ed.). *The urban challenge in Africa. Growth and management of its large cities*. New York: United Nations Press.

Swyngedouw, E. (1996). "Reconstructing citizenship, the re-scaling of the state and the new authoritarianism: Closing the Belgian mines." *Urban Studies,* 33: pp. 1499–521.

———. (1992). "The Mammon quest. 'Glocalisation', interspatial competition and the monetary order: the construction of new scales." In M. Dunford and G. Kafalas (eds.). *Cities and regions in the New Europe*. London: Belhaven Press.

Terlouw, P. (1992). *The regional geography of the world system: External arena, periphery, semiperiphery, core*. Utrecht: Netherlands Geographical Studies.

United Nations Center on Transnational Corporations (1988). *Transnational corporations in world development: Trends and prospects*. New York: United Nations.

Veseth, M. (1998). *Selling globalization. The myth of the global economy*. Boulder: Lynn Rienner.

World Bank (1994). *Adjustment in Africa: Reforms, results and the road ahead*. New York: Oxford University Press.

10

The Effects of Economic Globalization: Land Use and Land Values in Mumbai, India[1]

Jan Nijman

The "margins" of the global political economy may be defined as those areas that are relatively disconnected from the world economy. Of course, at the dawn of the twenty-first century, no world region is entirely detached from global developments. Some areas, however, are more integrated than others. I focus in this chapter on one important dimension of the globalization process: the diffusion of a transnational liberal ideology. The premise of this chapter is that the embrace of liberalization by governments in formerly more closed national economies leads into a highly critical phase of national economic development. This is due to potentially massive rescaling of the local/national market to global configurations. The term "transitional economy" has often been reserved for formerly communist states in Eastern Europe and the Soviet Union, or for a country such as South Africa since the end of apartheid. It has also applied to many other countries in Latin America, Africa, and Asia, whose governments have embarked on substantial economic reform policies.

I concentrate on a case study of market dynamics in the context of liberalization: the real estate market in Mumbai, India. It shows the potentially dramatic effects of the specific ways in which this transition toward a "free market" is engineered, pointing both to the powerful forces of global capital and highly consequential policy decisions by local governments. In the past decade, Mumbai's real estate market was characterized by extreme volatility, extravagantly high prices, and speculative market behavior. Huge profits were reaped and enormous losses were suffered. Excessive speculation meant that exchange values displaced use values of land and property, with questionable consequences for the quality of life in this city. As a direct and indirect result of the turbulent real estate market, many people were displaced (sometimes by high rents, sometimes by actual force). Moreover, a significant number of companies left Mumbai in search of more affordable locations. And, not least, a local government that was preoccupied with, and distracted by, the huge short-term stakes involved in the big business of development, risked losing sight of its long-term obligations to the community at large.

One question is to what extent this market turbulence should be attributed to the role of global capital or, more concretely, foreign agents, such as nonresident Indians and multinational corporations (MNCs). I document and explain here the making of Mumbai's volatile real estate market in the nineties. I do so against the background of present debates on liberalization, globalization, and their consequences. It is argued that the role of global capital must be understood in the context of the market and the regulatory environment, and that such an analysis should include the wider cast of players involved in that market. This chapter is not intended as a debate on the general vices or virtues of global capitalism. Instead, I argue that domestic forces and state intervention play a key role in the particular expression of global capitalism in any given local context. From a practical point of view, a focus on malleable local conditions may be more fruitful than one that deals with the elusive and uncontrollable forces of global capital.

Turbulence in Mumbai's real estate market

In 1996, Mumbai was reported to have the world's highest real estate prices (*Economist* 1996a, 1996b). The rise had been meteoric. Within five years from 1991, prices in the central business districts (CBDs) had risen between four to six times their previous levels. In June 1996, office rents had become more than twice the going rates in Paris or Frankfurt, and they were well beyond the cost of office space in established high-cost centers like New York, London, Tokyo, or Hong Kong.

This trend was not to last. In the latter part of 1996 and in 1997, prices came plummeting down again and have shown a consistent decline ever since. For many in the real estate business in this city, it has been a roller coaster ride. This kind of extreme turbulence is absent in the "mature" real estate markets of New York or London, where prices are much more stable, at a structurally high level. Mumbai's experience is even unusual in comparison with other major cities in so-called emerging markets, such as Kuala Lumpur, Jakarta, Sao Paolo, or Moscow.

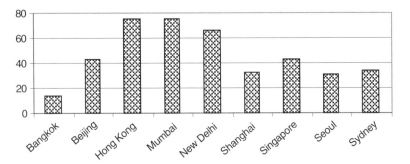

Figure 10.1   Net office rents in prime business areas in selected Asian cities, 1998. US$/sq. ft./yr.
Source: Cushman & Wakefield, 1998a

To be sure, Mumbai is still an expensive city from a global comparative perspective and a very expensive one by Asian standards. As Figure 10.1 shows, prices in 1998 were on a par with those of Hong Kong, and they are still much higher than in places like Singapore, Beijing, and Sydney. Indeed, in view of the comparative importance of these cities in the global economy, Mumbai real estate still seems extraordinarily expensive.

The city's real estate market is in part a reflection of trends in India as a whole. All major cities in India witnessed a sharp rise of values between 1991 and 1996 and a significant decline in subsequent years. However, in Mumbai the trends were much more extreme than elsewhere. Mumbai's peak values were about one-third above those in Delhi and about six times as high as in Chennai and Bangalore (Figure 10.2).

When considering the movements of the market in Mumbai, it is important to note the big differences in real estate values across the metropolitan area (Figure 10.3). The most expensive area is Nariman Point, on the southwestern tip of the peninsula, with additional centers to the east and southeast in Cuffe Parade, the Fort area, and Ballard Estate near the old port. Nariman Point covers land that was reclaimed from the Arabian Sea in 1960s and was built up mostly in the seventies and eighties. Thus, it is close to the old (colonial) parts of the city, but has a very different, modern, appearance with many highrise buildings. When Mumbai made headlines in the global media as the most expensive city in the world, it was largely due to the exorbi-

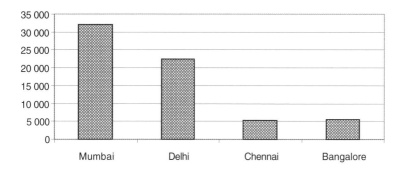

Figure 10.2 Peak values of prime office rentals in four Indian cities in 1995/1996, Rs/sq. ft./yr.
Source: Colliers Jardine, 1998

tant prices in Nariman Point. The southernmost part of the city functions as the CBD and houses a large number of big companies,
financial institutions, multinationals, and government agencies.

Secondary business areas that are less expensive are clustered about
eight kilometres to the north in Worli, Prabhadevi, and Lower Parel.
These areas have a concentration of industrial firms (Indian and
foreign) and of back office activities of companies that often have their
corporate headquarters in the CBD. More suburban and cheaper areas
include Bandra-Kurla and Andheri. The Bandra-Kurla complex was
planned to relieve pressure in the city, but development has been
rather slow. Andheri-Kurla used to form part of the industrial core area
of Mumbai. Recently, manufacturing has been moving further away,
freeing up space for offices. Andheri East, in particular, has witnessed
plenty of new construction. In the more remote suburbs, prices are
again considerably lower. These areas include Jogeshwari, Goregaon,
Kandivili, and Borivili in the northwest, and Sion, Chembur, Navi
Mumbai, and Panvel in the northeast. In these areas, office rents hover
around one-tenth of the values in Nariman Point. Part of the explanation for the steep gradient of land values (in terms of distance from the
CBD) lies in the inordinate amount of travel time in this extremely
congested city.

Compared to many large cities around the world, commercial and
residential land use is quite mixed in Mumbai. In this chapter, I focus
mainly on commercial real estate. For the purpose of clarity, it should

154

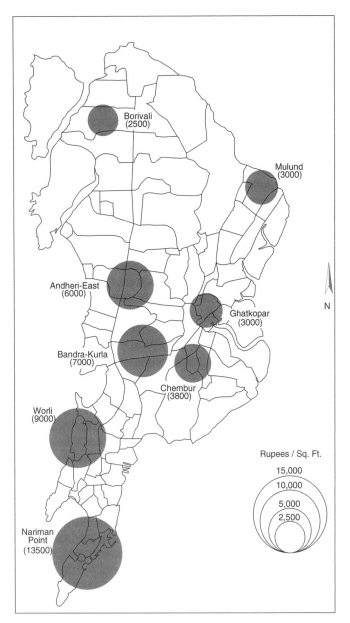

Figure 10.3 Commercial real estate values (rentals) across selected area in Greater Mumbai, 1998
Source: *Bombay Times*, 1998; *Property Times*, 1998

be noted that the residential real estate market was about as volatile as its commercial counterpart, and that they were closely connected. It was said in early 1995 that the most expensive piece of real estate in the world was a building under construction in Nariman Point – the Centre for the Performing Arts – that serves mostly residential purposes. By the time construction was finished, the market had imploded and the building suffered from high vacancy rates.

The residential market is also similarly patterned in a geographic sense. The most expensive residential areas are in the south and along the western seaboard stretching out to the north, including Cuffe Parade, Malabar Hill, Altamount Road, Peddar Road, and Worli. With the shift of corporate activity to the north due to high land values in the south, residential interest in the north has increased as well. There has been rapidly increasing demand in areas like Bandra, Andheri, and Juhu in recent years.

The turbulence of the real estate market was greatest in the prime business areas, where prices rose to the highest levels and where the decline was also the sharpest. Figure 10.4, showing the market movements for five different areas in Greater Mumbai, depicts the turbulence of the market and also the growing differentiation among various areas in the island city. At the beginning of the decade, prices in primary, secondary, and suburban locations were fairly close together, but they quickly drifted apart as prices increased. Presently, prices are converging again, but the difference between the south and other loca-

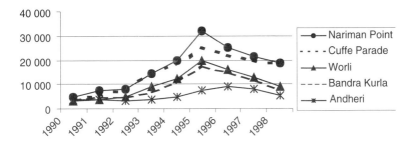

Figure 10.4 Capital values of office space in prime business areas of Greater Mumbai from 1990 to 1998, Rs/sq. ft./yr.
Source: Colliers Jardine, 1998; Cushman & Wakefield, 1998b

tions is still much more substantial than it was a decade ago. For the purpose of explaining the turbulence that has characterized the Mumbai real estate market, we need to focus in particular on the area where turbulence was the most salient: the CBDs in the southern tip of the city.

Blame globalization?

It is tempting to speculate about the relationship between the volatile real estate market and the implementation of national liberalization measures in India. One argument is that liberalization facilitates globalization as it increases exposure to the world economy. Thus, these unleashed global forces have had a destabilizing effect on the Mumbai real estate market. For example, Sujata Patel argued that "liberalization has led to the entry of global financial and real estate companies into the city. Land and housing prices have escalated." (Patel, 1996, p. xxxiii). In a similar vein, the *Financial Times* stated recently that "many multinational companies decided they had to be in India. Bombay, the commercial capital, was the obvious choice. The newcomers paid whatever it took to acquire the tiny supply of usable offices and apartment" (Guha, 1999, p. 32).

There does indeed seem to be a correlation in Mumbai between the presence of foreign capital, partially in the form of foreign companies, and the real estate market. Mumbai houses more foreign companies than any other city in India. Figure 10.5 shows the number of foreign-owned MNCs in Mumbai, Delhi, Chennai, and Bangalore. A comparison with Figure 10.2 suggests a relationship between the presence of large foreign companies on the one hand and the value of real estate and turbulence of the market in these four cities on the other. A closer look at the geography of MNCs within Greater Mumbai lends further credence to this relationship. Foreign-owned companies are highly concentrated in precisely those areas in the south where real estate is the most expensive and where market turbulence has been the most extreme (Figure 10.6). Nariman Point, in particular, provides the kind of atmosphere and environment that is quite typical of CBDs around the world, which explains its appeal to the management of many foreign companies (*Statesman Weekly*, 1997).

Is the volatility of Mumbai's real estate market during the past decade, then, an example of the kind of economic destabilization of local and national markets caused by the entry of uncontrolled global capital? Is

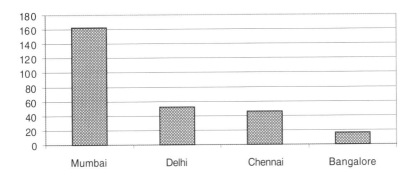

Figure 10.5 The number of large MNCs in four Indian cities, 1998. (Only firms with registered foreign ownership or with a minimum of 25 percent equity are selected. Small and lesser known firms may not be included).
Source: Center for the Monitoring of the Indian Economy (CMIE), 1998

this the kind of global "casino capitalism" that has free play once the state retreats from the market, the kind that can destabilize national and local economies (Strange, 1986)? The Asian crisis that escalated in the fall of 1997 was an event that triggered elaborate discussion, all around the world, on the alleged importance of state interference in the movement of global capital. In particular, there was considerable controversy about the role of foreign investors in the making of the crisis in Malaysia, as global capital massively fled that country to go elsewhere. Indeed, at the time some Indian commentators viewed these developments, and the relative tranquility of the Indian economy amidst this pan-Asian crisis, as evidence of the virtues of India's regulated and insulated environment (*Financial Express*, 1998).

The turbulent movements in the real estate market in Mumbai and other Indian cities that started around 1991 certainly appear to be related in some way to the liberalization and deregulation schemes that the Indian government embarked upon at the time. However, to simply attribute the volatility of the market to globalization, global capital, or foreign MNCs is to miss a large part of the picture and to distort the facts. For example, many multinationals were at the time not legally permitted to own real estate. That is not to say that global capital had no part in the sharp market movements at that time. Rather, it is to say that matters were more complex: they involved a range of domestic, foreign, public, and private actors, and they were closely related to changes in the regulatory environment.

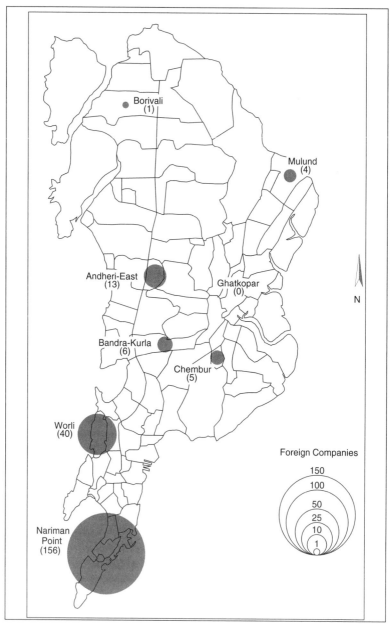

Figure 10.6 The geographical distinction of 606 foreign companies in Greater Mumbai by pin (zip) code area, 1998

A closer look at the market: the deregulation of demand

The steep rise of real estate values from 1991 to 1996 (Figure 10.4) is in principle explained by a growing imbalance of demand and supply. In other words, during the first half of the decade demand for high-quality office space must have increasingly exceeded supply. At least three important causes of an increase in demand can be identified.

First, the introduction of reforms and liberalization measures in 1991 and subsequent years led to major changes in the political and economic climate across India. In the country's entrepreneurial circles and among (potential) foreign investors there existed considerable optimism and growing expectations about the prospect of doing business in India. Because general indicators of the Indian economy were looking up during these years, foreign investments continued to pour in. More important, this mood of optimism about the Indian market among foreign *and* domestic businesses led to a growing willingness to pay dearly for office space in the most prized localities.

Second, many different sectors and dimensions of the Indian economy were subject to reform and deregulation after 1991, and special measures were taken to liberalize foreign investment in real estate. Most notably, in 1993 the Foreign Exchange and Regulation Act (FERA) of 1973 was modified to allow nonresident Indians (NRIs) and overseas corporate bodies (OCBs; foreign companies that are at least 60 percent owned by NRIs) to buy and own real estate. The legislative changes also opened up a possibility for other foreign companies (with the exclusion of foreign banks) to own real estate under restricted circumstances. This requires, however, often laborious and lengthy application procedures for special permits through the Reserve Bank of India. The large majority of foreign firms in Mumbai are still housed in rental properties.

The legislative changes were particularly significant in the residential real estate market, where wealthy NRIs (many residing in the United States or West Europe) were offered an opportunity to purchase a pied-à-terre in what many considered a lucrative market. In a retrospective analysis, the *Bombay Times* observed that "with NRIs investing large amounts with developers and raising the limits at income tax property auctions, prices spiralled" (*Bombay Times*, 1998, p. 1). Thus, in the early and mid-nineties, reports abounded of transactions of a US$1million-plus transactions for fashionable apartments in Malabar Hill and similar areas, often said to involve NRIs. Many other areas, less expensive and further away from the city, were affected as well. Some development projects were entirely geared to NRIs, such as the so-called Seawoods Estate in the northwestern suburbs of Greater Mumbai.

Given the mix of residential and commercial land uses in Mumbai, there is likely to have been a spillover effect of residential demand into the commercial real estate sector, driving up prices. Whatever the actual records of transactions looked like at the time, the prevailing market discourse was exceedingly bullish. In the marketplace, perception can be everything, at least for a brief period of time. In the early to mid-nineties, there was much talk in the city about increased demand by NRIs and foreign corporations. Whether these claims were exaggerated or not (they probably were), they tended to lead to higher prices. Indeed, the real estate and developer business communities served themselves well – for a short while – by talking the market up.[2]

Finally, there is an exogenous factor that is likely to have contributed to increased demand, one that is not directly related to deregulation of the real estate market. The crash of the stock market in April 1992 (related to the notorious "Bombay Scam") may have led to a shift of funds from the equity market into real estate, thereby fueling demand. It is difficult to track such capital shifts from equity to real estate, but the timing of capital flight out of the equity market coincided with the early phases of the steep rise of real estate prices. Thus, this factor may indeed have been quite important. There is no question that confidence of investors in the stock market had been shaken. The main market indices fell by about 33 percent, and it took nearly two years for the stock market to climb back to the level prior to the crash.[3] Furthermore, most of these capital flows were controlled within India, not abroad. Portfolio investment in the Indian equity markets was only effectively deregulated *after* the crash of 1992. Foreign institutional investors (FIIs), such as investment trusts and pension funds, only started entering the stock market in large numbers in late 1992 and 1993. Only 8 FIIs were registered with the Securities and Exchange Board of India through 1992. The number had risen to 131 by the end of 1993 (updated listings are available from the Bombay Stock Exchange). Thus, capital fleeing the market in the wake of the crash must have been predominantly under domestic control.

These changes in the demand of real estate applied generally across India, but they were particularly felt in the major cities, and most of all in Mumbai.[4] As the country's major business hub, financial center, and main gateway to the global economy, it received disproportionate attention from foreign investors, NRIs, Indian companies, and residents. The importance of the financial and producer services sector in

Mumbai also implied a high premium on office space in the already crowded CBDs.

A closer look at the market: the continued regulation of supply

While demand increased, the supply of real estate across, and particularly in, Mumbai remained low, causing prices to escalate. The general culture of real estate in India, in combination with the geographical limitations of Mumbai, played a part in this, but the most important explanation for the constrained supply was related to the regulatory environment in India and the state of Maharashtra.

If rising demand on the real estate market came in part from abroad, supply is of course an intrinsically domestic matter. In that sense, the real estate markets in India during those years formed the scene of a meeting of global (demand) and local (supply) forces. They provided an interesting contrast in the form of fast and detached global capital versus immobile and intrinsically valuable land that often lacked an established exchange value. Across India, real estate is still rarely transactable because people view it as a life-long asset only to be sold under the most dire, or extremely lucrative, circumstances. Real estate often stays in the family for many generations. This culture is reflected in the absence of established financial institutions in the real estate market.[5] Until recently, Indian banks did not provide loans to buy real estate, and mortgages were rarely available (the situation has only changed slightly in the past few years). In 1998, it was estimated that less than 8 percent of real estate transactions involved a financial institution. The bulk of existing real estate, therefore, is the full property of the owner and carries no costs like mortgage interest. This, in turn, implies less incentive to sell.

The second explanation that may be offered for the restricted supply of real estate in Mumbai relates to the city's geography. The Arabian Sea and Thane Creek pose natural limits to this peninsular city. Congestion is particularly acute in the narrow southern part of the city, where the CBD is located. Since the early seventies, city and state planners have pursued policies to reclaim land from the sea and to redirect urban growth to the mainland, in Navi Mumbai. These efforts have had only partial success (see, for example, Guha, 1996; Shaw, 1995). In comparisons of Mumbai's real estate market with that in other major cities in India, these geographic constraints are often mentioned, and clearly they should not be dismissed. However, there are vast areas in Greater Mumbai that are presently not developed for a number of reasons relating to legislation, regulation, speculation, and politics (D'Monte, 1997).

The third and most important explanation for restricted supply in the real estate market lies in the regulatory environment. There are many ways in which legislation constrains supply, including zoning laws, stipulations about the size limits of transactable plots, rent controls, and building laws (including labor laws). The most important, for our purpose, are the Urban Land Ceiling Act (ULCRA) and the rent control laws.

The ULCRA entails a limit of 500 square meters to the size of transactable plots in urban areas. Further, residential plots may not be converted to commercial use (Donkins, 1995, p. iv). In reality, larger plots have been bought and sold, and conversions have occurred, but via the back door. The law is generally believed in the city to have induced widespread corruption and bribery, including the involvement of organized crime. Notwithstanding such violations, the law has had a dampening effect on supply in the real estate market.

Rent controls, too, have had a suppressing effect on supply, in both the residential and the commercial markets. Landowners are reluctant to rent their property out, and when they do, they require extremely high deposits to cover themselves in view of the legal protection of tenants. Rent controls have therefore contributed to widespread deliberate vacancies of dwellings by owners, "owing to the fear that they would come under the mischief of Rent Control if they were let out" (Sukhthankar, 1998, p. 13). In 1998 it was estimated that some 40 000 apartments were sitting empty due to rent control laws (*Economist* 1998, p. 70; see also Kamdar, 1997). Rent control is also said to contribute to neglect and dilapidation of buildings and dwellings, thereby reducing the pool of high-quality space. Ongoing rent controls and rapidly rising market values result in absurd contrasts. In some parts of the city, tenants may be paying 200 rupees a month (about US$5) for an apartment worth $750,000 on the market (De Bellaigue, 1999).

The ULCRA and rent control laws have come under heavy criticism from the pro-reform lobby in India,[6] and some reforms have been implemented recently. In December 1998, the Maharashtra state government approved a new office location policy that allows conversion of some residential and industrial areas into commercial space. This decision was hailed by builders, developers, and mill landowners but criticized by activists (*Times of India*, 1998a). The ULCRA was repealed by the central government in New Delhi in January 1999, but the

Maharashtra state government has yet to follow (*Times of India*, 1999). Finally, the rent control laws have undergone only small and rather insignificant changes. For example, the Maharashtra state government approved in May 1998 a 5 percent maximum rent increase, far too little to bring these rents within the range of market values.

Casino capitalism

The steep rise of real estate values in the early nineties was without historical precedent in Mumbai or the rest of India. It was more than a mere increase of prices; it was a dramatic change in the way the real estate market worked. As pointed out earlier, the culture of real estate in India is traditionally such that most land enters the market only under very unusual circumstances. As a consequence, much real estate in India has no "going" market value. The partial opening up of Mumbai's market in the first half of the nineties meant that the market had to find the "right" price of Mumbai real estate. That price was escalating upward due to the much talked-about scarcity of office space in the city, in combination with rapidly increasing demand, an equally popular topic of conversation. The search for a stable market level was complicated by the entry of global capital, because Mumbai was now compared not only to places like Delhi or Pune but also to New York or Hong Kong. Thus, when Nariman Point became as expensive as Manhattan and five times as expensive as Bangalore, who was to say that this was not "normal"?

In these circumstances, where the sky appeared to be the limit, demand became increasingly speculative in nature. The market was more and more driven by speculative exchange value, not by use-value. Peak prices in 1995 and 1996 were often paid for so-called notional real estate, the kind that only existed on paper and that had not (yet) been built. Notional transactions made up about 75 percent of the total number of transactions in 1995 and concerned options to real estate that still had to be developed but in many cases never materialized. Nevertheless, some notional real estate changed hands many times until the bubble burst in 1996. In other words, approximately 75 percent of all real estate investment at the time was speculative and not for end-use, which resulted in artificially high and ultimately unsustainable price levels. Most of this notional real estate was (supposed to be developed) in the suburbs, places such as Worli, Bandra-Kurla, and Andheri-Kurla. Foreign capital, NRIs, and MNCs were involved in this speculative demand for real estate, but they were not the only players. Domestic Indian companies, realtors, and developers, along with local governments and public agencies, played a critical part as well.

With hindsight, it is clear that the general slowdown of the Indian economy around 1995 and 1996 provided the broader context for a decline. Around the middle of the decade, it appeared as if the Indian economy had started to run out of steam. Growth figures were down, as were many other basic indicators. This was in part attributed to the pace of policies of liberalization and reform, which was allegedly not fast enough. Also, a number of foreign investors appear to have overestimated the quick and sizable profits to be made from the much talked-about growing Indian middle class.[7] Whatever the reasons, the economy was slowing down, profits were stagnating, inflation was up, and optimism in the corporate sector was down. When the government decided to raise interest rates in late 1995 to dampen inflation, the result was credit tightening and a further squeeze of demand in real estate markets around the country.

As soon as the tide turned, in 1996, the majority of investors in real estate whose ventures were merely speculative opted out and in doing so contributed to a downward spiral. The spectacular rise during the early nineties had been unprecedented, and the same was true for the dramatic downturn that started in 1996. The search for the "right" price of Mumbai real estate had started to move down the spectrum. The fall was very sharp at first and then continued in a more gradual fashion. Between 1996 and 1998, real estate prices in Mumbai fell by over 40 percent and have somewhat stabilized during the past year or so.

The development and promotion of cheaper office sites in Greater Mumbai during the peak years also helped to create the conditions for a reversal in the market as they constituted new (if belated) supply. Since the mid-nineties there has been a shift of corporate activity and offices from the CBDs to secondary sites such as Worli and Lower Parel, and to suburbs such as Andheri and Bandra-Kurla. In some cases, only front offices remained in the CBDs. Andheri, in particular, has emerged as a popular alternative site for office locations, taking advantage of high-quality new accommodations, a good location (adjacent to the Santa Cruz free trade zone), and rapidly expanding cultural and social amenities for newly arriving middle-class residents (*Times of India,* 1998b, 1998c).

A number of manufacturing firms have moved out of the southern areas of the city toward Thane or even further away. Increasingly, the traditional CBDs show a concentration of firms in the financial and producer services sector, as well as headquarters of large manufacturing corporations. There is also evidence of companies shifting operations out of the Mumbai region altogether, to Pune or to sites outside Maharashtra. This shift is often related to the high cost of land, congestion, and high labor costs in Mumbai. A recent study pointed out that this trend has undermined Mumbai's competitive position vis-à-vis sites like Pune, Bangalore, and Hyderabad (Indian Market Research, 1998). Thus, recent developments in the real estate market have contributed to growing differentiation and specialization of Mumbai's economic geography and, at a larger scale, to the emergence of new economic centers and the consolidation of regional economies like the Mumbai–Pune corridor (see Shaw, 1999). For these reasons, along with expected further deregulation of the supply side of the market, it is very unlikely that real estate prices will return to the levels of 1995. Many buyers who made their purchase during the peak years are faced with enormous losses. Some continue to sit on their devalued property in lingering denial of their misfortune.

Conclusion

In India, and elsewhere, debates on the effects of globalization show a tendency to overestimate the importance and autonomy of global forces and to underestimate the significance of local and national actors. There can be little doubt that global connections played a critical part in the turbulence and high price levels that characterized Mumbai's real estate market in the nineties. But here, too, the relative importance of global actors must be understood in the context of the wider cast of players in the market.

NRIs played an active part in driving up demand in the residential market, *alongside* resident Indians from Mumbai and elsewhere in India. While the influx of demand by NRIs was a hotly debated topic, domestic (speculative) demand was rarely in the news. It is questionable whether NRIs were the main actors in the growing number of notional real estate transactions in 1994 and 1995 that played such an important part in the market's speculative and turbulent nature. At the same time, it seems likely that the influx of NRI investments increased local speculative interest in real estate investment, thereby accelerating overall demand.

In a more general sense, the developments in Mumbai's real estate market illustrate that a focus on the distinction between global and (by implication) local capital is potentially misleading. For the movements of the market, it makes no difference whether a buyer is an NRI or a local Mumbaikar. Moreover, the escalation of real estate prices was in part caused by the flow of funds of domestic rather than foreign capital.

The most *active* players in the residential and commercial market were the real estate businesses and property developers. These were almost all Indian (domestic) and local companies, some with a long history in the Mumbai region.[8] They saw an opportunity for exorbitant profits and seized it. The upward escalation of prices in the early to mid-nineties was in their interest, and most probably they were actively promoting the trend.

The role of MNCs was important but quite passive compared to some of the other actors. Most large MNCs in Mumbai in the early and mid-nineties had been in the area since the eighties or long before that. Many did not change their location during the turbulent years of the real estate market. In a sense, they were "just" sitting there, willing and able to pay the rapidly increasing rents. Even in this respect, they were not alone, but in the company of many large and prosperous Indian corporations.

The movers and shakers of the market appear to have been the local Indian real estate companies, developers, and state and national governments. If the metaphor of casino capitalism applied to Mumbai's real estate market, it was government that functioned as the management of that casino. The Indian government and Maharashtra state government, with the introduction of highly unbalanced deregulation measures, opened the door to increased foreign (and domestic) demand while keeping supply at abnormally low levels. In retrospect, it seems clear that these unbalanced reforms created the fundamental conditions for a market that was to get out of control. Further, once prices spiraled up, the government did not appear to take any steps to correct these imbalances. A number of local and other Indian authors and analysts have criticized the Maharashtra state government for acting on behalf of the local building industry and property developers.[9] It is indeed hard to avoid the impression that at times the government's actions and inactions regarding the regulatory environment of the real estate market were inspired by these ties. According to these critics, it would not have been the first time that the state government acted on behalf of local capital, developers, and the construction industry.

It makes little sense to blame the turbulent developments in Mumbai's real estate market on global capital or, more concretely, on

MNCs. Nor should this chapter be understood as an exercise in sin-
gling out domestic agents as the culprits. Rather, the experience of the
real estate market in Mumbai shows the importance of evenhanded liberalization packages that create the conditions for a local–global transition. Questions of "How much liberalization?" or "How much
globalization?" obfuscate the importance of the exact nature of deregulation measures and their consequences. It is not so much a matter of
whether central or state governments engaged in too much, or too
little, reform. In the case of the real estate market, one might say that
there was either too much deregulation on the demand side of the
market or too little on the supply side. From an abstract ideological
point of view, one may argue for either one or the other. From the
practical point of view of maintaining market stability and avoiding
excesses of speculative and destructive market behavior, it is the inherent balance of liberalization schemes that matters most

Notes

1 This study is part of a research project on the urban effects of globalization
in Greater Mumbai, sponsored by the National Geographic Society (Grant
6023–97) and the National Science Foundation (Grant BCS 9730920). An
earlier version of this chapter was published in *The Economic and Political
Weekly*, 35 (2000).
2 The lack of market transparency and information is a common contributing
cause to so-called bubbles in real estate markets, and probably played its part
in the case of Mumbai's extreme experience. The effect is often compounded
by "perverse incentives" on the part of participants in the property business
who stand to profit from inflated prices (see Herring and Wachter, 1999).
3 The main indices of the Bombay Stock Exchange (BSE) reached the same high
levels again in February 1994. The volatility of the stock exchange, in the
context of liberalization and deregulation, is a study in its own right. For the
movement of BSE indices during these years (see *BSE Index Numbers*, 1997).
4 There were also some measures of deregulation at the local level. The
Maharashtra state government prohibited the establishment of new offices
in Greater Mumbai from 1971 to 1991 (with the main exception of the Santa
Cruz Export Processing Zone). After this regulation was revoked, new
demand for office space probably entered the market.
5 This relative lack of involvement of the banking and finance sectors in the
real estate business saved these sectors from a potential crisis once prices
came tumbling down. Generally, the collapse of real estate booms is linked
to crises in banking systems (see Herring and Wachter, 1999).
6 See Joshi and Little, 1996, 209–10; Jalan, 1996. Also, according to some
observers, developers used the ULCRA, rent control, and other regulations to
generate a discourse that would result in and legitimize higher prices (see
Narayanan, 1997).

7 In management circles of TNCs in Mumbai, it is generally said that many companies were hurt after they overestimated the purchasing power and size of the emerging Indian middle class (see also Varma, 1998).
8 There is a small number of foreign-controlled real estate agencies that probably have a disproportionately large clientele among TNCs (such as Cushman and Wakefield, and Colliers Jardine). But the overwhelming majority of realtors and even more of property developers, are Indian. For example, of the forty-four companies dealing with commercial properties that are included in the *Prowess Database* of the CMIE (1998), only one has foreign ownership.
9 For example, the state government did not live up to promises to move government offices and employment from Mumbai's CBDs to Navi Mumbai, which would have suppressed real estate values in the city. The government is also said to have favored the building industry and developers by allowing designated new developments in the city, such as the Back Bay reclamation scheme. The construction industry and property developers are often believed to have strong ties to Mumbai's notorious underworld. For such critiques of the Maharashtra state government, see, for example, Guha, 1996; D'Monte, 1997; Narayanan, 1997; Kamdar, 1997; Shaw, 1995.

References

Bombay Times (1998). Supplement to *The Times of India.* "City looks up as prices dip", May 28, pp. 1, 5.
BSE Index Numbers. (1997). Mumbai: The Stock Exchange.
CMIE (Center for the Monitoring of the Indian Economy). (1998). *Prowess Database.*
Colliers Jardine (1998). *Bulletin: India property highlights.* April. Mumbai: Colliers Jardine India, Research and Consultancy Division.
Cushman & Wakefield (1998a). *Asian property update.* Quarterly Report, Fourth Quarter (November). Hong Kong: Cushman and Wakefield Research and Consultancy.
Cushman & Wakefield (1998b). *Prime commercial office locations in Mumbai.* (June 1). Mumbai.
De Bellaigue, Christopher (1999). "Bombay at war." *New York Review of Books,* April 22, 48–50.
D'Monte, Darryl (1997). "Redevelopment of Mumbai's cotton textile mill land: Opportunity lost." Paper presented at Seminar on Work and Workers in Mumbai. Mumbai, November 27–29.
Donkins, Richard (1995). "Property prices hit the roof." *Financial Times* (Survey on Maharashtra), June 19, p. iv.
Economist. (1998). "Housing finance in India", June 13, p. 70.
Economist. (1996a). "Emerging market indicators". February 24, p. 112.
———. (1996b). "Emerging market indicators." August 31, p. 84.
Financial Express (1998). "Casino capitalism", April 3.
Guha, Krishna (1999). "Stuck in a rut for four years." *The Financial Times,* May 23, 1999.
Guha, Swapna Banerjee (1996). "Urban development process in Bombay: Planning for whom?" In Sujata Patel and Alice Thorner (eds.). *Bombay: Metaphor for modern India* (pp. 100–20). Bombay: Oxford University Press.

Herring, Richard J. and Susan M. Wachter. (1999). *Real estate booms and banking Busts – An international perspective*. Occasional Paper 58. Washington, DC: Group of Thirty.

Indian Market Research Bureau (1998). *Project shift*. Report on a study prepared for Bombay First. Mumbai.

Jalan, Bimal (1996). *India's economic policy. Preparing for the twenty-first century*. New Delhi: Penguin Books India.

Joshi, Vijay and I. M. D. Little. (1996). *India's economic reforms, 1991–2001*. Oxford: Clarendon Press.

Kamdar, Mira (1997). "Bombay/Mumbai. The postmodern city." *World Policy Journal*, 14, pp. 75–88.

Narayanan, Harini (1997). "The plot thickens: Rhetoric and reality in the context of the Urban Land (Ceiling and Regulation) Act 1976 and its application in Mumbai." Paper presented at Seminar on Work and Workers in Mumbai. Mumbai, November 27–29.

Patel, Sujata (1996). "Bombay's urban predicament." In Sujata Patel and Alice Thorner (eds.). *Bombay: Metaphor for modern India*. Bombay: Oxford University Press.

Property Times (1998). (Supplement to *The Times of India*). Mumbai property prices: February, 1998.

Shaw, Annapurna (1995). "Satellite town development in Asia: The case of New Bombay, India." *Urban Geography*, 16, pp. 254–71.

Shaw, Annapurna (1999). "Emerging patterns of urban growth in India." *Economic and Political Weekly*, April 17–24.

Statesman Weekly (1997). "Paving the way for MNCs in south Mumbai", May 5.

Strange, Susan (1986). *Casino capitalism*. Oxford: Blackwell.

Sukhthankar, D. M. (1998). "Relax rent control in Mumbai." *The City* (A Publication of Bombay First), 1 (2), 13.

Times of India (1999). "Urban Land Ceiling Act repealed", January 12.

Times of India (1998a). "Housing activists condemn office location policy, builders hail it", December 24.

Times of India (1998b). "Andheri – An emerging alternative", February 1.

Times of India (1998c). "Suburbia takes on new sheen as growth in south Mumbai stagnates", September 13.

Varma, Pavan K. (1998). *The great Indian middle class*. New Delhi: Penguin Books India.

11
Globalization and Financial Crises in Seoul, South Korea

Yeong-Hyun Kim

Seoul has captured international attention with two major events. One was the 1988 Seoul Olympics, and the other was the financial crisis from November 1997 through 1998. While the Olympics served as the most favorable opportunity for Seoulers to promote their country's phenomenal economic growth, the crisis revealed the dark side of Korea's success story. The same high-rise office buildings that were described as the symbol of the Korean economic miracle have become emblematic of the corrupted relationship between government and businesses. Seoul, envisioning itself as an emerging world city for much of the 1990s, has lost its competitive edge by revealing structural weaknesses and practical faults in its globalization process.

As the world's view of Seoul has changed after the financial crisis, Seoul's view of the world, particularly globalization, has also significantly changed. Excitement about globalization, widespread among Seoulers in the early 1990s, has quickly faded away, and worries, discontents and anger have come in their stead. Numerous new plans and visions have been proposed with hopes of not repeating the crisis. The city has shown various – at many times contradictory – reactions to globalization in its recovery process from the recent economic turmoil. Its government and policy makers have taken a pro-globalization stance by opening up its stock market, for example, but civic campaigns criticizing the consumption of foreign products have contributed to the recent sharp fall in Korea's importing of consumer goods. The globalizing side of Seoul has developed along with plenty of signs of deglobalizing, antiforeign sentiments. I examine Seoul's contradictory positions to globalization after the financial crisis of 1997–8 that forced the Korean government to seek $58.4 billion in aid arranged by the International Monetary Fund (IMF).

Globalization is not a process that makes different places around the globe alike (Jameson and Miyoshi, 1998; Sassen, 1998; Short and Kim, 1999). Individual places have developed various forms and processes of globalization according to their economic strength, ethnic composition, political projects, and historical connections with the outside world. A variety of local settings have been identified as the major sources of diversifying globalization processes around the world (Cox, 1997; Mander and Goldsmith, 1996). Many case studies have focused on different characteristics among places to argue for the pluralistic nature of globalization. The local has often been identified as a source of continuity (Hannerz, 1996). Various dimensions of globalization, however, can be observed in a place by different local institutions, sectors, movements, classes, jobs, and ethnicities, each distinct in terms of international connectedness, exposure to other cultures, and commitment to the place and its tradition. Each has its own reading of globalization. Different aspects of globalization – whether good, bad, real, exaggerated, avoidable, or inevitable – are likely to be emphasized by different groups, and different understandings lead to disintegrated, discontinued (re)actions to globalization in a place. In this chapter I argue for a new way to conceptualize the local that develops multiple relationships with the global.

When the Korean economy enjoyed a boom after the Olympics, particularly in the early 1990s, globalization meant an opportunity for Seoul to become a world city. The city's semiconductor industry and internationally known multinationals seemed to help Seoulers envisage their city positioned next to New York, Tokyo, and London. After the Asian financial crisis in late 1997, however, people's reading of globalization suddenly changed. It was seen as the investors who suddenly pulled out their investment, as the IMF that imposed its austere restructuring measures, and as the foreign banks that bought insolvent local banks. Seoul portrayed itself as an innocent victim of globalization with little knowledge of the evil nature of global forces. These anti-globalization sentiments prevailed among Seoulers in late 1997 and into 1998, when the city suffered the worst of the crisis.

Seoul has been reinventing itself through the extensive restructuring program guided by the IMF. The city has bounced back from the aftereffects of the economic crisis since 1999 (*Economist*, 1999), although a complete restructuring may take much longer. In Seoul there are contesting groups with different views of globalization. Some argue for the inevitability of a more globalized Seoul to improve its competitiveness in the global economy. Others make a long list of troubles that globalization and its byproducts, such as the financial crisis, have brought to their lives. The issues of transparency and accountability have created heated debates about the relationship between Korean values and international standards, without clear definition of either term. Seoul appears very fragmented in the recovery process; the effects of the crisis and subsequent restructuring have been very unequal among peoples, jobs, and businesses. It is not easy to conclude which way Seoul is heading in the post-crisis era, because the city seems to be globalizing and deglobalizing at the same time. I examine a variety of views among Seoulers on globalization and the restructuring in the post-crisis era. This case study of Seoul, a city that is clearly revealing an acute tension between globalizing and deglobalizing trends, enables me to argue that a place has far more diverse relationships with global-ization than many researchers suppose.

The local in the plural

The phrase "globalization in the plural" has raised interest about local contexts in the globalization literature. Local factors, whether they resist, embrace, or surrender to global forces, have been at the core of debates on globalization over the past few years. Two arguments can be outlined.

First, a growing body of literature has addressed the endurance of the national and local in the age of globalization (Cox, 1997; Mander and Goldsmith, 1996; Weiss, 1998). Nation–states have not died, nor have national boundaries lost their significance in international transac-tions. The world economy still remains very nonintegrated and should be called an "inter-national" economy rather than a "globalized" one (Hirst and Thompson, 1996; Thompson, 1999). Local cultures are resilient to global cultures, most often represented by US culture (Jameson and Miyoshi, 1998). Local cultures may be more or less trans-formed by the import of massive quantities of American cultural prod-ucts, but they have not been completely displaced.

Second, a number of works employing a global framework to look at the local level have focused on the interplay of the global and the local (Grundy-Warr, Laurie and Marvin, 1999, Peachey, and Perry, 1999). The local is not being swept away by the global or the foreign; rather it plays an important role in diversifying globalization processes across the world. The global and the local interact in complex ways, and in particular instances the global can be subsumed in the local areas. For instance US cultural traits themselves are subject to change, as they are planted outside their territories. McDonald's hamburgers, for example, are served with teriyaki sauce, under the name of Teriyaki McBurgers, in their Japanese restaurants (McDonald's Corporation, 1999).

Much of the literature on the global–local nexus has found local factors critical of the diversity of globalization processes. Few, with two notable exceptions (Sassen, 1995, 1998; Tomlinson, 1999), however, have noticed that the local has multiple faces when it is globalizing. Sassen (1995, 1998) notes the ongoing tension between denationalizing economic space and renationalizing political discourse in most developed countries. Criticizing the economic definitions of globalization, Tomlinson (1999) argues for the multidimensionality of globalization including economic, political, social, interpersonal, technological, environmental, and cultural categories. Although they both point out the sheer complexity of the empirical reality of globalization, their claims lack empirically grounded works at a microscale.

The globalization of a place carries considerable differences in sectors (economic, cultural and political), times (boom and bust), institutions (government, multinationals, and small firms), and class (transnational business class to unskilled workers). While each of these factors is likely to have a distinct relationship with globalization, much of the globalization literature assumes a place has only one view of globalization, which is very often either helpless submission or vigorous resistance (Hirst and Thompson, 1996). A city that is highly global in economic terms can be focused culturally on the local. Tokyo is an emergent world city and its economy has led the globalization of the world economy, yet its ethnic composition is not so diverse as to be named a cosmopolitan center (Machimura, 1998). An institution sometimes maintains very inconsistent opinions about globalization; medium-sized firms in Seoul, for example, that have long protested the market invasion of high-profile American multinationals have had vast investment assets in neighboring, less developed countries (Y. Kim, 1998). With this diversity and complexity, the local should not be seen as a constant and steady space in relation to globalization. I thus argue here for "the local in the plural," while much of the literature has focused on globalization in the plural.

The existence of heterogeneous discourses in a city is not new in urban studies. The lives, landscapes, and economies of the underrepresented have attracted mounting attention (King, 1996; Sassen, 1991; Zukin, 1995), but these studies' findings are very much based on multiethnic cities where substantial differences between ethnic groups have long existed. In the case of Seoul, almost all residents share the same language, history, and ethnicity, all essential to the formation of a fairly continual, homogeneous space masking any minor, potential variations. The city, however, has revealed noticeable discontinuities and contradictions in the recent restructuring process aimed at globalizing and opening up the economy under the advisement of the IMF since the 1997 financial crisis. Since Seoul has not been known as a city of difference, the recent rise of different voices and visions makes it an appropriate setting for studying the local in the plural within the explanation of globalization in the plural.

How does globalization take place in the local? A few different scenarios can be identified while leaving ample room for others. The local meets the foreign, for instance, through the opening up of borders. The foreign is becoming deeply embedded in the local, and it is no longer meaningful to differentiate the two. The local moves beyond its territory physically or symbolically and starts contacting, competing, and mingling with the foreign. The local may undergo significant changes by these processes, and the transformed, deterritorialized local factors will have certain influences back on their original place. The globalization of a place should be seen as a set of processes through which the local, the deterritorialized foreign, and the deterritorialized local are influencing and subsequently changing one another. This way of theorizing globalization at the local allows us to make a stronger argument about diversity. Globalization is not a threat to diversity around the world; rather it is a process bringing to more differences the local through increasing transnational connections.

Governments, firms, and traditional cultures whose controls have been significantly undermined by the penetration of external factors have represented the local in many case studies (Bhalla, 1998; Mander and Goldsmith, 1996). The concept of local should be more inclusive. A closer look at a place reveals countless locals: some hampered by globalization, some facilitating the globalization process, some using globalization ideas for their own political and economic gains, some newly created by globalization, and some restructuring themselves for globalization. Once we admit the diversity of the local, it becomes much clearer that globalization does not proceed at the expense of the local; parts of the local may well benefit from globalization.

The diverse and fragmented local in relation to globalization can be better understood with an example drawn from Tokyo, a predominant world city that still maintains a high level of cultural unity. The city's distinguished status in the world economy can be seen in the gigantic cluster of corporate headquarters and financial firms in its main business districts, such as Shinzuku and Ginza. It is not necessary for many Japanese firms to follow global trends; instead they lead global business moves and create new waves. Japan, meanwhile, is one of the few countries whose traffic system requires cars in the left lane and the driver's seat on the right side of the car. The Japanese market has never been easy for foreign car manufacturers to penetrate. Although consumers in Tokyo have been very loyal to local products, an increasing number of young Japanese are buying American or German luxury cars that can be easily spotted on the street by their different arrangement of seats. They buy the BMWs that are not customized to the Japanese traffic system. While I was undertaking fieldwork in Tokyo in the summer of 1999, many young BMW drivers in Ginza seemed to enjoy being different from the majority – "globalized otherness" in Shields's term (1997). As globalization takes place in Tokyo, these different aspects of the city – economic dominance, local traffic rules, and globalized consumption patterns – all matter.

The local interacts with the global not in a unified way, but in multiple ways. The fragmented and inconsistent nature of the local is reinforced and heightened by the further development of globalization processes. Cities that had limited contacts with the outside world throughout their history, such as Seoul and Tokyo, have recently witnessed a considerable growth of "otherness," "elsewhereness," and "globalness" in their cultures, economic practices, and political discourses. This increased multiplicity at the local level in turn adds to the diversity and complexity of globalization. In the following sections, I examine Seoul's globalization process over the past decade. Although the direction of the city's globalization has never been agreed on, the recent financial crisis and the economic hardship that followed have greatly diversified Seoulers' readings of globalization.

Seoul's excitement about globalization

Seoul has been a Korean-only city for a very long time. Unlike Hong Kong and Singapore, it has not served as a focal point of international trade. Capital movement across its borders was controlled heavily until the early 1990s, when the Korean government began to show a commitment to opening up its capital market. Without any notable history of immigration, Seoul's ethnic composition has been solely Korean, and it thus has not celebrated ethnic areas or festivals, which many of the world cities have done for decades. As the dominant international gateway of Korea, however, Seoul went through tremendous changes in the 1990s. Prompted by extensive financial liberalization in the early 1990s, the Korean economy has expanded and deepened its connection to other countries' economies. Seoul has led the country's globalization process, because it is where much of foreign investment flows to Korea have settled, and where most Korean multinationals are based. In addition, since the Seoul Olympics in 1988, the increasing exposure of local culture to the outside world has lowered the cultural barriers experienced by the city for centuries. The Olympics were a key factor in the dramatic rise of Seoul's international orientation in the 1990s (Y. Kim, 1998).

Cities use international sports events to build up their claim to world city status. Just as Atlanta hosted the Centennial Olympic Games in pursuit of heightened international visibility (Rutheiser, 1996), Seoul held the 1988 Summer Olympics and will co-stage the 2002 World Cup with Tokyo. The Seoul Olympics made a clear statement of Korea's economic success to the world via the global reach of Olympic broadcasts (Kim, 1997). Seoul projected a (post)modern, prospering, and vibrant city image which aimed at eliminating the old perception of the Korean War (Larson and Park, 1993; Tomlinson, 1996). The Seoul Olympics helped Seoul reinvent itself as the center of an emerging economy in Asia instead of as an emblem of the Cold War. The numerous international events in association with the 1988 Games provided Seoul with an unprecedented opportunity to claim its world city-ness.

The Seoul Olympics also played a significant role in opening up Seoulers' eyes to the wider world. Hosting 160 national teams and hundreds of thousands of tourists from many parts of the world allowed Seoulers to taste other cultures as much as it allowed others to experience Seoul. Since Seoul was not a cosmopolitan city by any means, this exposure to the Other began to challenge the traditional notion of Korean-ness generally associated with, for instance, ethnic purity, family bonding, and patriotism. I do not intend to conclude that Seoul's local cultural traits have been dismissed by the excessive entry of foreign cultures during and after the Olympics. It is the case, however, that part of the cultural changes in the 1990s stemmed from Seoulers' exposure to cultures of union way had little or no experience before.

One of the most prominent cultural changes after the Olympics was the rising interest in others around the world. A big rush into foreign language institutes was observed, and interest about the outside world increased, forcing the government to remove restrictions on international travel that had been imposed for decades to prevent significant capital flight. There was an explosive growth of overseas travel among college students after the Games. Since few had been allowed to tour overseas for a long time, it was considered a bonus for ordinary Seoulers. Thanks to the booming national economy after the mid-1980s, they could afford expensive international travel, which entailed expansion not only of their physical space but of their representational space. According to Robertson (1992) and Tomlinson (1999), increased international connection is a very important source of change in the nature of the local (localities). The local culture began to be viewed through others. In an interview, a US lawyer who worked for New York-based multinationals in Seoul for more than a decade stated that:

> Seoul is still extremely homogenous. It's not near New York or London. I'm not talking about the percentage of foreigners that you just did. What I mean is attitude. The way they look at me. Basically they're racists. In a different way from those in the US. Few have met foreigners in their lifetime. They are very impatient about different ways of doing. But, as you said, the Olympics made a huge change. It's true. It became much easier to work here after the Games. Most of my clients got to know about Seoul through the Olympics. Now more people speak English of course. I can see their efforts to learn "international" ways of doing business. But you know what? They're still very Korean. It won't change soon. (Interview, winter 1998)

The heightened international visibility of Seoul after the Games, coupled with a labor shortage in the local manufacturing sector, contributed to the sheer growth of foreign workers. Before the Olympics, the presence of foreigners, mostly represented by Chinese Koreans and American army personnel, carried little significance, as Chinese descendants were assimilated into the mainstream long ago and US soldiers resided in largely restricted areas. Except for a very limited number of visitors, such as language instructors, business people, and tourists, it had been rare to encounter foreigners on the street. Some variations in Seoul's ethnic homogeneity, however, began to be detected around the late 1980s. Migrant workers from Southeast Asia and China flocked into Seoul. Small local manufacturing firms, who had suffered both the deindustrialization of the Seoul economy and the surge of wages, welcomed these workers.

To legalize the employment of foreign workers, the Korean government began the Industrial Training Program in 1993 (Y. Kim, 1998), through which it would grant foreign workers short-term stay visas (two to three years) on the condition they were hired in small and medium-sized firms and that they leave after their contracts expired. Foreign workers were recruited directly from their home countries by Korean recruitment offices set up throughout developing Asian countries. In 1996 more than 60 000 foreign workers came to Korea through the program, and most of them were employed in Seoul. Many of the trainees stayed illegally after their contracts expired, but it is difficult to estimate the exact numbers. Approximately 200 000 foreigners worked legally and illegally in Seoul in the mid-1990s. The number grew from a few thousand before the Olympics. The remittance sent by foreign workers in Korea to their own countries, according to the Korean Ministry of Labor (1997), increased from $26.3 million in 1990 to $179.7 million in 1996. Compared to other world cities, such as New York, where more than a third of the residents are foreign born (Sontag and Dugger, 1998), however, Seoul is still homogeneous, as the US lawyer noted earlier.

In the 1990s the Seoul economy attracted a large amount of capital from all around the globe (Table 11.1). With the subsequent decline of Seoul's manufacturing sector in the 1990s (Kim, 1996; Lee and Kim, 1995), service industries became major recipients of this increasing foreign direct investment. The foreign investors favored hotel industries, finance, commerce, and insurance. The rise of portfolio and other investments, which led to the excess of short-term loans and subsequently the financial crisis in later years, gave rise to a significant foreign financial presence in Seoul's urban economy. Citibank set up its first Seoul branch in 1988 and added eight more branches during the next decade. Except for the years immediately following the financial crisis in late 1997, much of the 1990s saw a sharp increase in the inflows of foreign money into Seoul. The rapid emergence of new financial districts in the southeastern part of the city (named *Kangnam*) symbolized the effects of financial liberalization in the early 1990s and the following massive influx of international capital. (Six of the nine Citibank buildings are located at these newly developed business districts in the Kangnam area.)

The ten years between the Olympics and the financial crisis saw marked changes in Seoul's economy and culture. The city underwent deindustrialization as many manufacturing firms moved to China, Southeast Asia, and Eastern Europe. The upsurge of wages, compounded by the launching of militant unions, contributed to the flight of labor-intensive industries from Seoul. The service industry, particu-

Table 11.1 Foreign direct investment in Seoul, 1982–98

	FDI flows ($ million)				
	1982	1987	1992	1998	
Manufacturing	133.3 (22.7)	291.7 (19.0)	512.8 (17.5)	1,064.1 (12.4)	
Services	451.8 (76.9)	1,245.8 (80.9)	2,421.4 (82.5)	7,115.5 (85.1)	
hotel	212.1	872.9	1,186.8	1,700.9	
finance	146.6	216.8	605.4	1,351.2	
commerce and trade	0.4	11.5	178.6	1,005.7	
retail and whole	0.5	16.6	61.0	833.6	
insurance	3.0	4.4	181.9	287.7	
Total*	587.4 (100.0)	1,539.2 (100.0)	2,934.9 (100.0)	8,365.2 (100.0)	

* FDI flows in the agricultural and mining industries are not listed, but are included in the total.
Source: International Economic Policy Bureau, Ministry of Finance and Economy, Korea

larly financial services funded by foreign capital, rapidly rose to prominence during this period. The industries that could not move abroad
started hiring cheap foreign workers. Even if the foreign population in
Seoul was still small compared to other big cities around the world,
Seoulers in the 1990s began to sense diversity. Their cultural exposures
to the Other have also been expanded by their increasing contacts with
foreigners through business, travel, and media. An Olympic city was
on the verge of being a world city in the mid-1990s, or at least so
Seoulers thought.

Financial crisis and deglobalizing sentiments

The financial crisis that crippled the Korean economy in November
1997 was a shock to both the world and the people in the region.
There were some worries about the sustainability of Asia's fast-growing
economies (Krugman, 1998; Young, 1994, 1995), but at the same time
much of the literature in development studies repeatedly reinforced
the success stories of Asian economies (E. Kim, 1998; Leipziger, 1997;
Thompson, 1998). The crisis generated a large body of literature examining the causes of the sudden collapse of these exemplary economies,
including the crony relationships between their governments, banks,
and businesses (Krugman, 1998). Their financial liberalization policies
in the early 1990s turned out to be ill-prepared and poorly managed
(Chang, 1998; Chang, Park, and Yoo, 1998; Smith, 1998). Large current
account deficits prior to the crisis made the Asian economies highly
vulnerable to short-term financial flows and their sudden reversals
(Fisher, 1998; Garnaut, 1998; World Bank, 1998). Speculative investment, called the "hedge fund" has been criticized (Radelet and Sachs,
1999; Wade, 1998a). The IMF, which bailed out the crisis economies,
was disapproved of for its untimely interventions and austere restructuring measures (Kapur, 1998; Singh and Weisse, 1999; Wade, 1998b).
The search for explanations is still going on.

    While scholars have been scrutinizing the direct and indirect sources
of the crisis, many Seoulers have suffered arguably the toughest times
since the Korean War. The period between November 1997 and the
beginning of 1999 (or the end of 1998) was the worst. A succession of
corporate bankruptcies left numerous workers jobless in Seoul, a city
whose unemployment rate had remained around 2 percent for years. A
total of 9894 local companies were put out of business in the fourteen
months to the end of 1998 (Seoul Metropolitan Government, 1999a).
And from November 1997 to January 1998 there were more than 1200

bankruptcies each month. Seoul's unemployment rate increased to almost 10 percent by July 1998 (Seoul Metropolitan Government, 1999a). Those fortunate enough to keep their jobs have had to tolerate a severe cut, around 30 percent on average, in their salaries. With less than half of females being economically active, most households, which depended on a single male income earner, have been severely affected by these layoffs and pay cuts. Although Korea has not gone through the nightmare that Indonesia experienced, the social consequences of the economic recession have been very threatening.

The widespread economic hardships have resulted in a striking number of broken homes. In Seoul, divorce had traditionally been more or less socially unacceptable. Many young couples, however, decided to end their marriages during the economic contraction. Fewer than 10 percent of marriages ended up in divorce until the 1980s. The divorce rate grew quickly in the 1990s with the introduction of Western lifestyles and the empowerment of women in the household and at work. In 1996, Seoul had 256 couples married and 54 couples divorced per day (Seoul Metropolitan Government, 1999b). While the number of newlyweds has declined, the number of divorced persons has increased dramatically since 1997, the print when Seoul fell into economic turmoil. In 1997 there was an average of 209 marriages and 46 divorces each day. In 1998 a mere 176 couples got married and 68 couples divorced each day. The rise of single-parent families, a problem that many Western countries have dealt with for decades, has become a new social problem in Seoul.

The difficulties that the economic recession brought to Seoulers have been acute, and the IMF's restructuring program has made the crisis even more painful to bear. Under the conditions of the biggest bailout package in its history, the IMF requested Korea to follow its traditional macroeconomic adjustment measures.[1] The austere IMF program has turned out to be the wrong medicine for an ailing Korean economy. Some argue that the international institution actually worsened the economic mess by shutting out foreign investors' confidence, creating massive layoffs, doubling interest rates, and tightening bank loans in the first few months of crisis management (Kapur, 1998; Singh and Weisse, 1999; Wade, 1998b). In an effort to transform the Korean economy into a more open, accountable, and transparent one, the IMF lifted all the barriers to free transnational capital flows in May 1998 following a 50 percent removal in November 1997.

Deglobalizing sentiment was extremely strong between late 1997 and 1998. Economic and social stresses caused by the crisis were attributed to both the IMF's restructuring program and the government, which did not resist the unbearable request. During this time, Seoulers seemed to consider the IMF as a representative of global investors, who had long wanted the Korean market to open up, rather than as a rescuer of their economy which was on the brink of collapse. When the government announced the complete termination of barriers to free trade and capital flows, the IMF was compared in the media to the likes of George Soros, whose speculative investments made many developing countries' stock markets highly vulnerable.

The financial crisis was commonly called "the IMF crisis" among Seoulers. Recovery from the crisis was understood as "overcoming the IMF," as if the international monetary agency was responsible for the country's economic troubles (Shim and Lee, 1998). The buying rush of foreign companies in bankrupted or newly privatized industries was viewed as a severe threat to Seoul's economic sovereignty.

Seoul high school students burned Western clothing in public places to condemn spending on imported luxury goods (Pollack, 1997). Countless civic groups were in the streets to assert the need to cut back on consumption, particularly of foreign products, which were perceived as contributing to the foreign debt problem that necessitated the IMF's bailout and restructuring. Gas stations refused to sell gas to foreign-car drivers. Some restaurants even put signs on the door declaring that the drivers of foreign cars were not to be served (Cho, 1998). A local shoemaking company criticized foreign-brand-loving youth by adding the question "Do your wear dollars?" at the end of its advertisement (*Korea Herald*, 1998).

The economic slump and deglobalizing sentiments slowed down local people's international travel, which had risen markedly in the first half of the 1990s (Figure 11.1). The financial crisis raised serious concerns among Koreans about the waste of hard-earned dollars by unnecessary international travel. The Kimpo airport, the main gateway of Seoul, had been packed with Koreans on package tours up until 1997, but became almost empty for several months following the crisis.

Another deglobalizing trend could be seen in the number of foreign workers in Seoul. The number of illegal migrant workers, which had surged in the first half of the 1990s, declined dramatically as the economic turmoil shut down job prospects (Nam, 1999). Foreigners paying their visa dues numbered 115 058 at the end of 1996, but this fell to 74 236 in 1998, the year the Korean economy went through the worst point of its downturn.[2] Depreciation of the Korean currency affected directly the real income of foreign workers. In addition, a con-

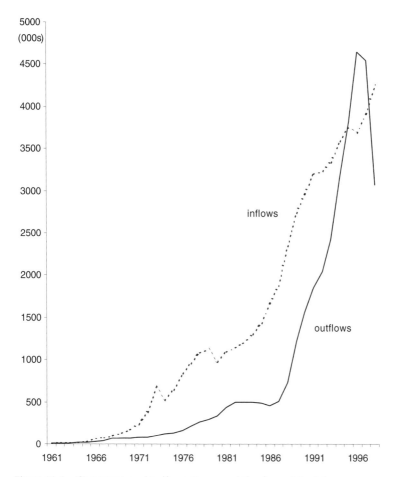

Figure 11.1   Overseas travel to/from Korea and the financial crisis
Source: Korea National Tourism Organization, 1999

siderable number of small-sized manufacturing firms, which were major employers of low-paid foreign laborers, were put out of business during and after the crisis. Local workers became highly xenophobic when they found themselves competing with foreigners in a dwindling job market. As signs of life have reemerged in the Korean economy since the beginning of 1999, however, the foreign population in Seoul has been on the rise again (*Korea Herald*, 1999).

Contradictory views of globalization

Deglobalization has not been the sole trend in crisis-laden Seoul. There has, of course, been remorse among Seoulers about the corruption and closed market that weakened the country's competitiveness in the world economy. The IMF restructuring programs forced Korea to be wide open to global capital flows. No matter what Seoulers feel about foreign products or companies, they have to deal with the foreign on a daily basis. Some factors of the foreign have become so deeply embedded in the local that Seoulers are getting used to its presence. Japanese cars and electronics, for example, which the Korean government long refused to import, have received a warm welcome in Seoul. Foreign banks, such as Citibank, have enjoyed a rapid increase in customers in their Seoul offices. Hamburgers, chicken fajitas, and pizzas have become young school children's favorite lunch menus.

With the debt crisis under control and the economy recovering quickly in 1999 (Figure 11.2), local people's reactions to globalization have become even more ambiguous. Some have shown very favorable attitudes to the changes of Seoul, while others have mourned the weakening of Korean-ness, which was considered the core of economic success in previous decades. The perceived threat to local businesses and traditions from outside has been mounting among some concerned Seoulers, but others have begun to truly enjoy the availability of "globalized" choices. With the removal of regulations on trade, wealthier consumers can afford upscale commodities, and small-sized hi-tech start-ups have been strongly favored by investors, restructured banks and the reform-driven government (C. Lee, 1999; Lee and Biers, 1998).

Many, including the government, have argued that a far-reaching restructuring is inevitable to improve the city's and the country's competitiveness in a globalizing world. Unlike Indonesia, which has tried to avoid any forced globalization processes, Korea has more or less focused on the opportunities that the IMF's restructuring could bring to it in the long term (Mathews, 1998). Indeed, part of the restructuring has been initiated by the local. Logos and slogans promoting Seoul's further globalization can be found throughout the city. For decades there have been slogans, such as "A Better Seoul," to mobilize civic participation in the development process of the capital city. During the Olympic period, "Olympic city-ness" was emphasized time after time. Seoulers were strongly encouraged by the government to nurture a mind-set appropriate for "world city residents" in the early 1990s. Since the crisis, however, the English phrase "global citizen" has gained currency. *Chosun Ilbo*, the

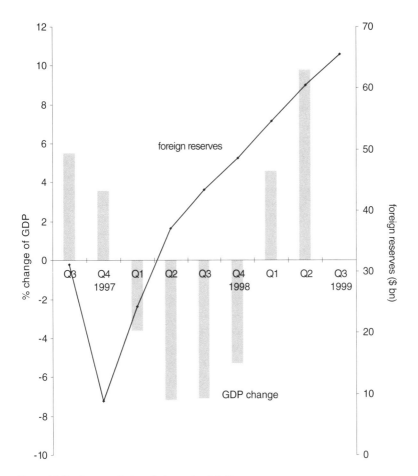

Figure 11.2 Economic trends in post-crisis Korea
Source: National Statistical Office, Korea 1999

most widely read local newspaper, has a daily column entitled "Global Etiquette, Global Citizen!" (*Chosun Ilbo*, 1999). As its title implies, the column is devoted to suggestions, experiences, and stories relating to the new Seoulers who are highly globally minded and foreigner friendly. While discouraged from buying foreign cars, Seoulers are expected to be friendly to foreigners. The launch of the Seoul Foreign Investment and Trade Services (FITS) Center in 1998 confirms that part of Seoul, particularly the government and entrepreneurs, have taken opening up as inevitable. The city has tried to put an end to the forced globalization era, and it now takes on globalization in a much more aggressive fashion. Compared to Seoulers' hostile reactions to the foreign during the months shortly following the financial crisis, the city's aggressive promotion of foreign investment shows that Seoulers have learned from the bitter experience of lacking foreign currency in late 1997.

While Seoul has tried to rearm itself with restructuring mainly focused on a foreigner-friendly image, there is still discontent. The unskilled working class has been the biggest victim of the economic turmoil, because the restructuring program allows employers to lay off their workers. There have been many strikes, street protests, and bitter jokes – for example, IMF as the acronym for "I'M Fired" – demonstrating local people's resistance to any further shake-ups of their lives. Many small firms have been ousted by the tightened availability of bank loans. Large numbers of small investors in the stock market have lost their retirement funds and savings as countless companies have failed. The fast rise of the homeless in Seoul shows how tough the situation has been for the working class during the crisis time. Those who have lost their jobs, companies or homes do not conceal their hatred for the IMF and their resentment toward the government for not keeping its pledge of social welfare to the underprivileged.

Government employees have also identified themselves as victims of the restructuring. Under IMF guidance, the state at all levels has changed into a much smaller, more efficient and high-tech informed structures. Many government workers have been transferred into different departments while others have been forced to take early retirement, neither situation imaginable in pre-crisis times.

Seoulers seem aware of the need for economic restructuring in terms of business–government relationships, greater transparency and accountability for corporations (particularly large conglomerates, named *Chaebols*), and prudential regulations on banking practices. However, clear rumbles of discontent have been heard from those who see themselves as the victims of the restructuring. These differences have embodied, and reflect, the contradictions, fragmentations, and inconsistencies in Seoul's post-crisis restructuring process.

Conclusion

While much of the globalization literature has focused on differences among places, I argue that differences within a place are also important considerations. A closer look at the local level reveals that a place accommodates a variety of groups with different views of globalization, distinct experiences, and multifaceted practices. Many studies have considered the local as either helplessly Americanizing or vigorously resisting, yet the globalization of a place proceeds in many different ways, not in a unified way; some are substantially integrated into global trends, while others remain in local, traditional forms. Some groups within a place want an acceleration of globalization, while others fear what globalization may bring. Given the different priorities, exposures, wishes and ideas, fragmentation, contradictions, and inconsistencies in reactions to global forces are inevitable.

The diversity in Seoul refers to a complex mix of globalizers, deglobalizers, nationalists, conformists, labor unions, multinationals, Americanized elites, Korean-ness advocates, foreigner-friendly shops, small businesses, protectionists, neoliberalists, xenophobes, and global citizens. Each of these elements has had distinct views, and taken action, in the restructuring process since the recent financial crisis, which has played a critical role in integrating Seoul fully into the global economy and politics. Seoul has not been completely submissive to the IMF's requests. Labor unions, for example, have refused to listen to the international agency's restructuring advice; some consumers have been pleased with the removal of regulations on the import of foreign cars; many others have shown their determination to stick to local products in a difficult time. The crisis has in part caused a breakdown of the frame of reference within which Seoulers viewed their economic success, strong government, traditional culture, and social coherence. The increasing influx of different values, practices, and lifestyles has added variations to the very homogeneous city, and the financial crisis and resulting economic hardship in recent years have immensely heightened those variations among Seoulers. Seoul's connection to the outside world has deepened dramatically and has expanded. Countless deterritorialized foreign factors have entered the city in recent years, transforming many local settings. Local people, firms, and cultures have increasingly moved beyond their physical and imaginational boundaries. The global and the local have intertwined in complex and diverse ways.

Notes

1   The IMF-supported program of Korea's economic reform featured (1) a firm exit policy for financial institutions, strong market and supervisory discipline, and independence for the central bank; (2) a tax increase; (3) dismantling of the nontransparent and inefficient ties among the government, banks, and businesses; (4) trade liberalization; (5) capital account liberalization; (6) labor market reform to facilitate the redeployment of labor; and (7)

publication and dissemination of key economic and financial data (IMF, 1998; Lane *et al.*, 1999).
2   According to Nam (1998), there were 262 000 foreigners, legal and illegal, in Korea in November 1997 just prior to the crisis; more than 40 percent of them left the country over the next nine months.

References

Bhalla, A. S. (ed.). (1998). *Globalization, growth and marginalization.* New York: St. Martin's Press.
Chang, Ha-Joon (1998). "Korea: The misunderstood crisis." *World Development*, 26 (8), pp. 1555–61.
Chang, Ha-Joon, Hong-Jae, Park and Chul Guye Yoo (1998). "Interpreting the Korean crisis: Financial liberalization, industrial policy and corporate governance." *Cambridge Journal of Economics*, 22 (6), pp. 735–46.
Cho, Yoon-Jung (1998). "Rough times ahead for owners of foreign vehicles." *Korea Herald*, March 13 (http://www.Koreaherald.co.kr).
Chosun Ilbo (1999). "Global etiquette, global citizen!" (http://global.chosun.com/)
Cox, Kevin R. (ed.). (1997). *Spaces of globalization: Reasserting the power of the local.* New York: Guilford Press.
Economist (1999). "Asia's economies: On their feet again?" August 21, pp. 16–18.
Fisher, Stanley (1998). "The Asian crisis: A view from the IMF." (http://www.imf.org/external/np/speeches/1998/012298.htm)
Garnaut, Ross (1998). "The East Asian crisis." In Ross H. McLeod and Ross Garnaut (eds.). *East Asia in crisis: From being a miracle to needing one?*, pp. 3–27. London: Routledge.
Grundy-Warr, Carl, Karen Peachey, and Martin Perry, (1999). "Fragmented integration in the Singapore–Indonesian Border Zone: Southeast Asia's 'Growth Triangle' against the global economy." *International Journal of Urban and Regional Research*, 23 (2), pp. 304–28.
Hannerz, Ulf (1996). *Transnational connections: Culture, people, places.* London: Routledge.
Hirst, Paul and Grahame Thompson (1996). *Globalization in question: The international economy and the possibilities of governance.* Cambridge: Blackwell.
International Economic Policy Bureau, Ministry of Finance and Economy, Republic of Korea (1999). "Distribution of foreign direct investment by region and industry."
International Monetary Fund (IMF) (1998). "The IMF's response to the Asian crisis." (http://www.imf.org/External/np/exr/facts/asia.HTM)
Jameson, Fredric and Masao Miyoshi (eds.). (1998). *The cultures of globalization.* Durham: Duke University Press.
Kapur, Devesh (1998). "The IMF: A cure or a curse?" *Foreign Policy*, 111, pp. 114–29.
Kim, Eun Mee (ed.). (1998). *The four Asian tigers: Economic development and the global political economy.* San Diego: Academic Press.
Kim, Hun (1996). "Outward foreign direct investment and the deindustrialization," *KDB Monthly Bulletin* (in Korean), 491 (October), pp. 1–39.
Kim, Yeong-Hyun (1998). Globalization, urban changes and Seoul's dreams: A global perspective on contemporary Seoul. Ph.D. dissertation, Syracuse University.

———. (1997). "Interpreting the Olympic landscape in Seoul: The politics of sports, spectacle and landscape." *Journal of the Korean Geographical Society*, 32 (3), pp. 387–402.

King, Anthony D. (ed.). (1996). *Re-presenting the city: Ethnicity, capital and culture in the 21st-century metropolis*. New York: New York University Press.

Korea Herald (1999). "Illegal foreign workers on the rise." September 13. (http://www.Koreaherald.co.kr/news/1999/09/_02/19990913_0211.htm)

———. (1998). "Companies publicizing their goods as 100 percent domestic products." (http://www.Koreaherald.co.kr)

Korea National Tourism Organization (1999). *Visitor arrivals, Korean departures, international tourism receipts and expenditures, 1961–1998*. (http://www.knto. or.kr/index_1.html)

Krugman, Paul (1998). "Asia: What went wrong: Sources of volatility in Asian financial markets. *Fortune*, March 2, pp. 32–3.

——— (1994). "The myth of Asia's miracle." *Foreign Affairs*, 73 (6), pp. 62–78.

Lane, Timothy, Atish Ghosh, Javier Hamann, Steven Phillips, Marianne Schulze-Ghattas, and Tsidi Tsikata (1999). *IMF-supported programs in Indonesia, Korea, and Thailand: A preliminary assessment*. Occasional Paper 178. Washington, DC: International Monetary Fund.

Larson, James F. and Heung-Soo Park. (1993). *Global television and the politics of the Seoul Olympics*. Boulder: Westview Press.

Laurie, P. and J. Marvin (1999). "Globalisation, neoliberalism, and negotiated development in the Andes: Water projects and regional identity in Cochabamba, Bolivia." *Environment and Planning A*, 31 (8), pp. 1401–15.

Lee, Charles S. (1999). "Wanted: New vision – South Korea looks to hi-tech services." *Far Eastern Economic Review*, June 10, 14.

Lee, Charles S. and Dan Biers, (1998). "Remaking Korea Inc." *Far Eastern Economic Review*, April 30, pp. 10–13.

Lee, Gun Young and Kim, Hyun Sik (eds.). (1995). *Cities and nation: Planning issues and policies of Korea*. Seoul: Korea Research Institute for Human Settlements.

Leipziger, Danny M. (1997). *Lessons from East Asia*. Ann Arbor: University of Michigan Press.

McDonald's Corporation (1999). "McDonald's around the world: Konnichi Wa." (http://www.mcdonalds.com/surftheworld/asia/japan/index.html)

Machimura, Takashi (1998). "Symbolic use of globalization in urban politics in Tokyo." *International Journal of Urban and Regional Research*, 22 (2), pp. 183–94.

Mander, Jerry and Edward Goldsmith (eds.). (1996). *The Case against the global economy and for a turn toward the local*. San Francisco: Sierra Club Books.

Mathews, John A. (1998). "Fashioning a new Korean model out of the crisis: The rebuilding of institutional capabilities." *Cambridge Journal of Economics*, 22 (6), pp. 747–59.

Ministry of Labor, Republic of Korea (1997). "Rapid rise of foreign workers' remittances." (http://www.molab.go.kr)

Nam, Kung-Duk (1999). "Foreign workers are leaving Korea." *Korea Economic Daily*, September 2.. (http://search.ked.co.kr/)

National Statistical Office, Republic of Korea (1999). "Major economic indicators." (http://www.nso.go.kr/stat/majorecono/econo.htm)

Pollack, Andrew (1997). "Frugal Koreans rush to rescue their rapidly sinking economy." *New York Times*, December 18, A1, D9.

Radelet, Steven and Jeffrey Sachs (1999). "What have we learned, so far, from the Asian financial crisis?" (http://www.stern.nyu.edu/~nroubini/asia/AsiaHomepage.html)

Robertson, Roland (1992). *Globalization: Social theory and global culture*. London: Sage Publications.

Rutheiser, Charles (1996). *Imagineering Atlanta: The politics of place in the city of dreams*. London: Verso.

Sassen, Saskia (1998). *Globalization and its discontents: Essays on the new mobility of people and money*. New York: New Press.

—— (1995). *Losing control? Sovereignty in an age of globalization*. New York: Columbia University Press.

—— (1991). *The global city: New York, London, Tokyo*. Princeton: Princeton University Press.

Seoul Metropolitan Government (1999a). "The latest economic trends of Seoul." (http://econo.metro.seoul.kr)

——. (1999b). "One day in Seoul." (http://www.metro.seoul.kr/eng/yearbook_fr.html)

Shields, R. (1997). "Ethnography in the crowd: The body, sociality and globalization in Seoul." (http://www.carleton.ca/~rshields/focaal.html)

Shim, Jae Hoon and Charles S. Lee (1998). "Unlocking the citadel." *Far Eastern Economic Review*, March 26, pp. 10–12.

Short, John Rennie and Yeong-Hyun Kim (1999). *Globalization and the city*. New York: Longman.

Singh, Ajit and Bruce A. Weisse (1999). "The Asian model: A crisis foretold?" *International Social Science Journal*, 160, pp. 203–15.

Smith, Heather (1998). "Korea." In Ross H. McLeod and Ross Garnaut (eds.). *East Asia in crisis: From being a miracle to needing one?* (pp. 66–84). London: Routledge.

Sontag, Deborah and Celia W. Dugger (1998). "The new immigrant tide: A shuttle between worlds." *New York Times*, July 19, 1, pp. 28–30.

Thompson, Grahame (1999). "Introduction: Situating globalization." *International Social Science Journal*, 160, pp. 139–52.

——. (ed.). (1998). *Economic dynamism in the Asia-Pacific: The growth of integration and competitiveness*. London: Routledge.

Tomlinson, Alan (1996). "Olympic spectacle: Opening ceremonies and some paradoxes of globalization." *Media, Culture and Society*, 18 (4), pp. 583–602.

Tomlinson, John (1999). *Globalization and culture*. Chicago: University of Chicago Press.

Wade, Robert (1998a). "From 'miracle' to 'cronyism': Explaining the great Asian slump." *Cambridge Journal of Economics*, 22 (6), pp. 693–706.

——(1998b). "The Asian debt-and-development crisis of 1997–?: Causes and consequences." *World Development*, 26 (8), pp. 1535–553.

Weiss, Linda (1998). *The myth of the powerless state*. Ithaca: Cornell University Press.

World Bank (1998). *World Development Report*. NY: Oxford University Press.

Young, Alwyn (1995). "The tyranny of numbers: Confronting the statistical realities of the East Asian growth experience." *Quarterly Journal of Economics*, 60 (3), pp. 641–80.

—— 1994. "Lessons from the East Asian NICs: A contrarian view." *European Economic Review*, 38, pp. 964–73.

Zukin, S. (1995). *The cultures of cities*. Cambridge: Blackwell.

Part IV
Conclusions

12
Conclusions: Ordering a Chaotic Concept Based on Evidence from the Margins

Richard Grant and John Rennie Short

The contributors in this volume have placed various aspects of globalization in particular locales. They showed that it is misleading to subsume everything under the rubric of globalization, while at the same time it is unhelpful to deny the very existence of globalization. Contemporary developments in the margins are best understood by the multiple relationships that the local arena forms with the global. From these studies of the globalization phenomena, we can conclude that globalization in the margins is better understood as the complex result of many different processes rather than a distinctive casual process in its own right. Globalizations in the plural rather than a singular notion of globalization better captures the diversity and complexities of local experiences.

Grounding the study of globalization from the perspective of marginal areas provides us with a refractive lens to examine globalization from inside out as well as the more conventional outside in. Drawing from the studies in the volume we can make some general observations about globalizations in the margins:

1) Globalization is both a structural and local structuring phenomenon in each marginal setting;
2) Globalization embodies not so much an evening out of economic and social development levels across the global, but more a deepening and reorganization of existing patterns of uneven geographical development based on the degree of exposure to the global economy;
3) Globalization shapes new local geographies. Some places, such as Nariman Point in Mumbai, Cantonments in Accra, Kangman in Seoul, and various gated communities, are hitched to the global economy

while the majority of areas are ditched, including the shanty towns of Lima, Accra, Mumbai and rural areas in the interior of particular states, such as Northern Indian villages. At the same time, no area is entirely excluded from the global economy. Graffiti used for advertising commodities in rural villages in Rajasthan embody global images and messages about global consumption standards;

4) In a globalization environment there are highly gendered contours of global restructuring;

5) Despite the intentions of global capitalists and international financial institutions, economic globalization rarely, if ever, involves the full structural integration and strategic integration across the globe. Contrary to the dominant narrative, the global economic system is a highly dispersed, fragmented and highly mediated entity at the margins; and

6) The current global expansion is characterized by an unprecedented geographical disjuncture between production and consumption, investment and production, work and market.

We have used the term 'margins' deliberately to convey the sense of a space away from a global core. The 'margins' is an important term for conceptualizing the combination of global and local. The combinations vary over time and across space. In some instances, global forces are foregrounded, for example, the spread of the Asian financial crisis to Seoul. At other times, local historical factors are much more important than contemporary global economic patterns in shaping spatial and social differentiation. Pellow illustrated this in her case study of Sabon Zongo. In other locales, domestic forces and state intervention can be more salient in the particular expression of global capitalism in a given local contest, for instance, the real estate market in Mumbai in the 1990s. We purposely employ the notion of the margins to move beyond the three-tier structure of core, periphery and semi-periphery in world-systems analysis and the state centric analysis that dominates development studies and the social sciences in general. Identifying the processes that predominantly operate at one scale does not adequately capture the complexity of the contemporary global–local nexus. Globalization is not just about one scale becoming more important than the rest, it is far more about changes in the very nature of the relationships among scales. The notion of the margins indicates that this integration and exposure to the global economy is often on unequal terms. Furthermore, the circuits of global capital can weakly connect with large parts of the global economy and be highly selective in terms of the integration of particular spaces and individuals along the margins. The notion of the margins puts the emphasis on a level of imbrication between global and local processes rather than simply viewing the places as peripheral or excluded from globalization forces. Importantly, the margins captures a sense of the hyper-differentiation of globalization across space. This hyper-differentiation is as salient as the hypermobilty of capital that has been well documented in the globalization literature. It also resembles the hypermobilty of capital in that it signifies the increased volatility of participating in the global economy.

The contributors identify many of the processes that are transforming areas on the margins. A useful way to think about globalization processes is to divide them into *inward* and *outward* connectivity. Processes identified in inward connectivity include:

1) Openings for actors other than nation–states in cross-border dynamics, particularly new global corporate actors and those collectivities whose experience of membership has not been subsumed fully under nationhood and its modern conception such as minorities, immigrants, first-nation people and many feminists (see Sassen's arguments in Chapter 2);
2) Opportunities for foreign direct investment, enhancing market share for global commodities, and for foreign companies in areas that are the particular foci of liberalization policies, such as gateway cities and financial centers (see Chapters 9, 10 and 11), which leads to an internationalization of national economic spaces by capital from a variety of international sources;
3) The denationalization of specific types of national setting, particular global cities and particular areas within those cities that have high exposure to global capital (see Chapters 2 and 10);
4) The tension between the requirements of capital, in general, and the interest of specific capitalists, depends on specific accumulation strategies and contingent on particular national and local contexts and historical relationships (Chapters 7 and 8);
5) An acceleration in the quantities available of global commodities that are marketed and advertised using global selling techniques but tailored to an increasingly differentiated local market;
6) The construction of a modern subjectivity and the relationship between media, migration, capital and imagination in creation of globalization representations (see Chapters 3 and 6); and
7) The dominant corporate global culture finds a local geographical expression in only part of the city in the margins. This global space

of precision and authority is clearly demarcated and articulated with the external economy. In the process, non-corporate spaces are more articulated with the local and national economies and inscribed with "otherness," and thereby devalued.

Processes identified as outward connectivity include: the policy elites, local media, place promoters and cosmopolitans in the margins seeking to promote a liberal market approach in their home states; flows from the margins to the center of money, resources, cuisine, art, music, models, fantasy coffins, and so on; the dominance of localization processes which restrict globalization in districts in cities in the margins, the so called slums or zongos that Pellow identified in Chapter 8; opportunities for domestic company collaborations with foreign companies in joint-venture arrangements and opportunities for local stock markets to list global companies on their exchanges; the intensification of exposure to the global economy that can cut both ways in terms of individual's (see Chapter 11 on the Asian financial crisis); resistance to globalization can sometimes take the form of isolated efforts where the struggle for daily survival is more paramount than political organization (see Hays-Mitchell's discussion in Chapter 7); and opportunities for anti-global movements to involve transnational collaboration from textile workers to environmental organization (see Robertson's analysis in Chapter 3).

Globalization processes offer a horizon of action for specific actors, but there is an inequality in terms of opportunities. Globalization has given more opportunities for the wealthy to make more money quickly. These individuals have utilized technology to move large sums of money around the globe quickly (buy real estates and establish foreign companies) and to speculate ever more efficiently. Unfortunately, this same technology makes little or no impact on the lives of the poor and provides them with few opportunities. If anything, globalization results in more social exclusion and leads to a burgeoning gap between the rich and poor. In many ways this is epoch making. Prior to the globalization era, the division between the rich and poor meant the need to talk and seek compromise and agreement, but this is less the case today. According to Bauman (1998, pp. 44–5) "it is not quite clear (anymore) what the new globalized rich and the new globalized poor would talk about, why they should feel the need to compromise and what sort of agreed modus coexistendi they would be inclined to seek." Bauman (1998, p. 45) goes on to note that the "globalizing and the localizing trends are mutually reinforcing and inseparable, but their respective products are increasingly set apart and the distance between then keeps growing, while reciprocal communication comes to a standstill."

Glocalization(s)

The extent of globalization depends on the exposure to the global economy as well as on complex connections among sub-global process and localization. This interface is better conceptualized as glocalization. As we outlined in the previous section, we are convinced that it is far more accurate to employ a relational understanding to globalization as opposed to a territorial one. The territorial logic in the regulation of economic life, for example, is prone to defend one spatial scale of organization against another or to seek a neat conceptualization of processes operating at the local, national and global scales. Swyngedouw (1997, p. 140) has made an important contribution by emphasizing that the global and local scales should be conceptualized as "simultaneous rather than hierarchical and thus without theoretical or empirical priority in the analysis of social life." Accordingly, a relational logic puts the emphasis on identifying which hybrid network locks together for a particular issue in a particular location. As Nijman noted in his study of the real estate market in Mumbai, if the metaphor of casino capitalism applied to Mumbai's real estate market, then it was the government that functioned as the management of the casino and it was NRIs, locals and MNCs who speculated, and who, in the process, shaped land-use and the new economic geography of the city.

Glocalization in the margins is based on the interdependence and intermingling and different permutations of global, national and local logics that result in a greater hybridation and perforation of economic and social life. Glocalization refers to the local variants of global processes whereby the occurrence, synthesis, dissipations, integration and decomposition are anything but accidental and even less are rectifiable. In the margins, the local global scene needs to be viewed as a matrix of possibilities, from which highly varied selections and combinations are made. Glocalization captures the highly individual ways that the global and local can be mediated in the margins.

We present five different illustrations of glocalization based on the case studies of particular marginal areas. We highlight each of the glocalizations in their own right but at the same time we acknowledge that different and multiple glocalizations are possible.

First, separate and distinct identities are woven together based on the selection and combination of characteristics from global and local culture. Moreover, the local industry of cultural differentiation turns into a globally determined characteristic of many aspects of life. There can be paradoxes in the identities that are created in a globalized world. As King noted in Chapter 6, social spatial and cultural identities are being made from outside as well as inside. The identity on the margins can be exported to the center, and identities in the center can be traded to the margins, whereby identity can be then formed in dialectical relation (and reaction) to each other. A globalization, sourced in the modernity of the center, allows the possibilities for new identities in the margins. The vehicles for these cultural flows are immigrants, electronic images, affluent tourism, global consumption standards and the media.

Second, corporate advertising strategies imbricate the global and local to enhance business success. The coexistence of opportunities for both globalization and localization is a distinguishing feature of advertising glocalization in the margins. Bhatia's research discussed in Chapter 5, shows that wall advertising in rural India employed an explicit strategy to glocalize the products of global companies. Glocalization is achieved by the mixing of two languages and scripts in a single advertisement for a global product. The mixing can involve portions of the advertisement in the so-called global English language, while another portion of the advertisement is in Hindi, Urdu or various local dialects. Some advertisers use color rather than linguistic means to advertise their global products locally. An advertisement by Pennzoil bridged the localization–globalization gap by sharing logographic properties of the products and by maintaining a common color scheme.

Third, foreign companies use a glocal strategy to embed themselves in local markets. Grant's research on foreign companies in Accra, analyzed in Chapter 9, illustrates that many foreign companies today, especially the larger ones, pursue a strategy of glocalization to embed their companies in the margins. These companies explicitly pursue this strategy to enhance their business and to distance themselves from the behavior of foreign companies in a different era (the colonial era) when they were regarded as "foreign impositions." The glocalization strategy of foreign companies can involve the formation of joint-ventures with local capitalists, listing foreign companies on local stock markets, historicizing foreign company involvement in the local economy and inventing a local consumer tradition. Guinness Ghana was a good example of a joint venture arrangement that employed all aspects of this glocal strategy.

Fourth, glocalization captures the new and diverging opportunities for spatial mobility in the margins. There has always been an elite in the margins that lived global lives as opposed to the local lives of most residents. Since the intensification of globalization, there have been greater opportunities for the elites, as well as an emerging middle class, to use time and money to annul the limitations of space. For the affluent and cosmopolitans, space has lost its constraining qualities and is easily traversed in real and virtual terms. The Internet offers opportunities for the middle class, and particularly the young middle class, to use the email and the net to dislocate themselves from their local settings and forge identities that are not based on their localities. For many in the margins, however, opportunities have not been altered. They are stuck in place; space is not controlled, it is controlling. According to Bauman (1998, p. 45) "the depravation of the poor is made more painful by the obtrusive media display of space conquest, foreign travel and the virtual accessibility of distances unreachable in the non-virtual reality." A great divide is now present in that some inhabit the globe while others are chained to place.

Finally, an aspect of glocalization that was alluded to in many of the chapters is how individuals in the margins use their subjective interpretative sphere to construct what is "foreign" and what is local, and even to differentiate between the two. Globalization is actively interpreted and re-represented as well as passively experienced. Research on consumption and on global signs and global symbols is still in a preliminary stage of exploration. According to Waters (1995, p. 156), material exchanges localize and symbolic exchanges are theorized as globalizing the world economy. We suggest that both realms of exchanges are highly mediated by glocalizations and the end result is far less predictable. It is possible that there are great differences at the individual level based on the extent of glocalizations, as well as individual characteristics that include personality, consumption patterns, lifestyle, global connections, local ties, and so forth. The end result, we think, might be more divided subcultures in an increasingly uneven and fragmented global geography.

Globalization and development in the twenty-first century: (re)placing geography

Since the introduction of liberalization policies in the 1980s, the relatively stable geography of the world economy has been scattered like so many jigsaw puzzle pieces. Globalization is a word and an idea that cloaks the array of complex and profound changes that have taken place since then. We have made a start in the process of placing the pieces back. The authors in their various contributions argue that there is not a disjuncture between the global economy and geography but rather a replacement of geography. We have not witnessed the "end of geography" (O'Brien, 1992) as some have speculated. Smith (1997, p. 188) describes globalization as producing "satanic geographies, of uneven development" that "represent a striking spatialization of class, and race, gender and national relations that make global production a social process." This new geography of uneven development is part of a long historical process.

The built environment in the margins, a product of the colonial and post-colonial eras, is a major contingency factor is shaping the contemporary geography of globalization in the margins. As Cox (1997, p. 5) notes "those conditions, those social relations that result in enduring commitments to particular places, which can in turn be sources of competitive advantages and to serve to reinforce other commitments." Capital is not as mobile, nor labor as immobile, as many globalization proponents would argue. Place is grounded from below, and has a dynamic and porous boundary around it, without closing out the extra-local. It becomes important then to specify what is included in the making of marginal places in the organization of everyday life. In an effort to commence this intellectual project on globalization we argue that new geographies have to be written for the new world of globalization. A new project on globalization and place must examine the openness of places to the outside world, the localization effects, and the interplay of how the global becomes a product of the local as much as the local is remade by the global.

Much of the evidence we present on globalization in the margins is suggestive rather than conclusive. There is a real need to globalize the intellectual study of globalization. Above all, researchers need to return to fieldwork, but this time fieldwork should be informed by theory. More comparative fieldwork might be helpful in moving away from the former confines of area studies and the tendency to place areas in particular continental regions rather than (re) placing areas in terms of how they are integrated into the wider space economy. We can hypothesize that the changes that are proceeding in Mumbai are quite similar to the changes that are taking place in Accra, Lima and Seoul, but each in their own particular contexts with various glocalizations.

We offer six suggestions for globalizing the globalization project. First, there is a need for greater collaboration among scholars across the world in understanding globalization. Second, we need to use indigenous knowledges to better understand the notion of the margins. We strongly endorse Boroujerdi's call in Chapter 4 to indigenize the entire globalization project. Research on globalization has been bedeviled by a radically ethnocentric view from those who think themselves to be in the cockpit of globalization. More funding from global organizations for scholars based in the margins would be a start. Third, increasing opportunities for global funding should be combined with more collaboration among scholars in universities in North American and Europe and scholars in the margins. Fourth, leading researchers have an obligation to publish their work in journals and outlets in the margins and not just the leading journals in the center and the academy. Fifth, more data needs to be collected on various aspects of globalization in the margins, including: the synergies that develop between global and local companies, the enduring effects of hybridity on local and national culture, the role of class in the globalization era in the margins, and whether a middle class emerges, as well as the effects of global standards in corporate culture and the spread of global consumptions standards. Sixth, we need to be aware of the hegemony of the English language in globalization debates. We need to open up the debate to other voices, with different opinions in different languages.

The contributors have separated the boosterist discourse of globalization from the qualitative changes that are occurring on the margins. The task at hand is not to unthink globalization, but to unpack globalization so that it can be properly grounded and the globalization experience of most of the citizens of the world can be understood. Globalization research needs to be at the center of a broader intellectual effort devoted to understanding the nature and characteristics of the persistently varied and divergent forms of capitalism. It is also fundamentally important to ascertain whether globalization precludes alternative futures. We need to think of globalization as a set of processes not as an inevitable end state. Globalization is contested as well as experienced. It is not only the apparent contradictions between equalization and differentiation in the global economy and the contradictions of identity that make globalization such a rich topic for research; it is the alluring prospect that it is a story we know with an end that we can only imagine.

References

Bauman, Z. (1998). "On glocalization: or globalization for some, localization for some others." *Thesis Eleven* 54 pp. 37–49.
Cox, K. (ed.). (1997). *Spaces of globalization. Reasserting the power of the local*. New York: Guildford Press.

Jessop, B. (1999). "Some critical reflections on globalization and its (il)logic(s)." In K. Olds, P. Dicken, P. Kelly, L. Kong, and H. Yeung (eds). *Globalization and Asia-Pacific: contested territories*. London: Routledge.

Dicken, P. 2000. "Places and flows: situating international investment" *Oxford Handbook of Economic Geography*. Ed. G. Clark, M. Feldman and M. Gertler (Oxford University Press, New York). pp. 275–91.

Kelly, P. (1999). "The geographies and politics of globalization." *Political Geography* 23: pp. 379–400.

Mittlelman, J. (1996). *Globalization: critical reflections*. Boulder: Lynn Rienner.

Mittlelman, J. (2000). *The globalization syndrome. Transformation and resistance*. Princeton: Princeton University Press.

O' Brien, R. (1992). *Global Financial Integration: the End of Geography*. New York: Royal Institute of International Affairs and Council on Foreign Relations.

Smith, N. (1997). "The Satanic geographies of globalization: uneven development in the 1990s." *Public Culture* 10(1) pp. 1691–89.

Swyngedouw, E. (1997). "Neither global nor local: 'glocalization' and the politics of scales." In K. Cox (ed). *Spaces of globalization: reasserting the power of the local*. London: Guildford.

Waters, M. (1995). *Globalization*. New York: Routledge.

Index

Abel, C.   78
Abu-Lughod, J. L.   20
accountability   172
Accra   4, 193, 194, 198, 200
  Metropolitan Assembly   114
  Municipal Council   114, 118
  see also foreign companies and
    glocalization; migrant
    communities
Acquah, I.   140
Adabraka   115, 116, 117
advertising
  banner   59
  conventional   54
  corporate   198
  nonconventional   54, 55
  social development and services
    64, 65
  video van   56–7
  wall   54, 55, 56–7, 69, 70
  see also localization or
    globalization: rural advertising
    in India
affiliation part   67
affluent tourism   198
Afghanistan   12
Africa   42, 142, 150
African Americans   23
Afshar, H.   98
agglomeration   20
airport areas   112
Akan   115, 123, 124
Alatas, S. F.   41, 42
Aluuworks   143
AMA (Accra Metropolitan Assembly)
  121, 123, 125
Americanization   36–7
Amin, S.   40, 42
Anderson, P.   73
Annan, K.   26
anti-AIDS drugs   36
antiglobal movements   196

antiglobality   35
  and economism   27–31
  and global variety   33
  and homogenization thesis   31–2
  and marginality   34
antiglobalization   35, 131, 136, 171
antimodernism   27
antisystemic movements   30
Appaduri, A.   35, 74, 75, 76, 80 137,
  146
Aptheker, B.   96
architecture   76–7
Arn, J.   113, 118, 120
Ashanti Goldfields   140, 141, 143
Asia   34, 36, 42, 142, 150, 177, 178
Asian financial crisis   157, 194, 196
  South Korea   171, 172, 174, 175,
    178, 187
Atal, Y.   41
attention-getter   59, 63, 68
audience recall   58
Australia   152
autonomy   18
Axial Period (Jaspers)   29

Bakker, I.   96, 98
Bako, A. S.   124
Bako, M.   116, 118, 119, 120
Bako, S.   123
bankruptcies   180–1, 182
banner advertising   59
Baran, P.   42
Barber, B.   32
Barbour-Sackey, E.   120
Barboza, D.   32
Barthes, R.   79
Basch, L.   76
Baud, I.   99
Bauman, Z.   26, 196, 199
Baylis, J.   53
Berger, M.   99, 100
Bhalla, A. S.   174

Bhargava, C.   56
Bhatia, T.   53–70, 198
Biers, D.   184
bilingualism   68
Blanc, C.   76
Blankson, C.   114
Blumberg, R.   99, 100
body copy/main text   59
Body-Gendrot, S.   21
Bollywood   56
Boorstin, D. J.   45
Bornstein, D.   100
Boroujerdi, M.   4, 39–47, 201
Bosnia   142
Bourdieu, P.   41, 79, 87
Brand, R.   113, 124
Brazil   33, 34, 151
Breckenridge, C.   76, 77, 85
Bridges, G.   22
Bruijne, G.   99
Buchanan, P.   6
Burtless, G.   27
business linkages, global   139–44
Buvinic, M.   99, 100
Buzu   126

Cadbury   140, 142
Canada   130
   Organization of Development
      through Education (CODE)   147
capital   8, 9, 16, 93
   accumulation   99
   corporate   19
   flows   11
   global   20, 24
   globalization   21
   hypermobility   195
   internationalization   16
   Mumbai, India   166
capitalism   10, 41
   casino   163–5, 166, 197
   see also global capitalism
capitalist development   96
casino capitalism   163–5, 166, 197
Castells, M.   20
causality   12
Central America   28
central business districts   112
centrality, geography of   16

Cerelac   142
Césaire, A.   40
Chakrabarty, L.   73
Chang, H.-J.   180
Chardin, T. de   72
China   142, 152, 177, 178
Cho, Y.-J.   182
Chomsky, N.   53
Christianborg   114
Christianity   123
Chul Guye Yoo   180
Citibank   178, 184
citizenship   16
city, claims on   20–2
claims, formation of   15–24
   city, claims on   20–2
   localization of the global   17–19
   recovering place   15–17
   space of power   19–20
   urban landscape, inscription in
      22–3
Clark, J.   100
class   173
Clifford, J.   76
Clinton, B.   131
closed market   184
CNN   31, 54
Coca–Cola   140
Cohen, M.   133
Colliers Jardine   153, 155
colonialism   112–14
color schemes   59, 60, 64, 66, 69, 198
commercial products   55
competition   8
competitive model   66
competitive strategy   61–7
compounds   124–5
computers   11
conceptualization   66, 100
connectivity, inward and outward
      195, 196
consciousness   105
consumerism   56, 76–7, 143
contemporary   13
content-sensitive means   67
Cooke, P.   135
cooperation model   67–8
Copjec, J.   20
corporate advertising strategies   198

corruption 114, 184
Council of Muslim Chiefs 123
Cox, K. 11, 171, 172, 200
credit 101, 105
 cooperatives 101
 -extension programs 98–9
Creevey, L. 100
Crinson, M. 78
Crystal, D. 53
cuisine 34
cults 34
culture: homogenization thesis and
 antiglobalization 31
culture 12, 24
 economism and antiglobalization
 29
 homogenization thesis and
 antiglobalization 32
 Seoul, South Korea 177
 United States 12
culture, corporate 23
culture/cultural
 "alien" 28
 authenticity 41
 capital 41
 differentiation 126–7
 globalization 10, 134
 identities 198
 orientation 115
 phenomena 34
 processes 9–10
 trends 28
Cushman & Wakefield 152, 155
customs 10

Dagati 126
Dagomba 126
Dallmayr, F. 45
Dayal, R. 58
De Bellaigue, C. 162
de Mooij, M. 32, 54, 132, 136, 137
debt 93, 94
defining globalization 8–10
deglobalization 172, 180–3, 184
deindustrialization 178
delinquency 21
demand, deregulation of 159–61
denationalization 195
Dennis, C. 98

deregulation 17, 20, 21, 25
 Mumbai, India 157, 159, 166, 167
deterritorialization 174
devalorization 23
development
 agencies 100–1
 paradigms 95
 uneven 10–14
diasporic designs 76–7
Dicken, P. 137
difference 32
diversity 174
Divestiture Implementation
 Committee 139
divorce 181
D'Monte, D. 162
domestic forces 151, 194
Dominican Republic 12
Donkins, R. 162
Dovey, K. 79
dream cultures, constructed 76–7
dual citizenship 147
Dugger, C. W. 178
Dun & Bradstreet 133, 138
Dunford, M. 135
Dunn, S. 20
Dunning, J. 130, 137

Eade, J. 137
early modern 13
East Asia 36
Eastern Europe 28, 150, 178
Eckstein, S. 96
ecology 35
economic activity 15
economic dominance 175
economic globalization 10, 13, 15
 claims, formation of 16
 economism and antiglobalization
 30
 gender and resistance 93, 94, 96
 Ghana 131, 137, 146, 147
 inscription 22
 opposition and resistance to
 globalization 25
 and politics 24
 resistance and empowerment 107
 sociocultural consequences 26, 27
economic processes 9

Economic Recovery Program   114
economic reductionism   26
economic restructuring   96–8
  debt-related   94
  gender and resistance   95, 96
  resistance and empowerment   106
economic trends   28
economics   29
economism and antiglobalization
  27–31
"edge" cities   22, 111
education   115, 123–4, 137
Egypt   41
Electric Corporation   123
electronic
  communications   11
  images   198
  media   56
Elson, D.   96, 98
embeddedness   198
Emeagwali, G.   98
empowerment   18, 100–7
English language   53, 55, 56, 57, 61,
  62, 69, 70, 126
Enlightenment   42, 43
Enterprise Insurance   143
environment   26, 28
equity market   160
equity shares   142
ethnic homogeneity   177
Eurocentrism   39
Europe   7, 28, 36, 134, 140
  and Accra   113, 142
  economism and antiglobalization
    31
  immigration   17
  intellectuals/scholars   40
  non-resident Indians   159
  religiosity   34
  Sabon Zongo   112
  social sciences   39, 42
  see also Eastern Europe
evaluation   67, 68, 69
Evenson, N.   78
Ewe   123, 124, 126
exclusion   8, 132, 133
export processing zones   112

Fainstein, S.   21

Fan Milk   143
Fanon, F.   40
fashions   10
favoritism   114
Featherstone, M.   75
Feldman, S.   96
feminization   19
Ferguson, J.   75
Fernández-Baca, G.   97, 99
finance   8, 15
financial crises in Seoul, South Korea
  170–88
  and deglobalizing sentiments
    180–3
  globalization   175–80;
    contradictory views of
    184–6
  local in the plural   172–5
financial markets   41
FINCA-International   101
Fingleton, E.   53
Fisher, S.   180
foreign companies and glocalization
  in Accra   130–48
  activities of foreign companies
    137–9
  global business linkages   139–44
  intepretative sphere of globalization
    144–6
  reconceptualizing globalization in
    the margins   132–5
foreign direct investment   135, 138,
  140
  Mumbai, India   156, 159, 163
  Seoul, South Korea   176, 178, 179,
    186
Foreign Exchange and Regulation Act
  159
foreign institutional investors
  160
former Soviet Union   9, 150, 151
Foucault, M.   44
France   13, 22, 43, 111
Frank, A. G.   42
Frankfurt School   44
Fraser, C.   53
French West Africa   115
Friedmann, T. L.   5, 53, 136
Fukuyama, F.   11

Fulani   115, 116, 123, 126
Futa, A.   118

Ga   113, 115, 116, 118, 123, 124,
     126, 147
Gandhi, R.   77
Garnaut, R.   180
gender and resistance in Peru
     93–108
   economic restructuring and
     women's poverty   96–8
   marginalization   98–100
   nuancing gendered dimensions of
     global economic change
     94–6
   resistance and empowerment
     100–7
General Agreement on Tariffs and
   Trade   27
geographic dispersion   56
Gergen, K.   44
Germany   13, 130, 141, 142
Geschiere, P.   126
Ghana   4, 41, 111
   Broadcasting   126
   Free Zone Board   139
   Investment Promotion Center
     131, 139, 140
   Star beer   12
   Stock Exchange   143
   Telecom   123
   telephone directory   139
   see also Guinness Ghana; migrant
     communities in Accra:
     marginalization
Giddens, A.   22
global
   capital   151, 157, 161, 163, 166
   capitalism   36, 194
   cities   8; claims, formation of   15,
     16, 17; powerlessness and
     invisibility   19; as strategic
     space   23; and women   18
   communication   53
   consumption standards   198
   flows   133, 134, 137
   variety   32–5
globalization from above   36
globalization from below   36

"globalization in the plural"   172
globalized consumption patterns
     175
"globalized otherness"   175
globalution   5–6
globaphobia   6
globoccidentalism   13
glocalization   3, 12, 197–9, 200
   and codification   68
   homogenization thesis and
     antiglobalization   32
   rural advertising in India   54
   wall advertising   70
   see also foreign companies and
     glocalization
Goldsmith, E.   136, 171, 172, 174
Goodman, S.   53
government   137
Graddol, D.   53
Graham, S.   20
Gramsci, A.   45
Grant, R.   3–14, 111, 130–48,
     193–201
"greenfield" operation   141
Greenpeace   28
Grundy-Warr, C.   172
Grunshie   124
Guha, K.   156
Guha, S. B.   161
Guinness   140, 142
   Ghana   143–4, 146, 198
Gulf oil   61–2
Gupta, A.   75

Habermas, J.   44
habitus   41
Halimi, S.   31
Hannerz, U.   30, 32, 79, 171
Hausa   115, 116, 118, 120, 123, 124,
     126
Hays-Mitchell, M.   93–108, 196
header/captions   59
"hedge fund"   180
Heidegger, M.   45
Heineken   12, 143
Held, D.   13
Hindi language   55–7, 61–7, 69
Hindustan Lever   56
Hirst, P.   6, 130, 137, 172, 173

historical factors   194
historicizing   143, 198
Hite, R. E.   53
Hobsbawm, E.   31
Hoffmann, S.   39
homogenization   31–2, 33, 34, 54
Hondagneu-Sotelo, I.   18
Hong Kong   152, 175
Hong-Jae, P.   180
Hoogvelt, A.   53
housing estates   114
human rights   9
humankind   29

identity   20, 24, 31, 198
illogic   10–11
immigration   17, 18, 21, 22, 23, 28,
     198
import substitution   140
India   7, 41, 142, 198
   Bangalore   152, 153, 156, 157, 165
   Bombay   156
   Bombay Stock Exchange   160
   Chennai   152, 153, 156, 157
   Delhi   153, 156, 157
   Hyderabad   165
   Maharashtra   161, 162–3, 166
   Market Research Bureau   55
   New Delhi   152
   Pune   165
   Rajasthan   194
   Reserve Bank   159
   Securities and Exchange Board   160
   Thane   164
   "think local, act global"   44
   see also land use and land values;
        localization or globalization;
        postmodernism,
        transnationalism and Indian
        urbanity
indigenization   *see* subduing
     globalization
Indonesia   41, 151, 181, 184
Industrial Training Program   177–8
informales   98, 99, 101
informalization   17–18, 19
information technology   41
infrastructure   125
institutions   173

International Monetary Fund   27,
     33, 36, 112
   Seoul, South Korea   170, 171, 174,
        180, 181, 182, 184
international relations   29, 39
Internet   199
interpretation   146
investment trusts   160
invisibility   17, 18, 19, 22
   noncorporate   23
Ireland   111
Islam/Muslims   34, 45–7, 115, 118,
     123–4, 125
Italy   142

James, C. L. R.   40
James, J.   53
Jameson, F.   73, 171, 172
Jamestown   114
Japan   13, 17, 130, 134, 184
   Tokyo   22, 111, 173, 174–5
Jaspers, K.   29
Jencks, C.   73
Jethwaney, J.   58
joint ventures   141, 142, 143, 146,
     196, 198

Kafkalas, G.   135
Kamdar, M.   162
Kaneshie   114
Kanso, A.   53
Kanuri   115, 126
Kaplan, R. D.   5
Kapur, D.   180, 181
Kaul, P.   56
Kellogg's   62
Khondker, H.   27
Kierkegaard, S. A.   45
Kim, E. M.   180
Kim, H.   178
Kim, Y.-H.   10, 72, 170–88
King, A. D.   4–5, 20, 22, 72–89, 113,
     173, 198
knowledge indigenization   41,
     42–5
Kobrin, S. J.   27
Korea   4
   Ministry of Labor   178
   see also Seoul

Kotokoli   126
Krugman, P.   180
Kujala, A.   53
Kumasi Brewery   143
Kurien, C. T.   41
Kusno, A.   79

Labadi   114
labor   9, 20, 93
land use and land values in Mumbai,
    India   4, 5, 150–68, 194, 197,
    200
  Altamount Road   155
  Andheri   153, 155, 164
  Andheri-Kurla   163
  Ballard Estate   152
  Bandra   155
  Bandra-Kurla   153, 155, 163, 164
  Borivili   153
  casino capitalism   163–5
  Chembur   153
  continued regulation of supply
      161–3
  Cuffe Parade   152, 155
  deregulation of demand   159–61
  Fort area   152
  Goregaon   153
  Jogeshwari   153
  Juhu   155
  Kandivili   153
  Lower Pare   153, 164
  Malabar Hill   155, 159
  Nariman Point   152, 153, 155,
      156, 163, 193
  Navi Mumbai   153
  Panvel   153
  Peddar Road   155
  Prabhadevi   153
  Seawoods Estate   160
  Sion   153
  turbulence in real estate market
      151–6
  Worli   153, 155, 163, 164
language   53, 58, 60, 63, 65, 66, 68,
    70, 198
  allocation   61
  choice   55
  Ghana   126
  mixing   60

segregation   60
zongos   115
see also English; Hindi; linguistic
Larbi, W. O.   114
Larkin, B.   126
Larson, J. F.   176
Latin America   42, 93, 94, 95, 96, 99,
    150
see also Peru
Laurie, P.   172
Leaf, M.   79
Lebanon   142
Lee, C. S.   182, 184
Lee, G. Y.   178
Lee, R. D.   46
Lefebvre, H.   75
Lehtinen, U.   53
Leipziger, D. M.   180
liaison arrangement   141
liberalization   9, 10, 195, 199
  Ghana   111
  migrant communities and
      marginalization   112
  Mumbai, India   150, 151, 156,
      157, 159, 164, 167
  Seoul, South Korea   176, 178, 180
Liberia   147
Liechtenstein   142
Lin, J.   28
linguistic
  choices   60
  composition   61
  dispersion   56–7
  forms   57
  representational strategies   60
  systems   67
  terms   66
Lloyd, P.   114
loans   98
local economies   8
Local Government Law   114
local traffic rules   175
local–global interface   13
localization   32, 68, 69, 135, 137,
      196, 200
  of the global   17–19
  see also localization or globalization
localization or globalization: rural
      advertising in India   53–70

localization or globalization *(cont.)*
  competitive strategy   61–7
  content analysis and marketization
    of discourse   68–70
  cooperation model   67–8
  interpretation of global marketing
    in the margins   56–7
  wall advertisements   57–60
logic   10
logos   61, 69
Lycette, M.   99

Mabogunje, A. L.   113
McArthur, T.   53
McChesney, R.   53
Machimura, T.   173
macrodevelopment   131
macroeconomic indicators   133
Malaysia   151, 157
Malta Guinness   143
Mander, J.   136, 171, 172, 174
marginality
  and contemporary globality   33
  rural advertising in India   54
  socioeconomic phenomena   34
  United States   35
marginalization   98–100
  Ghana   130, 131, 133, 134
  see also migrant communities in
    Accra: marginalization
margins   7, 193–201
  Accra   132–5
  global marketing   56–7
  globalization and development in
    twenty-first century   199–201
  glocalization   197–9
  India   150
market reform   140
market-driven model   93
marketing, global   56–7
marketization   25, 130, 147
markets   93
Marvin, J.   20, 172
Marx, K.   29
material goods   10
Mathews, J. A.   184
Mauritius   142
Maxi-Malt   143
McDonald, H.   56

McDonald's   54, 173
media   198
Memmi, A.   40
Metcalf, T. R.   79
Meyer, B.   126, 145
Meyer, J. W.   35
microenterprise development   95,
    98, 99, 100, 106, 107, 108
Middle East   42
migrant communities in Accra:
    marginalization   111–28
  colonial city   112–14
  Sabon Zongo   121–5
  zongos, creation of   115–21
Milo   142
Minerals Commission   139
Ministry of Information and
    Broadcasting   58
mismanagement   114
Miyoshi, M.   171, 172
Mobil Oil Ghana   143
mobility   9
modern   13
modernity   41, 43, 45, 46
modernization   10
Molyneux, M.   94
Moser, C.   98
Mossi   126
Mottahedeh, R.   43
Mubai   *see* land use and land values
    in Mumbai
Mubarak, President   26
Mueller, B.   53
multiculturalism   16
Multilateral Agreement on
    Investment   27
multilaterals   142
multinational corporations   130,
    133, 137–8, 197
  Mumbai, India   151, 156, 157,
    160, 163, 166, 167
  Seoul, South Korea   171
Mutahhari, A. M.   46

Nam, K.-D.   182
nation-state   16, 29, 35, 172
national   12
National Council of Applied
    Economic Research   55

national economies   8
national-global   16
nationalism   35
Natrajan, I.   56
negotiation   137
Neiman Marcu   147
neoliberal restructuring   95, 107, 108
Nestlé   142, 146
Netherlands   142
New International Economic Order 42
new products   142
New Zealand   44
Nietzsche, F. W.   45
Nigeria   115
Nijman, J.   5, 150–68, 197
Nima   118, 120, 121
non-governmental organizations 55, 98, 121, 131
non-resident Indians   76–7, 80–5, 159, 160, 163, 165, 166, 197
North America   7, 34, 36
   see also Canada; United States
North American Free Trade Agreement   28
North Atlantic Treaty Organization 9
notional real estate   163
Nupe   115, 123

O'Brien, R.   11, 200
O'Connell, H.   98
Ohmae, K.   9
Oncu, A.   79, 80, 83
Onkvisit, S.   54
opposition   106
opposition and resistance to globalization   25–37
   contested symbol   25–6
   economism and antiglobalization 27–31
   global variety   32–5
   homogenization thesis and antiglobalization   31–2
oppression   94, 100
Organisation for Economic Cooperation and Development 138

otherness   23
overseas corporate bodies   159
overvalorization   23

Park, H.-S.   176
Patel, S.   156
Paterson Zochonis   143
patriarchy   95
Peachey, K.   172
Peil, M.   115
Pellow, D.   4, 111–28, 194, 196
Pennzoil   66, 198
pension funds   160
Pentecostalism   145, 146
people of color   21
Perry, M.   172
Persian   61
Peru   4, 194, 200
   see also gender and resistance in Peru
pharmaceutical corporations   36
physical properties   59, 69
Pioneer Tobacco   143
place   10, 11
   of exclusion   8
political
   globalization   13
   power, organization of   15
   processes   9
   trends   28
politicoeconomic globalization   25
politics   29
Pollack, A.   182
port areas   112
postmodernism   39
postmodernism, transnationalism and Indian urbanity   72–89
   architecture, property and consumerism   77–9
   consumption   79–80
   diasporic designs: constructed dream cultures and non–resident Indian   76–7
   imagination   74–6
   non-resident Indian   80–5
poverty   94, 96–8, 100
powerlessness   19
premodern   13
Presidente beer   12

privatization   20, 25
product information   69
product name   59, 60, 61, 62
production   93
property   76–7
    see also land use and land values

Radelet, S.   180
Raina, M.   78
Rakodi, C.   131
Ranger, T.   31
Rao, S. L.   56
Ratz, D.   54
Rawlings, J.   131, 147
Rayfield, J. R.   112
Razin, A.   53
real estate   *see* land use and land
    values
reconceptualizing globalization in the
    margins   132–5
recovering place   15–17
reforms   159, 164
regional economies   8
regulatory environment   136,
    162
religion   10, 28, 34, 146, 147
rent control laws   162–3
research   69
resistance   100–7
    see also gender and resistance;
        opposition and resistance
restructuring   194
    neoliberal   95, 107, 108
    Seoul, South Korea   172, 174, 186,
        187
    see also economic restructuring
Ritchie, M.   28
Ritzer, G.   32
Robertson, R.   3, 25–37, 54, 72, 75,
    132, 135, 136, 137, 177, 196
Rodrik, D.   6, 26
Rogerson, C.   131
Rotenberg, R.   125
Rousseau, J.-J.   45
rural advertising   *see* localization or
    globalization: rural advertising in
    India
Ruthleiser, C.   176
Ryans, J.   54

Sabon Zongo   111–12, 114, 116–18,
    120, 121–6, 194
Sachs, J.   180
Sachs, W.   35
Sadka, E.   53
Safi, L. M.   46
Sanskrit   61
Sartre, J.-P.   45
Sassen, S.   4, 15–24, 136, 171, 173,
    195
scale   12
Schiller, N. G.   76
Schoffield, H.   34
script   58, 60–2, 64–70, 198
Scriver, P.   78
Secretan, T.   147
sectors   173
self   29
self-identity   105
semiconductor industry   171
Senghore, L. S.   40
Sennett, R.   22
Seoul   200
    Asian Financial Crisis   194
    Foreign Investment and Trade
        Services   185
    Kangman   193
    Olympics   176, 177, 184
    see also financial crises in Seoul
September 11th attacks   36
service industry   55
service and social advertisements   62
services   8, 93
Shaw, A.   161, 165
Shaw, J.   54
Shayegan, D.   46
Shields, R.   175
Shim, J. H.   182
Short, J. R.   3–14, 72, 171,
    193–201
Simon, D.   130, 131, 134
Singapore   111, 152, 175
Singh, A.   180, 181
single-parent families   181
Sisala   124
Sklair, L.   84
slogans   59, 60, 62, 63
slums   196
Smith, H.   180

Smith, N. 200
Smith, S. 53
social cohesion 6
social and development campaigns 55
social development and service advertising 64, 65
social identities 198
Social and Rural Research Institute 55
social science 39, 40, 41, 47
Social Security Bank 143
socias 102–6
sociological subdivisions 123–4
solidarity group 101
Sontag, D. 178
Sorkin, M. 20
Soros, G. 182
Sorush, A. 46–7
South Africa 36, 150
South America 36
South Korea 142, 152
  see also financial crises in Seoul
Southeast Asia 177, 178
Southern Europe 28
sovereignty 15
space 199
space of power 19–20
space-time 11
Sparr, P. 96, 98
spatial
  compartmentalization 113
  identities 198
  mobility 199
  subdivisions 123–4
specialization 56
Spengler, O. 45
Spivak, G. 72
Standard Chartered Bank 143
standardization 33, 56
Star beer 12
state intervention 151, 157, 194
Strange, S. 157
strategies of glocalization 136, 146
structural adjustment 96–8, 100, 101, 105
  gender and resistance 107
  Ghana 111, 114, 131, 140
structural properties 59, 60

subduing globalization: indigenization movement 39–47
  knowledge indigenization 42–5
  risks and limitations: Islamic experiment 45–7
subheader 60
subjective interpretative sphere 199
Sufjic, D. 81
Sukhthankar, D. M. 162
Super Paper Products 143
supply, continued regulation of 161–3
Sweden 13
Switzerland 142
  World Economic Forum 26
Swyngedouw, E. 132, 135, 197

Taliban Islamic fundamentalism 12
Tanski, J. 96
telecommunications 11, 20
television 11
Terlouw, P. 130
text size 62–3
Thailand 152
"think and act both globally and locally at the same time" approach 67
"think global, act local" 6, 61–2, 63, 66
"think local, act global" 44
"think local, act local" 62–6
Third World
  debt 36, 93
  intellectuals/scholars 39, 40, 42, 43
  scientific and technological gap 47
  social science 41, 43
Third Worldism 40
Thompson, A. K. W. 116
Thompson, G. 56, 130, 137, 172, 173, 180
Thrift, N. 79
Time Warner 54
times 173
Tomlinson, A. 176
Tomlinson, J. 32, 173, 177

Toynbee, A.   73
trade   8
tradition   10, 31
training   101, 105
translocal communities   20
transnational corporations   15
transnational relations   28
transnationalism   146
   see also postmodernism,
      transnationalism and Indian
      urbanity
transnationalization of labor   20
transparency   172
transport costs   11
travel   11
Turkey   44
Twi   126

unemployment   180–1
UNESCO   55
Unilever   140
Unilever Ghana   143
Union of Needle Trades, Industrial
   and Textile employees   28
uniqueness   32
United Kingdom   7, 13, 43, 130
   and Ghana   115, 116, 140, 141,
      142, 143
   Gold Coast   113
   London   22, 111, 151
United Nations   26, 28
   Center on Transnational
      Corporations 138
United States   13, 134
   antiglobality   34
   companies in Ghana   142, 143
   culture   12, 172, 173
   economism and antiglobalization
      30, 31
   foreign policy   39
   immigration   17
   intellectuals/scholars   40
   Los Angeles   22
   marginality   35
   multinational corporations   130
   New York   22, 111, 151, 178
   nonresident Indians   159
   overseas investments   131
   religious fundamentalism   28

scholarship   43
social sciences   42
"think local, act global"   44
Urban Environmental Sanitation
   Project   120
Urban Land Ceiling Act   162
urban landscape, inscription in
   22–3
urban planning   114
urbanity   *see* postmodernism,
   transnationalism and Indian
   urbanity
Ussher Town   116
UTC Estates of Ghana   143
utility   69

valorization   19
values   10
Van Lieshout, M.   96
verbal cues   68
Veseth, M.   6, 134
video-van advertising   56–7
village-banking   101, 103
visual cues   60, 64, 68
Volta Garments   142

Wade, R.   1, 80, 181
wall advertising   54, 55, 56–7, 69, 70
Wallerstein, I.   29, 30
Wangara   115, 123, 126
Waring, M.   96
Waters, M.   199
Watson, J. L.   32
Watson, S.   22
Webb, R.   97, 99
Weber, M.   29
Weidemann, C.   99, 100
Weinstein, S.   31
Weiss, L.   172
Weisse, B. A.   180, 181
Welfare Organization   120
West Africa 5,   113, 140, 142
   see also Ghana
White, K.   99
Winch, P.   43
women   17, 18, 21, 23
   see also gender and resistance
World Bank   9, 27, 36, 112, 120
   Project Urban IV   121

World Economic Forum   26, 36
World Trade Organization   27, 35, 36

Yahaya, A.   120
Yoruba   115, 116, 123, 126
Young, A.   180

Zabrama   123, 124, 126
zongo   116
zongos   113, 120, 196
  creation of   115–21
Zukin, S.   173